Programming Computer Vision
with Python

Jan Erik Solem

O'REILLY®

Beijing · Cambridge · Farnham · Köln · Sebastopol · Tokyo

Programming Computer Vision with Python
by Jan Erik Solem

Published by O'Reilly Media, Inc., 1005 Gravenstein Highway North, Sebastopol, CA 95472.

O'Reilly books may be purchased for educational, business, or sales promotional use. Online editions are also available for most titles (*http://my.safaribooksonline.com*). For more information, contact our corporate/institutional sales department: (800) 998-9938 or *corporate@oreilly.com*.

Interior designer:	David Futato	**Project manager:**	Paul C. Anagnostopoulos
Cover designer:	Karen Montgomery	**Copyeditor:**	Priscilla Stevens
Editors:	Andy Oram, Mike Hendrickson	**Proofreader:**	Richard Camp
Production editor:	Holly Bauer	**Illustrator:**	Laurel Muller

June 2012   First edition

Revision History for the First Edition:

2012-06-11   First release

See *http://oreilly.com/catalog/errata.csp?isbn=0636920022923* for release details.

ISBN: 978-1-449-31654-9
[LSI]   [2012-08-17]

Table of Contents

Preface . . . . **vii**

1. Basic Image Handling and Processing **1**
    1.1   PIL—The Python Imaging Library   1
    1.2   Matplotlib   3
    1.3   NumPy   7
    1.4   SciPy   16
    1.5   Advanced Example: Image De-Noising   23
    Exercises   26
    Conventions for the Code Examples   27

2. Local Image Descriptors **29**
    2.1   Harris Corner Detector   29
    2.2   SIFT—Scale-Invariant Feature Transform   36
    2.3   Matching Geotagged Images   44
    Exercises   51

3. Image to Image Mappings **53**
    3.1   Homographies   53
    3.2   Warping Images   57
    3.3   Creating Panoramas   70
    Exercises   77

4. Camera Models and Augmented Reality **79**
    4.1   The Pin-Hole Camera Model   79
    4.2   Camera Calibration   84
    4.3   Pose Estimation from Planes and Markers   86
    4.4   Augmented Reality   89
    Exercises   98

5. Multiple View Geometry **99**

    5.1   Epipolar Geometry   99

    5.2   Computing with Cameras and 3D Structure   107

    5.3   Multiple View Reconstruction   113

    5.4   Stereo Images   120

    Exercises   125

6. Clustering Images **127**

    6.1   *K*-Means Clustering   127

    6.2   Hierarchical Clustering   133

    6.3   Spectral Clustering   140

    Exercises   145

7. Searching Images **147**

    7.1   Content-Based Image Retrieval   147

    7.2   Visual Words   148

    7.3   Indexing Images   151

    7.4   Searching the Database for Images   155

    7.5   Ranking Results Using Geometry   160

    7.6   Building Demos and Web Applications   162

    Exercises   165

8. Classifying Image Content **167**

    8.1   *K*-Nearest Neighbors   167

    8.2   Bayes Classifier   175

    8.3   Support Vector Machines   179

    8.4   Optical Character Recognition   183

    Exercises   189

9. Image Segmentation **191**

    9.1   Graph Cuts   191

    9.2   Segmentation Using Clustering   200

    9.3   Variational Methods   204

    Exercises   206

10. OpenCV **209**

    10.1   The OpenCV Python Interface   209

    10.2   OpenCV Basics   210

    10.3   Processing Video   213

    10.4   Tracking   216

    10.5   More Examples   223

    Exercises   226

A. Installing Packages **227**

    A.1   NumPy and SciPy   227

    A.2   Matplotlib   228

    A.3   PIL   228

    A.4   LibSVM   228

    A.5   OpenCV   229

    A.6   VLFeat   230

    A.7   PyGame   230

    A.8   PyOpenGL   230

    A.9   Pydot   230

    A.10 Python-graph   231

    A.11 Simplejson   231

    A.12 PySQLite   232

    A.13 CherryPy   232

B. Image Datasets **233**

    B.1   Flickr   233

    B.2   Panoramio   234

    B.3   Oxford Visual Geometry Group   235

    B.4   University of Kentucky Recognition Benchmark Images   235

    B.5   Other   235

C. Image Credits **237**

    C.1   Images from Flickr   237

    C.2   Other Images   238

    C.3   Illustrations   238

References **239**

Index **243**

Preface

Today, images and video are everywhere. Online photo-sharing sites and social networks have them in the billions. Search engines will produce images of just about any conceivable query. Practically all phones and computers come with built-in cameras. It is not uncommon for people to have many gigabytes of photos and videos on their devices.

Programming a computer and designing algorithms for understanding what is in these images is the field of computer vision. Computer vision powers applications like image search, robot navigation, medical image analysis, photo management, and many more.

The idea behind this book is to give an easily accessible entry point to hands-on computer vision with enough understanding of the underlying theory and algorithms to be a foundation for students, researchers, and enthusiasts. The Python programming language, the language choice of this book, comes with many freely available, powerful modules for handling images, mathematical computing, and data mining.

When writing this book, I have used the following principles as a guideline. The book should:

- Be written in an exploratory style and encourage readers to follow the examples on their computers as they are reading the text.
- Promote and use free and open software with a low learning threshold. Python was the obvious choice.
- Be complete and self-contained. This book does not cover all of computer vision but rather it should be complete in that all code is presented and explained. The reader should be able to reproduce the examples and build upon them directly.
- Be broad rather than detailed, inspiring and motivational rather than theoretical.

In short, it should act as a source of inspiration for those interested in programming computer vision applications.

Prerequisites and Overview

This book looks at theory and algorithms for a wide range of applications and problems. Here is a short summary of what to expect.

What You Need to Know

- Basic programming experience. You need to know how to use an editor and run scripts, how to structure code as well as basic data types. Familiarity with Python or other scripting languages like Ruby or Matlab will help.
- Basic mathematics. To make full use of the examples, it helps if you know about matrices, vectors, matrix multiplication, and standard mathematical functions and concepts like derivatives and gradients. Some of the more advanced mathematical examples can be easily skipped.

What You Will Learn

- Hands-on programming with images using Python.
- Computer vision techniques behind a wide variety of real-world applications.
- Many of the fundamental algorithms and how to implement and apply them yourself.

The code examples in this book will show you object recognition, content-based image retrieval, image search, optical character recognition, optical flow, tracking, 3D reconstruction, stereo imaging, augmented reality, pose estimation, panorama creation, image segmentation, de-noising, image grouping, and more.

Chapter Overview

Chapter 1, "Basic Image Handling and Processing"
Introduces the basic tools for working with images and the central Python modules used in the book. This chapter also covers many fundamental examples needed for the remaining chapters.

Chapter 2, "Local Image Descriptors"
Explains methods for detecting interest points in images and how to use them to find corresponding points and regions between images.

Chapter 3, "Image to Image Mappings"
Describes basic transformations between images and methods for computing them. Examples range from image warping to creating panoramas.

Chapter 4, "Camera Models and Augmented Reality"
Introduces how to model cameras, generate image projections from 3D space to image features, and estimate the camera viewpoint.

Chapter 5, "Multiple View Geometry"
Explains how to work with several images of the same scene, the fundamentals of multiple-view geometry, and how to compute 3D reconstructions from images.

Chapter 6, "Clustering Images"
> Introduces a number of clustering methods and shows how to use them for grouping and organizing images based on similarity or content.

Chapter 7, "Searching Images"
> Shows how to build efficient image retrieval techniques that can store image representations and search for images based on their visual content.

Chapter 8, "Classifying Image Content"
> Describes algorithms for classifying image content and how to use them to recognize objects in images.

Chapter 9, "Image Segmentation"
> Introduces different techniques for dividing an image into meaningful regions using clustering, user interactions, or image models.

Chapter 10, "OpenCV"
> Shows how to use the Python interface for the commonly used OpenCV computer vision library and how to work with video and camera input.

There is also a bibliography at the back of the book. Citations of bibliographic entries are made by number in square brackets, as in [20].

Introduction to Computer Vision

Computer vision is the automated extraction of information from images. Information can mean anything from 3D models, camera position, object detection and recognition to grouping and searching image content. In this book, we take a wide definition of computer vision and include things like image warping, de-noising, and augmented reality.[1]

Sometimes computer vision tries to mimic human vision, sometimes it uses a data and statistical approach, and sometimes geometry is the key to solving problems. We will try to cover all of these angles in this book.

Practical computer vision contains a mix of programming, modeling, and mathematics and is sometimes difficult to grasp. I have deliberately tried to present the material with a minimum of theory in the spirit of "as simple as possible but no simpler." The mathematical parts of the presentation are there to help readers understand the algorithms. Some chapters are by nature very math-heavy (Chapters 4 and 5, mainly). Readers can skip the math if they like and still use the example code.

Python and NumPy

Python is the programming language used in the code examples throughout this book. Python is a clear and concise language with good support for input/output, numerics, images, and plotting. The language has some peculiarities, such as indentation

---

[1] These examples produce new images and are more image processing than actually extracting information from images.

and compact syntax, that take getting used to. The code examples assume you have Python 2.6 or later, as most packages are only available for these versions. The upcoming Python 3.x version has many language differences and is not backward compatible with Python 2.x or compatible with the ecosystem of packages we need (yet).

Some familiarity with basic Python will make the material more accessible for readers. For beginners to Python, Mark Lutz' book *Learning Python* [20] and the online documentation at *http://www.python.org/* are good starting points.

When programming computer vision, we need representations of vectors and matrices and operations on them. This is handled by Python's NumPy module, where both vectors and matrices are represented by the `array` type. This is also the representation we will use for images. A good NumPy reference is Travis Oliphant's free book *Guide to NumPy* [24]. The documentation at *http://numpy.scipy.org/* is also a good starting point if you are new to NumPy. For visualizing results, we will use the Matplotlib module, and for more advanced mathematics, we will use SciPy. These are the central packages you will need and will be explained and introduced in Chapter 1.

Besides these central packages, there will be many other free Python packages used for specific purposes like reading JSON or XML, loading and saving data, generating graphs, graphics programming, web demos, classifiers, and many more. These are usually only needed for specific applications or demos and can be skipped if you are not interested in that particular application.

It is worth mentioning IPython, an interactive Python shell that makes debugging and experimentation easier. Documentation and downloads are available at *http://ipython.org/*.

Notation and Conventions

Code looks like this:

```
# some points
x = [100,100,400,400]
y = [200,500,200,500]

# plot the points
plot(x,y)
```

The following typographical conventions are used in this book:

Italic
> Used for definitions, filenames, and variable names.

Constant width
> Used for functions, Python modules, and code examples. It is also used for console printouts.

Hyperlink
> Used for URLs.

Plain text
> Used for everything else.

Mathematical formulas are given inline like this $f(\mathbf{x}) = \mathbf{w}^T \mathbf{x} + b$ or centered independently:

$$f(\mathbf{x}) = \sum_i w_i x_i + b$$

and are only numbered when a reference is needed.

In the mathematical sections, we will use lowercase $(s, r, \lambda, \theta, \ldots)$ for scalars, uppercase $(A, V, H, \ldots)$ for matrices (including I for the image as an array), and lowercase bold $(\mathbf{t}, \mathbf{c}, \ldots)$ for vectors. We will use $\mathbf{x} = [x, y]$ and $\mathbf{X} = [X, Y, Z]$ to mean points in 2D (images) and 3D, respectively.

Using Code Examples

This book is here to help you get your job done. In general, you may use the code in this book in your programs and documentation. You do not need to contact us for permission unless you're reproducing a significant portion of the code. For example, writing a program that uses several chunks of code from this book does not require permission. Selling or distributing a CD-ROM of examples from O'Reilly books does require permission. Answering a question by citing this book and quoting example code does not require permission. Incorporating a significant amount of example code from this book into your product's documentation does require permission.

We appreciate, but do not require, attribution. An attribution usually includes the title, author, publisher, and ISBN. For example: "*Programming Computer Vision with Python* by Jan Erik Solem (O'Reilly). Copyright © 2012 Jan Erik Solem, 978-1-449-31654-9."

If you feel your use of code examples falls outside fair use or the permission given above, feel free to contact us at *permissions@oreilly.com*.

How to Contact Us

Please address comments and questions concerning this book to the publisher:

O'Reilly Media, Inc.
1005 Gravenstein Highway North
Sebastopol, CA 95472
(800) 998-9938 (in the United States or Canada)
(707) 829-0515 (international or local)
(707) 829-0104 (fax)

We have a web page for this book, where we list errata, examples, links to the code and data sets used, and any additional information. You can access this page at:

oreil.ly/comp_vision_w_python

To comment or ask technical questions about this book, send email to:

bookquestions@oreilly.com

For more information about our books, courses, conferences, and news, see our website at *http://www.oreilly.com*.

Find us on Facebook: *http://facebook.com/oreilly*

Follow us on Twitter: *http://twitter.com/oreillymedia*

Watch us on YouTube: *http://www.youtube.com/oreillymedia*

Safari® Books Online

Safari Safari Books Online (*www.safaribooksonline.com*) is an on-demand digital library that delivers expert content in both book and video form from the world's leading authors in technology and business.

Technology professionals, software developers, web designers, and business and creative professionals use Safari Books Online as their primary resource for research, problem solving, learning, and certification training.

Safari Books Online offers a range of product mixes and pricing programs for organizations, government agencies, and individuals. Subscribers have access to thousands of books, training videos, and prepublication manuscripts in one fully searchable database from publishers like O'Reilly Media, Prentice Hall Professional, Addison-Wesley Professional, Microsoft Press, Sams, Que, Peachpit Press, Focal Press, Cisco Press, John Wiley & Sons, Syngress, Morgan Kaufmann, IBM Redbooks, Packt, Adobe Press, FT Press, Apress, Manning, New Riders, McGraw-Hill, Jones & Bartlett, Course Technology, and dozens more. For more information about Safari Books Online, please visit us online.

Acknowledgments

I'd like to express my gratitude to everyone involved in the development and production of this book. The whole O'Reilly team has been helpful. Special thanks to Andy Oram (O'Reilly) for editing, and Paul Anagnostopoulos (Windfall Software) for efficient production work.

Many people commented on the various drafts of this book as I shared them online. Klas Josephson and Håkan Ardö deserve lots of praise for their thorough comments and feedback. Fredrik Kahl and Pau Gargallo helped with fact checks. Thank you all readers for encouraging words and for making the text and code examples better. Receiving emails from strangers sharing their thoughts on the drafts was a great motivator.

Finally, I'd like to thank my friends and family for support and understanding when I spent nights and weekends on writing. Most thanks of all to my wife Sara, my long-time supporter.

## CHAPTER 1

Basic Image Handling and Processing

This chapter is an introduction to handling and processing images. With extensive examples, it explains the central Python packages you will need for working with images. This chapter introduces the basic tools for reading images, converting and scaling images, computing derivatives, plotting or saving results, and so on. We will use these throughout the remainder of the book.

1.1 PIL—The Python Imaging Library

The *Python Imaging Library* (*PIL*) provides general image handling and lots of useful basic image operations like resizing, cropping, rotating, color conversion and much more. PIL is free and available from *http://www.pythonware.com/products/pil/*.

With PIL, you can read images from most formats and write to the most common ones. The most important module is the Image module. To read an image, use:

```
from PIL import Image

pil_im = Image.open('empire.jpg')
```

The return value, *pil_im*, is a PIL image object.

Color conversions are done using the convert() method. To read an image and convert it to grayscale, just add convert('L') like this:

```
pil_im = Image.open('empire.jpg').convert('L')
```

Here are some examples taken from the PIL documentation, available at *http://www .pythonware.com/library/pil/handbook/index.htm*. Output from the examples is shown in Figure 1-1.

Convert Images to Another Format

Using the save() method, PIL can save images in most image file formats. Here's an example that takes all image files in a list of filenames (*filelist*) and converts the images to JPEG files:

Figure 1-1. Examples of processing images with PIL.

```
from PIL import Image
import os

for infile in filelist:
  outfile = os.path.splitext(infile)[0] + ".jpg"
  if infile != outfile:
    try:
      Image.open(infile).save(outfile)
    except IOError:
      print "cannot convert", infile
```

The PIL function **open()** creates a PIL image object and the **save()** method saves the image to a file with the given filename. The new filename will be the same as the original with the file ending ".jpg" instead. PIL is smart enough to determine the image format from the file extension. There is a simple check that the file is not already a JPEG file and a message is printed to the console if the conversion fails.

Throughout this book we are going to need lists of images to process. Here's how you could create a list of filenames of all images in a folder. Create a file called *imtools.py* to store some of these generally useful routines and add the following function:

```
import os

def get_imlist(path):
  """ Returns a list of filenames for
    all jpg images in a directory. """

  return [os.path.join(path,f) for f in os.listdir(path) if f.endswith('.jpg')]
```

Now, back to PIL.

Create Thumbnails

Using PIL to create thumbnails is very simple. The **thumbnail()** method takes a tuple specifying the new size and converts the image to a thumbnail image with size that fits within the tuple. To create a thumbnail with longest side 128 pixels, use the method like this:

```
pil_im.thumbnail((128,128))
```

Copy and Paste Regions

Cropping a region from an image is done using the `crop()` method:

```
box = (100,100,400,400)
region = pil_im.crop(box)
```

The region is defined by a 4-tuple, where coordinates are (left, upper, right, lower). PIL uses a coordinate system with (0, 0) in the upper left corner. The extracted region can, for example, be rotated and then put back using the `paste()` method like this:

```
region = region.transpose(Image.ROTATE_180)
pil_im.paste(region,box)
```

Resize and Rotate

To resize an image, call `resize()` with a tuple giving the new size:

```
out = pil_im.resize((128,128))
```

To rotate an image, use counterclockwise angles and `rotate()` like this:

```
out = pil_im.rotate(45)
```

Some examples are shown in Figure 1-1. The leftmost image is the original, followed by a grayscale version, a rotated crop pasted in, and a thumbnail image.

1.2 Matplotlib

When working with mathematics and plotting graphs or drawing points, lines, and curves on images, `Matplotlib` is a good graphics library with much more powerful features than the plotting available in PIL. `Matplotlib` produces high-quality figures like many of the illustrations used in this book. `Matplotlib`'s `PyLab` interface is the set of functions that allows the user to create plots. `Matplotlib` is open source and available freely from *http://matplotlib.sourceforge.net/*, where detailed documentation and tutorials are available. Here are some examples showing most of the functions we will need in this book.

Plotting Images, Points, and Lines

Although it is possible to create nice bar plots, pie charts, scatter plots, etc., only a few commands are needed for most computer vision purposes. Most importantly, we want to be able to show things like interest points, correspondences, and detected objects using points and lines. Here is an example of plotting an image with a few points and a line:

```
from PIL import Image
from pylab import *

# read image to array
im = array(Image.open('empire.jpg'))

# plot the image
imshow(im)

# some points
x = [100,100,400,400]
y = [200,500,200,500]

# plot the points with red star-markers
plot(x,y,'r*')

# line plot connecting the first two points
plot(x[:2],y[:2])

# add title and show the plot
title('Plotting: "empire.jpg"')
show()
```

This plots the image, then four points with red star markers at the x and y coordinates given by the *x* and *y* lists, and finally draws a line (blue by default) between the two first points in these lists. Figure 1-2 shows the result. The show() command starts the figure GUI and raises the figure windows. This GUI loop blocks your scripts and they are paused until the last figure window is closed. You should call show() only once per script, usually at the end. Note that PyLab uses a coordinate origin at the top left corner as is common for images. The axes are useful for debugging, but if you want a prettier plot, add:

```
axis('off')
```

This will give a plot like the one on the right in Figure 1-2 instead.

There are many options for formatting color and styles when plotting. The most useful are the short commands shown in Tables 1-1, 1-2 and 1-3. Use them like this:

```
plot(x,y) # default blue solid line

plot(x,y,'r*') # red star-markers

plot(x,y,'go-') # green line with circle-markers

plot(x,y,'ks:') # black dotted line with square-markers
```

Image Contours and Histograms

Let's look at two examples of special plots: image contours and image histograms. Visualizing image iso-contours (or iso-contours of other 2D functions) can be very

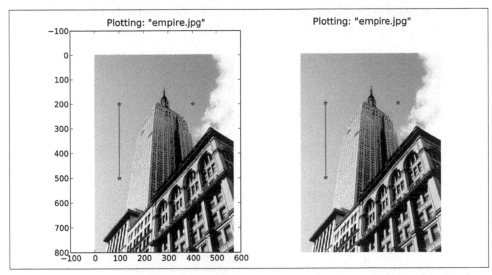

Figure 1-2. Examples of plotting with Matplotlib. *An image with points and a line with and without showing the axes.*

Table 1-1. Basic color formatting commands for plotting with PyLab.

Color	
'b'	blue
'g'	green
'r'	red
'c'	cyan
'm'	magenta
'y'	yellow
'k'	black
'w'	white

Table 1-2. Basic line style formatting commands for plotting with PyLab.

Line style	
'-'	solid
'- -'	dashed
':'	dotted

Table 1-3. Basic plot marker formatting commands for plotting with PyLab.

Marker	
'.'	point
'o'	circle
's'	square
'*'	star
'+'	plus
'x'	x

useful. This needs grayscale images, because the contours need to be taken on a single value for every coordinate [*x*, *y*]. Here's how to do it:

```
from PIL import Image
from pylab import *

# read image to array
im = array(Image.open('empire.jpg').convert('L'))

# create a new figure
figure()
# don't use colors
gray()
# show contours with origin upper left corner
contour(im, origin='image')
axis('equal')
axis('off')
```

As before, the PIL method convert() does conversion to grayscale.

An image histogram is a plot showing the distribution of pixel values. A number of bins is specified for the span of values and each bin gets a count of how many pixels have values in the bin's range. The visualization of the (graylevel) image histogram is done using the hist() function:

```
figure()
hist(im.flatten(),128)
show()
```

The second argument specifies the number of bins to use. Note that the image needs to be flattened first, because hist() takes a one-dimensional array as input. The method flatten() converts any array to a one-dimensional array with values taken row-wise. Figure 1-3 shows the contour and histogram plot.

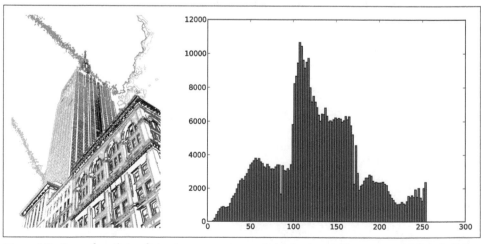

Figure 1-3. Examples of visualizing image contours and plotting image histograms with Matplotlib.

Interactive Annotation

Sometimes users need to interact with an application, for example by marking points in an image, or you need to annotate some training data. PyLab comes with a simple function, ginput(), that lets you do just that. Here's a short example:

```
from PIL import Image
from pylab import *

im = array(Image.open('empire.jpg'))
imshow(im)
print 'Please click 3 points'
x = ginput(3)
print 'you clicked:',x
show()
```

This plots an image and waits for the user to click three times in the image region of the figure window. The coordinates $[x, y]$ of the clicks are saved in a list x.

1.3 NumPy

NumPy (*http://www.scipy.org/NumPy/*) is a package popularly used for scientific computing with Python. NumPy contains a number of useful concepts such as array objects (for representing vectors, matrices, images and much more) and linear algebra functions. The NumPy array object will be used in almost all examples throughout this book.[1] The array object lets you do important operations such as matrix multiplication, transposition, solving equation systems, vector multiplication, and normalization, which are needed to do things like aligning images, warping images, modeling variations, classifying images, grouping images, and so on.

NumPy is freely available from *http://www.scipy.org/Download* and the online documentation (*http://docs.scipy.org/doc/numpy/*) contains answers to most questions. For more details on NumPy, the freely available book [24] is a good reference.

Array Image Representation

When we loaded images in the previous examples, we converted them to NumPy array objects with the **array()** call but didn't mention what that means. Arrays in NumPy are multi-dimensional and can represent vectors, matrices, and images. An array is much like a list (or list of lists) but is restricted to having all elements of the same type. Unless specified on creation, the type will automatically be set depending on the data.

The following example illustrates this for images:

```
im = array(Image.open('empire.jpg'))
print im.shape, im.dtype

im = array(Image.open('empire.jpg').convert('L'),'f')
print im.shape, im.dtype
```

---

[1] PyLab actually includes some components of NumPy, like the array type. That's why we could use it in the examples in Section 1.2.

The printout in your console will look like this:

```
(800, 569, 3) uint8
(800, 569) float32
```

The first tuple on each line is the shape of the image array (rows, columns, color channels), and the following string is the data type of the array elements. Images are usually encoded with unsigned 8-bit integers (uint8), so loading this image and converting to an array gives the type "uint8" in the first case. The second case does grayscale conversion and creates the array with the extra argument "f". This is a short command for setting the type to floating point. For more data type options, see [24]. Note that the grayscale image has only two values in the shape tuple; obviously it has no color information.

Elements in the array are accessed with indexes. The value at coordinates i, j and color channel k are accessed like this:

```
value = im[i,j,k]
```

Multiple elements can be accessed using array slicing. *Slicing* returns a view into the array specified by intervals. Here are some examples for a grayscale image:

```
im[i,:] = im[j,:]       # set the values of row i with values from row j
im[:,i] = 100           # set all values in column i to 100
im[:100,:50].sum()      # the sum of the values of the first 100 rows and 50 columns
im[50:100,50:100]       # rows 50-100, columns 50-100 (100th not included)
im[i].mean()            # average of row i
im[:,-1]                # last column
im[-2,:] (or im[-2])    # second to last row
```

Note the example with only one index. If you only use one index, it is interpreted as the row index. Note also the last examples. Negative indices count from the last element backward. We will frequently use slicing to access pixel values, and it is an important concept to understand.

There are many operations and ways to use arrays. We will introduce them as they are needed throughout this book. See the online documentation or the book [24] for more explanations.

Graylevel Transforms

After reading images to NumPy arrays, we can perform any mathematical operation we like on them. A simple example of this is to transform the graylevels of an image. Take any function f that maps the interval $0 \ldots 255$ (or, if you like, $0 \ldots 1$) to itself (meaning that the output has the same range as the input). Here are some examples:

```
from PIL import Image
from numpy import *

im = array(Image.open('empire.jpg').convert('L'))

im2 = 255 - im # invert image
```

```
im3 = (100.0/255) * im + 100 # clamp to interval 100...200

im4 = 255.0 * (im/255.0)**2 # squared
```

The first example inverts the graylevels of the image, the second one clamps the intensities to the interval 100 . . . 200, and the third applies a quadratic function, which lowers the values of the darker pixels. Figure 1-4 shows the functions and Figure 1-5 the resulting images. You can check the minimum and maximum values of each image using:

```
print int(im.min()), int(im.max())
```

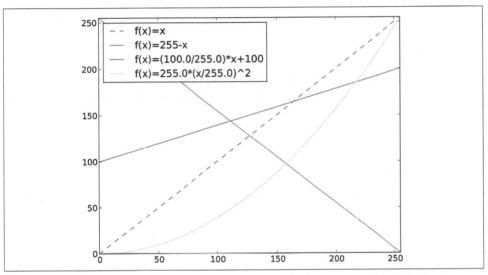

Figure 1-4. Example of graylevel transforms. Three example functions together with the identity transform showed as a dashed line.

Figure 1-5. Graylevel transforms. Applying the functions in Figure 1-4: Inverting the image with $f(x) = 255 - x$ (left), clamping the image with $f(x) = (100/255)x + 100$ (middle), quadratic transformation with $f(x) = 255(x/255)^2$ (right).

If you try that for each of the examples above, you should get the following output:

```
2 255
0 253
100 200
0 255
```

The reverse of the `array()` transformation can be done using the PIL function `fromarray()` as:

```
pil_im = Image.fromarray(im)
```

If you did some operation to change the type from "uint8" to another data type, such as *im3* or *im4* in the example above, you need to convert back before creating the PIL image:

```
pil_im = Image.fromarray(uint8(im))
```

If you are not absolutely sure of the type of the input, you should do this as it is the safe choice. Note that NumPy will always change the array type to the "lowest" type that can represent the data. Multiplication or division with floating point numbers will change an integer type array to float.

Image Resizing

NumPy arrays will be our main tool for working with images and data. There is no simple way to resize arrays, which you will want to do for images. We can use the PIL image object conversion shown earlier to make a simple image resizing function. Add the following to *imtools.py*:

```
def imresize(im,sz):
    """ Resize an image array using PIL. """
    pil_im = Image.fromarray(uint8(im))

    return array(pil_im.resize(sz))
```

This function will come in handy later.

Histogram Equalization

A very useful example of a graylevel transform is *histogram equalization*. This transform flattens the graylevel histogram of an image so that all intensities are as equally common as possible. This is often a good way to normalize image intensity before further processing and also a way to increase image contrast.

The transform function is, in this case, a *cumulative distribution function* (cdf) of the pixel values in the image (normalized to map the range of pixel values to the desired range).

Here's how to do it. Add this function to the file *imtools.py*:

```
def histeq(im,nbr_bins=256):
    """ Histogram equalization of a grayscale image. """
```

```
# get image histogram
imhist,bins = histogram(im.flatten(),nbr_bins,normed=True)
cdf = imhist.cumsum() # cumulative distribution function
cdf = 255 * cdf / cdf[-1] # normalize

# use linear interpolation of cdf to find new pixel values
im2 = interp(im.flatten(),bins[:-1],cdf)

return im2.reshape(im.shape), cdf
```

The function takes a grayscale image and the number of bins to use in the histogram as input, and returns an image with equalized histogram together with the cumulative distribution function used to do the mapping of pixel values. Note the use of the last element (index -1) of the cdf to normalize it between 0 . . . 1. Try this on an image like this:

```
from PIL import Image
from numpy import *

im = array(Image.open('AquaTermi_lowcontrast.jpg').convert('L'))
im2,cdf = imtools.histeq(im)
```

Figures 1-6 and 1-7 show examples of histogram equalization. The top row shows the graylevel histogram before and after equalization together with the cdf mapping. As you can see, the contrast increases and the details of the dark regions now appear clearly.

Averaging Images

Averaging images is a simple way of reducing image noise and is also often used for artistic effects. Computing an average image from a list of images is not difficult. Assuming the images all have the same size, we can compute the average of all those images by simply summing them up and dividing with the number of images. Add the following function to *imtools.py*:

```
def compute_average(imlist):
    """ Compute the average of a list of images. """

    # open first image and make into array of type float
    averageim = array(Image.open(imlist[0]), 'f')

    for imname in imlist[1:]:
        try:
            averageim += array(Image.open(imname))
        except:
            print imname + '...skipped'
    averageim /= len(imlist)

    # return average as uint8
    return array(averageim, 'uint8')
```

This includes some basic exception handling to skip images that can't be opened. There is another way to compute average images using the mean() function. This requires all images to be stacked into an array and will use lots of memory if there are many images. We will use this function in the next section.

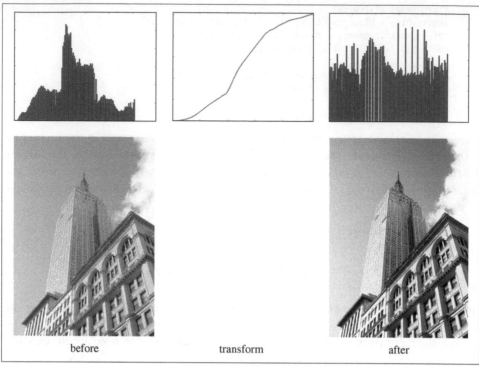

Figure 1-6. Example of histogram equalization. On the left is the original image and histogram. The middle plot is the graylevel transform function. On the right is the image and histogram after histogram equalization.

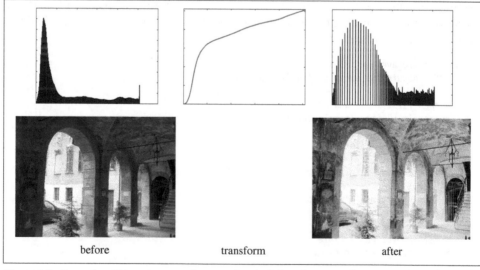

Figure 1-7. Example of histogram equalization. On the left is the original image and histogram. The middle plot is the graylevel transform function. On the right is the image and histogram after histogram equalization.

PCA of Images

Principal Component Analysis (PCA) is a useful technique for dimensionality reduction and is optimal in the sense that it represents the variability of the training data with as few dimensions as possible. Even a tiny 100×100 pixel grayscale image has 10,000 dimensions, and can be considered a point in a 10,000-dimensional space. A megapixel image has dimensions in the millions. With such high dimensionality, it is no surprise that dimensionality reduction comes in handy in many computer vision applications. The projection matrix resulting from PCA can be seen as a change of coordinates to a coordinate system where the coordinates are in descending order of importance.

To apply PCA on image data, the images need to be converted to a one-dimensional vector representation using, for example, NumPy's `flatten()` method.

The flattened images are collected in a single matrix by stacking them, one row for each image. The rows are then centered relative to the mean image before the computation of the dominant directions. To find the principal components, singular value decomposition (SVD) is usually used, but if the dimensionality is high, there is a useful trick that can be used instead since the SVD computation will be very slow in that case. Here is what it looks like in code:

```
from PIL import Image
from numpy import *

def pca(X):
  """ Principal Component Analysis
    input: X, matrix with training data stored as flattened arrays in rows
    return: projection matrix (with important dimensions first), variance
    and mean. """

  # get dimensions
  num_data,dim = X.shape

  # center data
  mean_X = X.mean(axis=0)
  X = X - mean_X

  if dim>num_data:
    # PCA - compact trick used
    M = dot(X,X.T) # covariance matrix
    e,EV = linalg.eigh(M) # eigenvalues and eigenvectors
    tmp = dot(X.T,EV).T # this is the compact trick
    V = tmp[::-1] # reverse since last eigenvectors are the ones we want
    S = sqrt(e)[::-1] # reverse since eigenvalues are in increasing order
    for i in range(V.shape[1]):
      V[:,i] /= S
  else:
    # PCA - SVD used
    U,S,V = linalg.svd(X)
    V = V[:num_data] # only makes sense to return the first num_data

  # return the projection matrix, the variance and the mean
  return V,S,mean_X
```

This function first centers the data by subtracting the mean in each dimension. Then the eigenvectors corresponding to the largest eigenvalues of the covariance matrix are computed, either using a compact trick or using SVD. Here we used the function range(), which takes an integer n and returns a list of integers $0 \ldots (n - 1)$. Feel free to use the alternative arange(), which gives an array, or xrange(), which gives a generator (and might give speed improvements). We will stick with range() throughout the book.

We switch from SVD to use a trick with computing eigenvectors of the (smaller) covariance matrix $X X^T$ if the number of data points is less than the dimension of the vectors. There are also ways of only computing the eigenvectors corresponding to the k largest eigenvalues (k being the number of desired dimensions), making it even faster. We leave this to the interested reader to explore, since it is really outside the scope of this book. The rows of the matrix V are orthogonal and contain the coordinate directions in order of descending variance of the training data.

Let's try this on an example of font images. The file *fontimages.zip* contains small thumbnail images of the character "a" printed in different fonts and then scanned. The 2,359 fonts are from a collection of freely available fonts.[2] Assuming that the filenames of these images are stored in a list, *imlist*, along with the previous code, in a file *pca.py*, the principal components can be computed and shown like this:

```
from PIL import Image
from numpy import *
from pylab import *
import pca

im = array(Image.open(imlist[0])) # open one image to get size
m,n = im.shape[0:2] # get the size of the images
imnbr = len(imlist) # get the number of images

# create matrix to store all flattened images
immatrix = array([array(Image.open(im)).flatten()
            for im in imlist],'f')

# perform PCA
V,S,immean = pca.pca(immatrix)

# show some images (mean and 7 first modes)
figure()
gray()
subplot(2,4,1)
imshow(immean.reshape(m,n))
for i in range(7):
  subplot(2,4,i+2)
  imshow(V[i].reshape(m,n))

show()
```

[2] Images courtesy of Martin Solli (*http://webstaff.itn.liu.se/~marso/*) collected and rendered from publicly available free fonts.

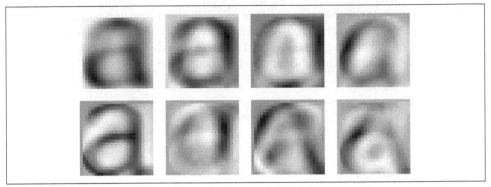

Figure 1-8. The mean image (top left) and the first seven modes; that is, the directions with most variation.

Note that the images need to be converted back from the one-dimensional representation using reshape(). Running the example should give eight images in one figure window like the ones in Figure 1-8. Here we used the PyLab function subplot() to place multiple plots in one window.

Using the Pickle Module

If you want to save some results or data for later use, the pickle module, which comes with Python, is very useful. Pickle can take almost any Python object and convert it to a string representation. This process is called *pickling*. Reconstructing the object from the string representation is conversely called *unpickling*. This string representation can then be easily stored or transmitted.

Let's illustrate this with an example. Suppose we want to save the image mean and principal components of the font images in the previous section. This is done like this:

```
# save mean and principal components
f = open('font_pca_modes.pkl', 'wb')
pickle.dump(immean,f)
pickle.dump(V,f)
f.close()
```

As you can see, several objects can be pickled to the same file. There are several different protocols available for the *.pkl* files, and if unsure, it is best to read and write binary files. To load the data in some other Python session, just use the load() method like this:

```
# load mean and principal components
f = open('font_pca_modes.pkl', 'rb')
immean = pickle.load(f)
V = pickle.load(f)
f.close()
```

Note that the order of the objects should be the same! There is also an optimized version written in C called cpickle that is fully compatible with the standard pickle module. More details can be found on the pickle module documentation page *http://docs.python.org/library/pickle.html*.

For the remainder of this book, we will use the `with` statement to handle file reading and writing. This is a construct that was introduced in Python 2.5 that automatically handles opening and closing of files (even if errors occur while the files are open). Here is what the saving and loading above looks like using `with()`:

```
# open file and save
with open('font_pca_modes.pkl', 'wb') as f:
    pickle.dump(immean,f)
    pickle.dump(V,f)
```

and:

```
# open file and load
with open('font_pca_modes.pkl', 'rb') as f:
    immean = pickle.load(f)
    V = pickle.load(f)
```

This might look strange the first time you see it, but it is a very useful construct. If you don't like it, just use the `open` and `close` functions as above.

As an alternative to using pickle, NumPy also has simple functions for reading and writing text files that can be useful if your data does not contain complicated structures, for example a list of points clicked in an image. To save an array x to file, use:

```
savetxt('test.txt',x,'%i')
```

The last parameter indicates that integer format should be used. Similarly, reading is done like this:

```
x = loadtxt('test.txt')
```

You can find out more from the online documentation *http://docs.scipy.org/doc/numpy/ reference/generated/numpy.loadtxt.html*.

Finally, NumPy has dedicated functions for saving and loading arrays. Look for `save()` and `load()` in the online documentation for the details.

1.4 SciPy

SciPy (*http://scipy.org/*) is an open-source package for mathematics that builds on NumPy and provides efficient routines for a number of operations, including numerical integration, optimization, statistics, signal processing, and most importantly for us, image processing. As the following will show, there are many useful modules in SciPy. SciPy is free and available at *http://scipy.org/Download*.

Blurring Images

A classic and very useful example of image convolution is *Gaussian blurring* of images. In essence, the (grayscale) image I is convolved with a Gaussian kernel to create a blurred version

$$I_\sigma = I * G_\sigma,$$

where * indicates convolution and G_σ is a Gaussian 2D-kernel with standard deviation σ defined as

$$G_\sigma = \frac{1}{2\pi\sigma}e^{-(x^2+y^2)/2\sigma^2}.$$

Gaussian blurring is used to define an image scale to work in, for interpolation, for computing interest points, and in many more applications.

SciPy comes with a module for filtering called `scipy.ndimage.filters` that can be used to compute these convolutions using a fast 1D separation. All you need to do is this:

```
from PIL import Image
from numpy import *
from scipy.ndimage import filters

im = array(Image.open('empire.jpg').convert('L'))
im2 = filters.gaussian_filter(im,5)
```

Here the last parameter of `gaussian_filter()` is the standard deviation.

Figure 1-9 shows examples of an image blurred with increasing σ. Larger values give less detail. To blur color images, simply apply Gaussian blurring to each color channel:

```
im = array(Image.open('empire.jpg'))
im2 = zeros(im.shape)
for i in range(3):
    im2[:,:,i] = filters.gaussian_filter(im[:,:,i],5)
im2 = uint8(im2)
```

Here the last conversion to "uint8" is not always needed but forces the pixel values to be in 8-bit representation. We could also have used

```
im2 = array(im2,'uint8')
```

for the conversion.

Figure 1-9. An example of Gaussian blurring using the `scipy.ndimage.filters` module: (a) original image in grayscale; (b) Gaussian filter with $\sigma = 2$; (c) with $\sigma = 5$; (d) with $\sigma = 10$.

For more information on using this module and the different parameter choices, check out the SciPy documentation of scipy.ndimage at *http://docs.scipy.org/doc/scipy/ reference/ndimage.html*.

Image Derivatives

How the image intensity changes over the image is important information and is used for many applications, as we will see throughout this book. The intensity change is described with the x and y derivatives I_x and I_y of the graylevel image I (for color images, derivatives are usually taken for each color channel).

The *image gradient* is the vector $\nabla I = [I_x, \ I_y]^T$. The gradient has two important properties, the *gradient magnitude*

$$|\nabla I| = \sqrt{I_x^2 + I_y^2},$$

which describes how strong the image intensity change is, and the *gradient angle*

$$\alpha = \arctan2(I_y, I_x),$$

which indicates the direction of largest intensity change at each point (pixel) in the image. The NumPy function arctan2() returns the signed angle in radians, in the interval $-\pi \ldots \pi$.

Computing the image derivatives can be done using discrete approximations. These are most easily implemented as convolutions

$$I_x = I * D_x \text{ and } I_y = I * D_y.$$

Two common choices for D_x and D_y are the *Prewitt filters*

$$D_x = \begin{bmatrix} -1 & 0 & 1 \\ -1 & 0 & 1 \\ -1 & 0 & 1 \end{bmatrix} \text{ and } D_y = \begin{bmatrix} -1 & -1 & -1 \\ 0 & 0 & 0 \\ 1 & 1 & 1 \end{bmatrix},$$

and *Sobel filters*

$$D_x = \begin{bmatrix} -1 & 0 & 1 \\ -2 & 0 & 2 \\ -1 & 0 & 1 \end{bmatrix} \text{ and } D_y = \begin{bmatrix} -1 & -2 & -1 \\ 0 & 0 & 0 \\ 1 & 2 & 1 \end{bmatrix}.$$

These derivative filters are easy to implement using the standard convolution available in the scipy.ndimage.filters module. For example:

```
from PIL import Image
from numpy import *
from scipy.ndimage import filters

im = array(Image.open('empire.jpg').convert('L'))
```

```
# Sobel derivative filters
imx = zeros(im.shape)
filters.sobel(im,1,imx)

imy = zeros(im.shape)
filters.sobel(im,0,imy)

magnitude = sqrt(imx**2+imy**2)
```

This computes x and y derivatives and gradient magnitude using the *Sobel filter*. The second argument selects the x or y derivative, and the third stores the output. Figure 1-10 shows an image with derivatives computed using the Sobel filter. In the two derivative images, positive derivatives are shown with bright pixels and negative derivatives are dark. Gray areas have values close to zero.

Using this approach has the drawback that derivatives are taken on the scale determined by the image resolution. To be more robust to image noise and to compute derivatives at any scale, *Gaussian derivative filters* can be used:

$$I_x = I * G_{\sigma x} \ \text{ and } \ I_y = I * G_{\sigma y},$$

where $G_{\sigma x}$ and $G_{\sigma y}$ are the x and y derivatives of G_σ, a Gaussian function with standard deviation σ.

The `filters.gaussian_filter()` function we used for blurring earlier can also take extra arguments to compute Gaussian derivatives instead. To try this on an image, simply do:

```
sigma = 5 # standard deviation

imx = zeros(im.shape)
filters.gaussian_filter(im, (sigma,sigma), (0,1), imx)

imy = zeros(im.shape)
filters.gaussian_filter(im, (sigma,sigma), (1,0), imy)
```

The third argument specifies which order of derivatives to use in each direction using the standard deviation determined by the second argument. See the documentation

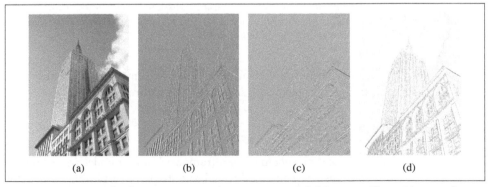

(a)   (b)   (c)   (d)

Figure 1-10. An example of computing image derivatives using Sobel derivative filters: (a) original image in grayscale; (b) x-derivative; (c) y-derivative; (d) gradient magnitude.

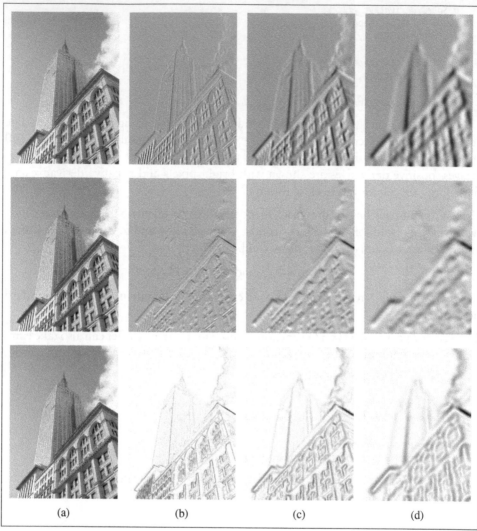

(a)   (b)   (c)   (d)

Figure 1-11. An example of computing image derivatives using Gaussian derivatives: x-derivative (top), y-derivative (middle), and gradient magnitude (bottom); (a) original image in grayscale, (b) Gaussian derivative filter with $\sigma = 2$, (c) with $\sigma = 5$, (d) with $\sigma = 10$.

for the details. Figure 1-11 shows the derivatives and gradient magnitude for different scales. Compare this to the blurring at the same scales in Figure 1-9.

Morphology—Counting Objects

Morphology (or *mathematical morphology*) is a framework and a collection of image processing methods for measuring and analyzing basic shapes. Morphology is usually applied to binary images but can be used with grayscale also. A *binary image* is an image in which each pixel takes only two values, usually 0 and 1. Binary images are often the result of thresholding an image, for example with the intention of counting objects or measuring their size. A good summary of morphology and how it works is in *http://en.wikipedia.org/wiki/Mathematical_morphology*.

Morphological operations are included in the `scipy.ndimage` module `morphology`. Counting and measurement functions for binary images are in the `scipy.ndimage` module `measurements`. Let's look at a simple example of how to use them.

Consider the binary image in Figure 1-12a.[3] Counting the objects in that image can be done using:

```
from scipy.ndimage import measurements,morphology

# load image and threshold to make sure it is binary
im = array(Image.open('houses.png').convert('L'))
im = 1*(im<128)

labels, nbr_objects = measurements.label(im)
print "Number of objects:", nbr_objects
```

This loads the image and makes sure it is binary by thresholding. Multiplying by 1 converts the boolean array to a binary one. Then the function `label()` finds the individual objects and assigns integer labels to pixels according to which object they belong to. Figure 1-12b shows the *labels* array. The graylevel values indicate object index. As you can see, there are small connections between some of the objects. Using an operation called binary opening, we can remove them:

```
# morphology - opening to separate objects better
im_open = morphology.binary_opening(im,ones((9,5)),iterations=2)

labels_open, nbr_objects_open = measurements.label(im_open)
print "Number of objects:", nbr_objects_open
```

The second argument of `binary_opening()` specifies the *structuring element*, an array that indicates what neighbors to use when centered around a pixel. In this case, we used 9 pixels (4 above, the pixel itself, and 4 below) in the y direction and 5 in the x direction. You can specify any array as structuring element; the non-zero elements will determine the neighbors. The parameter *iterations* determines how many times to apply the operation. Try this and see how the number of objects changes. The image after opening and the corresponding label image are shown in Figure 1-12c–d. As you might expect, there is a function named `binary_closing()` that does the reverse. We leave that and the other functions in `morphology` and `measurements` to the exercises. You can learn more about them from the `scipy.ndimage` documentation *http://docs.scipy.org/doc/scipy/reference/ndimage.html*.

---

[3] This image is actually the result of image "segmentation." Take a look at Section 9.3 if you want to see how this image was created.

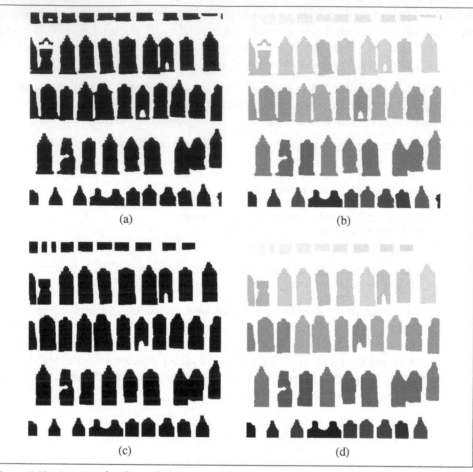

Figure 1-12. An example of morphology. Binary opening to separate objects followed by counting them: (a) original binary image; (b) label image corresponding to the original, grayvalues indicate object index; (c) binary image after opening; (d) label image corresponding to the opened image.

Useful SciPy Modules

SciPy comes with some useful modules for input and output. Two of them are `io` and `misc`.

Reading and writing .mat files

If you have some data, or find some interesting data set online, stored in Matlab's *.mat* file format, it is possible to read this using the `scipy.io` module. This is how to do it:

```
data = scipy.io.loadmat('test.mat')
```

The object *data* now contains a dictionary with keys corresponding to the variable names saved in the original *.mat* file. The variables are in array format. Saving to *.mat* files is equally simple. Just create a dictionary with all variables you want to save and use `savemat()`:

```
data = {}
data['x'] = x
scipy.io.savemat('test.mat',data)
```

This saves the array x so that it has the name "x" when read into Matlab. More information on `scipy.io` can be found in the online documentation, *http://docs.scipy .org/doc/scipy/reference/io.html*.

Saving arrays as images

Since we are manipulating images and doing computations using array objects, it is useful to be able to save them directly as image files.[4] Many images in this book are created just like this.

The `imsave()` function is available through the `scipy.misc` module. To save an array *im* to file just do the following:

```
from scipy.misc import imsave
imsave('test.jpg',im)
```

The `scipy.misc` module also contains the famous "Lena" test image:

```
lena = scipy.misc.lena()
```

This will give you a 512 × 512 grayscale array version of the image.

1.5 Advanced Example: Image De-Noising

We conclude this chapter with a very useful example, de-noising of images. Image *de-noising* is the process of removing image noise while at the same time trying to preserve details and structures. We will use the *Rudin-Osher-Fatemi de-noising model* (ROF) originally introduced in [28]. Removing noise from images is important for many applications, from making your holiday photos look better to improving the quality of satellite images. The ROF model has the interesting property that it finds a smoother version of the image while preserving edges and structures.

The underlying mathematics of the ROF model and the solution techniques are quite advanced and outside the scope of this book. We'll give a brief, simplified introduction before showing how to implement a ROF solver based on an algorithm by Chambolle [5].

The *total variation* (*TV*) of a (grayscale) image I is defined as the sum of the gradient norm. In a continuous representation, this is

$$J(I) = \int |\nabla I| d\mathbf{x}. \tag{1.1}$$

---

[4] All `PyLab` figures can be saved in a multitude of image formats by clicking the "save" button in the figure window.

In a discrete setting, the total variation becomes

$$J(I) = \sum_{\mathbf{x}} |\nabla I|,$$

where the sum is taken over all image coordinates $\mathbf{x} = [x, y]$.

In the Chambolle version of ROF, the goal is to find a de-noised image U that minimizes

$$\min_{U} \ ||I - U||^2 + 2\lambda J(U),$$

where the norm $||I - U||$ measures the difference between U and the original image I. What this means is, in essence, that the model looks for images that are "flat" but allows "jumps" at edges between regions.

Following the recipe in the paper, here's the code:

```python
from numpy import *

def denoise(im,U_init,tolerance=0.1,tau=0.125,tv_weight=100):
    """ An implementation of the Rudin-Osher-Fatemi (ROF) denoising model
        using the numerical procedure presented in eq (11) A. Chambolle (2005).

        Input: noisy input image (grayscale), initial guess for U, weight of
        the TV-regularizing term, steplength, tolerance for stop criterion.

        Output: denoised and detextured image, texture residual. """

    m,n = im.shape # size of noisy image

    # initialize
    U = U_init
    Px = im # x-component to the dual field
    Py = im # y-component of the dual field
    error = 1

    while (error > tolerance):
        Uold = U

        # gradient of primal variable
        GradUx = roll(U,-1,axis=1)-U # x-component of U's gradient
        GradUy = roll(U,-1,axis=0)-U # y-component of U's gradient

        # update the dual varible
        PxNew = Px + (tau/tv_weight)*GradUx
        PyNew = Py + (tau/tv_weight)*GradUy
        NormNew = maximum(1,sqrt(PxNew**2+PyNew**2))

        Px = PxNew/NormNew # update of x-component (dual)
        Py = PyNew/NormNew # update of y-component (dual)

        # update the primal variable
        RxPx = roll(Px,1,axis=1) # right x-translation of x-component
        RyPy = roll(Py,1,axis=0) # right y-translation of y-component

        DivP = (Px-RxPx)+(Py-RyPy) # divergence of the dual field.
```

```
    U = im + tv_weight*DivP # update of the primal variable

    # update of error
    error = linalg.norm(U-Uold)/sqrt(n*m);

    return U,im-U # denoised image and texture residual
```

In this example, we used the function `roll()`, which, as the name suggests, "rolls" the values of an array cyclically around an axis. This is very convenient for computing neighbor differences, in this case for derivatives. We also used `linalg.norm()`, which measures the difference between two arrays (in this case, the image matrices *U* and *Uold*). Save the function `denoise()` in a file *rof.py*.

Let's start with a synthetic example of a noisy image:

```
from numpy import *
from numpy import random
from scipy.ndimage import filters
import rof

# create synthetic image with noise
im = zeros((500,500))
im[100:400,100:400] = 128
im[200:300,200:300] = 255
im = im + 30*random.standard_normal((500,500))

U,T = rof.denoise(im,im)
G = filters.gaussian_filter(im,10)

# save the result
from scipy.misc import imsave
imsave('synth_rof.pdf',U)
imsave('synth_gaussian.pdf',G)
```

The resulting images are shown in Figure 1-13 together with the original. As you can see, the ROF version preserves the edges nicely.

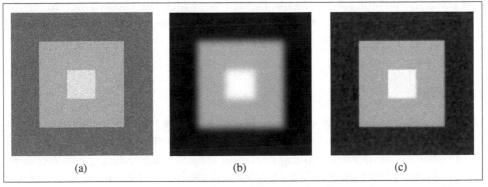

(a)   (b)   (c)

Figure 1-13. An example of ROF de-noising of a synthetic example: (a) original noisy image; (b) image after Gaussian blurring ($\sigma = 10$); (c) image after ROF de-noising.

(a)   (b)   (c)

Figure 1-14. An example of ROF de-noising of a grayscale image: (a) original image; (b) image after Gaussian blurring ($\sigma = 5$); (c) image after ROF de-noising.

Now, let's see what happens with a real image:

```
from PIL import Image
from pylab import *
import rof

im = array(Image.open('empire.jpg').convert('L'))
U,T = rof.denoise(im,im)

figure()
gray()
imshow(U)
axis('equal')
axis('off')
show()
```

The result should look something like Figure 1-14c, which also shows a blurred version of the same image for comparison. As you can see, ROF de-noising preserves edges and image structures while at the same time blurring out the "noise."

Exercises

1. Take an image and apply Gaussian blur like in Figure 1-9. Plot the image contours for increasing values of σ. What happens? Can you explain why?

2. Implement an *unsharp masking* operation (*http://en.wikipedia.org/wiki/Unsharp_masking*) by blurring an image and then subtracting the blurred version from the original. This gives a sharpening effect to the image. Try this on both color and grayscale images.

3. An alternative image normalization to histogram equalization is a *quotient image*. A quotient image is obtained by dividing the image with a blurred version $I/(I * G_\sigma)$. Implement this and try it on some sample images.

4. Write a function that finds the outline of simple objects in images (for example, a square against white background) using image gradients.

5. Use gradient direction and magnitude to detect lines in an image. Estimate the extent of the lines and their parameters. Plot the lines overlaid on the image.

6. Apply the `label()` function to a thresholded image of your choice. Use histograms and the resulting label image to plot the distribution of object sizes in the image.

7. Experiment with successive morphological operations on a thresholded image of your choice. When you have found some settings that produce good results, try the function `center_of_mass` in `morphology` to find the center coordinates of each object and plot them in the image.

Conventions for the Code Examples

From Chapter 2 and onward, we assume PIL, NumPy, and Matplotlib are included at the top of every file you create and in every code example as:

```
from PIL import Image
from numpy import *
from pylab import *
```

This makes the example code cleaner and the presentation easier to follow. In the cases when we use SciPy modules, we will explicitly declare that in the examples.

Purists will object to this type of blanket imports and insist on something like

```
import numpy as np
import matplotlib.pyplot as plt
```

so that namespaces can be kept (to know where each function comes from) and only import the pyplot part of Matplotlib, since the NumPy parts imported with PyLab are not needed. Purists and experienced programmers know the difference and can choose whichever option they prefer. In the interest of making the content and examples in this book easily accessible to readers, I have chosen not to do this.

Caveat emptor.

## CHAPTER 2

Local Image Descriptors

This chapter is about finding corresponding points and regions between images. Two different types of local descriptors are introduced with methods for matching these between images. These local features will be used in many different contexts throughout this book and are an important building block in many applications, such as creating panoramas, augmented reality, and computing 3D reconstructions.

2.1 Harris Corner Detector

The *Harris corner detection* algorithm (or sometimes the Harris & Stephens corner detector) is one of the simplest corner indicators available. The general idea is to locate interest points where the surrounding neighborhood shows edges in more than one direction; these are then image corners.

We define a matrix $\mathbf{M}_I = \mathbf{M}_I(\mathbf{x})$, on the points $\mathbf{x}$ in the image domain, as the positive semi-definite, symmetric matrix

$$\mathbf{M}_I = \nabla I \, \nabla I^T = \begin{bmatrix} I_x \\ I_y \end{bmatrix} [\, I_x \quad I_y \,] = \begin{bmatrix} I_x^2 & I_x I_y \\ I_x I_y & I_y^2 \end{bmatrix}, \tag{2.1}$$

whereas before ∇I is the image gradient containing the derivatives I_x and I_y (we defined the derivatives and the gradient on page 18). Because of this construction, $\mathbf{M}_I$ has rank one with eigenvalues $\lambda_1 = |\nabla I|^2$ and $\lambda_2 = 0$. We now have one matrix for each pixel in the image.

Let W be a weight matrix (typically a Gaussian filter G_σ). The component-wise convolution

$$\overline{\mathbf{M}}_I = W * \mathbf{M}_I \tag{2.2}$$

gives a local averaging of $\mathbf{M}_I$ over the neighboring pixels. The resulting matrix $\overline{\mathbf{M}}_I$ is sometimes called a *Harris matrix*. The width of W determines a region of interest around $\mathbf{x}$. The idea of averaging the matrix $\mathbf{M}_I$ over a region like this is that the eigenvalues will change depending on the local image properties. If the gradients vary in the region, the second eigenvalue of $\overline{\mathbf{M}}_I$ will no longer be zero. If the gradients are the same, the eigenvalues will be the same as for $\mathbf{M}_I$.

Depending on the values of ∇I in the region, there are three cases for the eigenvalues of the Harris matrix, $\overline{\mathbf{M}}_I$:

- If λ_1 and λ_2 are both large positive values, then there is a corner at $\mathbf{x}$.
- If λ_1 is large and $\lambda_2 \approx 0$, then there is an edge and the averaging of $\mathbf{M}_I$ over the region doesn't change the eigenvalues that much.
- If $\lambda_1 \approx \lambda_2 \approx 0$, then there is nothing.

To distinguish the important case from the others without actually having to compute the eigenvalues, Harris and Stephens [12] introduced an indicator function

$$\det(\overline{\mathbf{M}}_I) - \kappa \, \text{trace}(\overline{\mathbf{M}}_I)^2.$$

To get rid of the weighting constant κ, it is often easier to use the quotient

$$\frac{\det(\overline{\mathbf{M}}_I)}{\text{trace}(\overline{\mathbf{M}}_I)^2}$$

as an indicator.

Let's see what this looks like in code. For this, we need the `scipy.ndimage.filters` module for computing derivatives using Gaussian derivative filters as described on page 18. The reason is again that we would like to suppress noise sensitivity in the corner detection process.

First, add the corner response function to a file *harris.py*, which will make use of the Gaussian derivatives. Again, the parameter σ defines the scale of the Gaussian filters used. You can also modify this function to take different scales in the x and y directions, as well as a different scale for the averaging, to compute the Harris matrix.

```
from scipy.ndimage import filters

def compute_harris_response(im,sigma=3):
    """ Compute the Harris corner detector response function
        for each pixel in a graylevel image. """

    # derivatives
    imx = zeros(im.shape)
    filters.gaussian_filter(im, (sigma,sigma), (0,1), imx)
    imy = zeros(im.shape)
    filters.gaussian_filter(im, (sigma,sigma), (1,0), imy)

    # compute components of the Harris matrix
    Wxx = filters.gaussian_filter(imx*imx,sigma)
    Wxy = filters.gaussian_filter(imx*imy,sigma)
    Wyy = filters.gaussian_filter(imy*imy,sigma)

    # determinant and trace
    Wdet = Wxx*Wyy - Wxy**2
    Wtr = Wxx + Wyy

    return Wdet / Wtr
```

This gives an image with each pixel containing the value of the Harris response function. Now, it is just a matter of picking out the information needed from this image. Taking all points with values above a threshold, with the additional constraint that corners must be separated with a minimum distance, is an approach that often gives good results. To do this, take all candidate pixels, sort them in descending order of corner response values, and mark off regions too close to positions already marked as corners. Add the following function to *harris.py*:

```python
def get_harris_points(harrisim,min_dist=10,threshold=0.1):
    """ Return corners from a Harris response image
        min_dist is the minimum number of pixels separating
        corners and image boundary. """

    # find top corner candidates above a threshold
    corner_threshold = harrisim.max() * threshold
    harrisim_t = (harrisim > corner_threshold) * 1

    # get coordinates of candidates
    coords = array(harrisim_t.nonzero()).T

    # ...and their values
    candidate_values = [harrisim[c[0],c[1]] for c in coords]

    # sort candidates
    index = argsort(candidate_values)

    # store allowed point locations in array
    allowed_locations = zeros(harrisim.shape)
    allowed_locations[min_dist:-min_dist,min_dist:-min_dist] = 1

    # select the best points taking min_distance into account
    filtered_coords = []
    for i in index:
        if allowed_locations[coords[i,0],coords[i,1]] == 1:
            filtered_coords.append(coords[i])
            allowed_locations[(coords[i,0]-min_dist):(coords[i,0]+min_dist),
                    (coords[i,1]-min_dist):(coords[i,1]+min_dist)] = 0

    return filtered_coords
```

Now you have all you need to detect corner points in images. To show the corner points in the image, you can add a plotting function to *harris.py* using `Matplotlib` as follows:

```python
def plot_harris_points(image,filtered_coords):
    """ Plots corners found in image. """

    figure()
    gray()
    imshow(image)
    plot([p[1] for p in filtered_coords],[p[0] for p in filtered_coords],'*')
    axis('off')
    show()
```

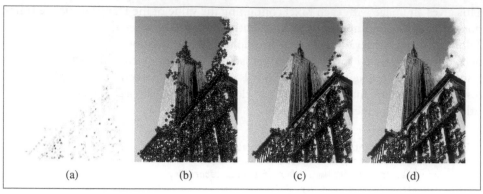

Figure 2-1. An example of corner detection with the Harris corner detector: (a) the Harris response function; (b–d) corners detected with threshold 0.01, 0.05, and 0.1, respectively.

Try running the following commands:

```
im = array(Image.open('empire.jpg').convert('L'))
harrisim = harris.compute_harris_response(im)
filtered_coords = harris.get_harris_points(harrisim,6)
harris.plot_harris_points(im, filtered_coords)
```

The image is opened and converted to grayscale. Then, the response function is computed and points selected based on the response values. Finally, the points are plotted overlaid on the original image. This should give you a plot like the images in Figure 2-1.

For an overview of different approaches to corner detection, including improvements on the Harris detector and further developments, see for example *http://en.wikipedia .org/wiki/Corner_detection*.

Finding Corresponding Points Between Images

The Harris corner detector gives interest points in images but does not contain an inherent way of comparing these interest points across images to find matching corners. What we need is to add a descriptor to each point and a way to compare such descriptors.

An *interest point descriptor* is a vector assigned to an interest point that describes the image appearance around the point. The better the descriptor, the better your correspondences will be. By *point correspondence* or *corresponding points*, we mean points in different images that refer to the same object or scene point.

Harris corner points are usually combined with a descriptor consisting of the graylevel values in a neighboring image patch together with normalized cross-correlation for comparison. An *image patch* is almost always a rectangular portion of the image centered around the point in question.

In general, *correlation* between two (equally sized) image patches $I_1(\mathbf{x})$ and $I_2(\mathbf{x})$ is defined as

$$c(I_1, I_2) = \sum_{\mathbf{x}} f(I_1(\mathbf{x}), I_2(\mathbf{x})),$$

where the function f varies depending on the correlation method. The sum is taken over all positions $\mathbf{x}$ in the image patches. For *cross-correlation*, the function is $f(I_1, I_2) = I_1 I_2$, and then $c(I_1, I_2) = I_1 \cdot I_2$, with $\cdot$ denoting the scalar product (of the row- or column-stacked patches). The larger the value of $c(I_1, I_2)$, the more similar the patches I_1 and I_2 are.[1]

Normalized cross-correlation is a variant of cross-correlation defined as

$$ncc(I_1, I_2) = \frac{1}{n-1} \sum_{\mathbf{x}} \frac{(I_1(\mathbf{x}) - \mu_1)}{\sigma_1} \cdot \frac{(I_2(\mathbf{x}) - \mu_2)}{\sigma_2}, \quad (2.3)$$

where n is the number of pixels in a patch, μ_1 and μ_2 are the mean intensities, and σ_1 and σ_2 are the standard deviations in each patch, respectively. By subtracting the mean and scaling with the standard deviation, the method becomes robust to changes in image brightness.

To extract image patches and compare them using normalized cross-correlation, you need two more functions in *harris.py*. Add these:

```python
def get_descriptors(image,filtered_coords,wid=5):
    """ For each point return, pixel values around the point
        using a neighbourhood of width 2*wid+1. (Assume points are
        extracted with min_distance > wid). """

    desc = []
    for coords in filtered_coords:
        patch = image[coords[0]-wid:coords[0]+wid+1,
                      coords[1]-wid:coords[1]+wid+1].flatten()
        desc.append(patch)

    return desc

def match(desc1,desc2,threshold=0.5):
    """ For each corner point descriptor in the first image,
        select its match to second image using
        normalized cross-correlation. """

    n = len(desc1[0])

    # pair-wise distances
    d = -ones((len(desc1),len(desc2)))
    for i in range(len(desc1)):
        for j in range(len(desc2)):
            d1 = (desc1[i] - mean(desc1[i])) / std(desc1[i])
            d2 = (desc2[j] - mean(desc2[j])) / std(desc2[j])
            ncc_value = sum(d1 * d2) / (n-1)
            if ncc_value > threshold:
                d[i,j] = ncc_value

    ndx = argsort(-d)
    matchscores = ndx[:,0]

    return matchscores
```

---

[1] Another popular function is $f(I_1, I_2) = (I_1 - I_2)^2$, which gives *sum of squared differences* (SSD).

The first function takes a square grayscale patch of odd side length centered around the point, flattens it, and adds to a list of descriptors. The second function matches each descriptor to its best candidate in the other image using normalized cross-correlation. Note that the distances are negated before sorting, since a high value means better match. To further stabilize the matches, we can match from the second image to the first and filter out the matches that are not the best both ways. The following function does just that:

```
def match_twosided(desc1,desc2,threshold=0.5):
  """ Two-sided symmetric version of match(). """

  matches_12 = match(desc1,desc2,threshold)
  matches_21 = match(desc2,desc1,threshold)

  ndx_12 = where(matches_12 >= 0)[0]

  # remove matches that are not symmetric
  for n in ndx_12:
    if matches_21[matches_12[n]] != n:
      matches_12[n] = -1

  return matches_12
```

The matches can be visualized by showing the images side-by-side and connecting matched points with lines using the following code. Add these two functions to *harris.py*:

```
def appendimages(im1,im2):
  """ Return a new image that appends the two images side-by-side. """

  # select the image with the fewest rows and fill in enough empty rows
  rows1 = im1.shape[0]
  rows2 = im2.shape[0]

  if rows1 < rows2:
    im1 = concatenate((im1,zeros((rows2-rows1,im1.shape[1]))),axis=0)
  elif rows1 > rows2:
    im2 = concatenate((im2,zeros((rows1-rows2,im2.shape[1]))),axis=0)
  # if none of these cases they are equal, no filling needed.

  return concatenate((im1,im2), axis=1)


def plot_matches(im1,im2,locs1,locs2,matchscores,show_below=True):
  """ Show a figure with lines joining the accepted matches
      input: im1,im2 (images as arrays), locs1,locs2 (feature locations),
      matchscores (as output from 'match()'),
      show_below (if images should be shown below matches). """

  im3 = appendimages(im1,im2)
  if show_below:
    im3 = vstack((im3,im3))
```

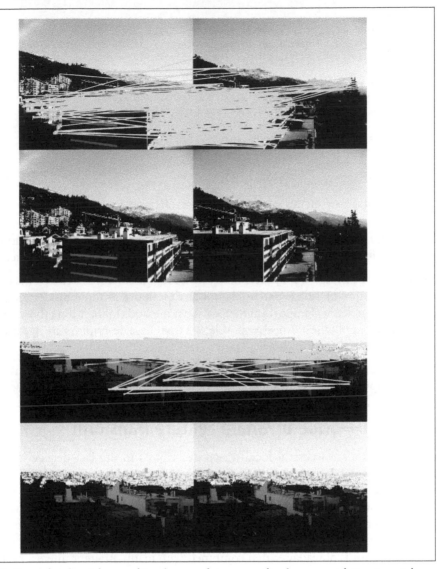

Figure 2-2. Example of matches resulting from applying normalized cross-correlation to patches around Harris corner points.

```
imshow(im3)

cols1 = im1.shape[1]
for i,m in enumerate(matchscores):
  if m>0:
    plot([locs1[i][1],locs2[m][1]+cols1],[locs1[i][0],locs2[m][0]],'c')
axis('off')
```

Figure 2-2 shows an example of finding such corresponding points using normalized cross-correlation (in this case, with 11 × 11 pixels in a patch) using the following commands:

```
wid = 5
harrisim = harris.compute_harris_response(im1,5)
filtered_coords1 = harris.get_harris_points(harrisim,wid+1)
d1 = harris.get_descriptors(im1,filtered_coords1,wid)

harrisim = harris.compute_harris_response(im2,5)
filtered_coords2 = harris.get_harris_points(harrisim,wid+1)
d2 = harris.get_descriptors(im2,filtered_coords2,wid)

print 'starting matching'
matches = harris.match_twosided(d1,d2)

figure()
gray()
harris.plot_matches(im1,im2,filtered_coords1,filtered_coords2,matches)
show()
```

If you only want to plot a subset of the matches to make the visualization clearer, substitute *matches* with, for example, *matches[:100]* or a random set of indices.

As you can see in Figure 2-2, there are quite a lot of incorrect matches. This is because cross-correlation on image patches is not as descriptive as more modern approaches. As a consequence, it is important to use robust methods for handling these correspondences in an application. Another problem is that these descriptors are not invariant to scale or rotation, and the choice of patch sizes affects the results.

In recent years, there has been a lot of development in improving feature point detection and description. Let's take a look at one of the best algorithms in the next section.

2.2 SIFT—Scale-Invariant Feature Transform

One of the most successful local image descriptors in the last decade is the *Scale-Invariant Feature Transform (SIFT)*, introduced by David Lowe in [17]. SIFT was later refined and described in detail in the paper [18] and has stood the test of time. SIFT includes both an interest point detector and a descriptor. The descriptor is very robust and is largely the reason behind the success and popularity of SIFT. Since its introduction, many alternatives have been proposed with essentially the same type of descriptor. The descriptor is nowadays often combined with many different interest point detectors (and region detectors for that matter) and sometimes even applied densely across the whole image. SIFT features are invariant to scale, rotation, and intensity and can be matched reliably across 3D viewpoint and noise. A brief overview is available online at *http://en.wikipedia.org/wiki/Scale-invariant_feature_transform*.

Interest Points

SIFT interest point locations are found using *difference-of-Gaussian* functions

$$D(\mathbf{x}, \sigma) = [G_{k\sigma}(\mathbf{x}) - G_\sigma(\mathbf{x})] * I(\mathbf{x}) = [G_{k\sigma} - G_\sigma] * I = I_{k\sigma} - I_\sigma,$$

where G_σ is the Gaussian 2D kernel described on page 16, I_σ the G_σ-blurred grayscale image, and k a constant factor determining the separation in scale. Interest points are the maxima and minima of $D(\mathbf{x}, \sigma)$ across both image location and scale. These candidate locations are filtered to remove unstable points. Points are dismissed based on a number of criteria, like low contrast and points on edges. The details are in the paper.

Descriptor

The interest point (keypoint) locator above gives position and scale. To achieve invariance to rotation, a reference direction is chosen based on the direction and magnitude of the image gradient around each point. The dominant direction is used as reference and determined using an orientation histogram (weighted with the magnitude).

The next step is to compute a descriptor based on the position, scale, and rotation. To obtain robustness against image intensity, the SIFT descriptor uses image gradients (compare that to normalized cross-correlation above, which uses the image intensities). The descriptor takes a grid of subregions around the point and for each subregion computes an image gradient orientation histogram. The histograms are concatenated to form a descriptor vector. The standard setting uses 4 × 4 subregions with 8 bin orientation histograms, resulting in a 128 bin histogram ($4*4*8 = 128$). Figure 2-3 illustrates the construction of the descriptor. The interested reader should look at [18] for the details or *http://en.wikipedia.org/wiki/Scale-invariant_feature_transform* for an overview.

Detecting Interest Points

To compute SIFT features for images, we will use the binaries available with the open source package VLFeat [36]. A full Python implementation of all the steps in the algorithm would not be very efficient and really is outside the scope of this book. VLFeat is available at *http://www.vlfeat.org/*, with binaries for all major platforms. The library

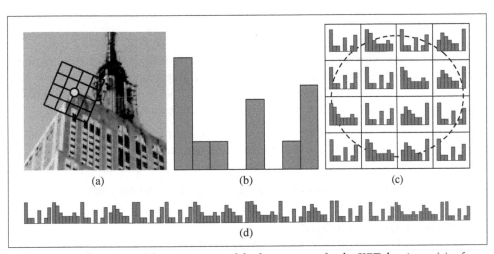

Figure 2-3. An illustration of the construction of the feature vector for the SIFT descriptor: (a) a frame around an interest point, oriented according to the dominant gradient direction; (b) an 8-bin histogram over the direction of the gradient in a part of the grid; (c) histograms are extracted in each grid location; (d) the histograms are concatenated to form one long feature vector.

is written in C but has a command line interface that we can use. There is also a Matlab interface and a Python wrapper (*http://github.com/mmmikael/vlfeat/*) if you prefer that to the binaries used here. The Python wrapper can be a little tricky to install on some platforms due to its dependencies, so we will focus on the binaries instead. There is also an alternative SIFT implementation available at Lowe's website, *http://www.cs.ubc .ca/~lowe/keypoints/* (Windows and Linux only).

Create a file *sift.py* and add the following function that calls the executable:

```python
def process_image(imagename,resultname,params="--edge-thresh 10 --peak-thresh 5"):
    """ Process an image and save the results in a file. """

    if imagename[-3:] != 'pgm':
        # create a pgm file
        im = Image.open(imagename).convert('L')
        im.save('tmp.pgm')
        imagename = 'tmp.pgm'

    cmmd = str("sift "+imagename+" --output="+resultname+
            " "+params)
    os.system(cmmd)
    print 'processed', imagename, 'to', resultname
```

The binaries need the image in grayscale .pgm format, so if another image format is used, we first convert to a temporary *.pgm* file. The result is stored in a text file in an easy-to-read format. The files look something like this:

```
318.861 7.48227 1.12001 1.68523 0 0 0 1 0 0 0 0 0 11 16 0 ...
318.861 7.48227 1.12001 2.99965 11 2 0 0 1 0 0 0 173 67 0 0 ...
54.2821 14.8586 0.895827 4.29821 60 46 0 0 0 0 0 0 99 42 0 0 ...
155.714 23.0575 1.10741 1.54095 6 0 0 0 150 11 0 0 150 18 2 1 ...
42.9729 24.2012 0.969313 4.68892 90 29 0 0 0 1 2 10 79 45 5 11 ...
229.037 23.7603 0.921754 1.48754 3 0 0 0 141 31 0 0 141 45 0 0 ...
232.362 24.0091 1.0578 1.65089 11 1 0 16 134 0 0 0 106 21 16 33 ...
201.256 25.5857 1.04879 2.01664 10 4 1 8 14 2 1 9 88 13 0 0 ...
  :
  :
```

Here, each row contains the coordinates, scale, and rotation angle for each interest point as the first four values, followed by the 128 values of the corresponding descriptor. The descriptor is represented with the raw integer values and is not normalized. This is something you will want to do when comparing descriptors. More on that later.

The example above shows the first part of the first eight features found in an image. Note that the two first rows have the same coordinates but different rotation. This can happen if several strong directions are found at the same interest point.

Here's how to read the features to NumPy arrays from an output file like the one above. Add this function to *sift.py*:

```python
def read_features_from_file(filename):
    """ Read feature properties and return in matrix form. """

    f = loadtxt(filename)
    return f[:,:4],f[:,4:] # feature locations, descriptors
```

Here we used the NumPy function loadtxt() to do all the work for us.

If you modify the descriptors in your Python session, writing the result back to feature files can be useful. The function below does this for you using NumPy's savetxt():

```
def write_features_to_file(filename,locs,desc):
  """ Save feature location and descriptor to file. """
  savetxt(filename,hstack((locs,desc)))
```

This uses the function hstack() that horizontally stacks the two arrays by concatenating the rows so that the descriptor part comes after the locations on each row.

Having read the features, visualizing them by plotting their locations in the image is a simple task. Just add plot_features() as below to your file *sift.py*:

```
def plot_features(im,locs,circle=False):
  """ Show image with features. input: im (image as array),
    locs (row, col, scale, orientation of each feature). """

  def draw_circle(c,r):
    t = arange(0,1.01,.01)*2*pi
    x = r*cos(t) + c[0]
    y = r*sin(t) + c[1]
    plot(x,y,'b',linewidth=2)

  imshow(im)
  if circle:
    for p in locs:
      draw_circle(p[:2],p[2])
  else:
    plot(locs[:,0],locs[:,1],'ob')
  axis('off')
```

This will plot the location of the SIFT points as blue dots overlaid on the image. If the optional parameter *circle* is set to "True", circles with radius equal to the scale of the feature will be drawn instead using the helper function draw_circle().

The following commands will create a plot like the one in Figure 2-4b with the SIFT feature locations shown:

```
import sift

imname = 'empire.jpg'
im1 = array(Image.open(imname).convert('L'))
sift.process_image(imname,'empire.sift')
l1,d1 = sift.read_features_from_file('empire.sift')

figure()
gray()
sift.plot_features(im1,l1,circle=True)
show()
```

To see the difference compared to Harris corners, the Harris corners for the same image are shown to the right (Figure 2-4c). As you can see, the two algorithms select different locations.

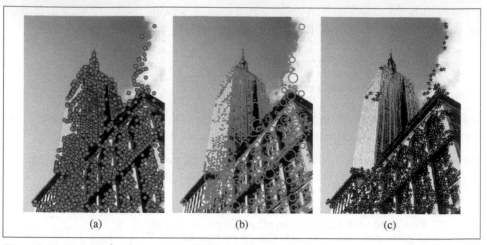

(a)   (b)   (c)

Figure 2-4. An example of extracting SIFT features for an image: (a) SIFT features; (b) SIFT features shown with circle indicating the scale of the feature; (c) Harris points for the same image for comparison.

Matching Descriptors

A robust criteria (also introduced by Lowe) for matching a feature in one image to a feature in another image is to use the ratio of the distance to the two closest matching features. This ensures that only features that are distinct enough compared to the other features in the image are used. As a consequence, the number of false matches is lowered. Here's what this matching function looks like in code. Add match() to *sift.py*:

```python
def match(desc1,desc2):
    """ For each descriptor in the first image,
        select its match in the second image.
        input: desc1 (descriptors for the first image),
        desc2 (same for second image). """

    desc1 = array([d/linalg.norm(d) for d in desc1])
    desc2 = array([d/linalg.norm(d) for d in desc2])

    dist_ratio = 0.6
    desc1_size = desc1.shape

    matchscores = zeros((desc1_size[0],1),'int')
    desc2t = desc2.T # precompute matrix transpose
    for i in range(desc1_size[0]):
        dotprods = dot(desc1[i,:],desc2t) # vector of dot products
        dotprods = 0.9999*dotprods
        # inverse cosine and sort, return index for features in second image
        indx = argsort(arccos(dotprods))

        # check if nearest neighbor has angle less than dist_ratio times 2nd
        if arccos(dotprods)[indx[0]] < dist_ratio * arccos(dotprods)[indx[1]]:
            matchscores[i] = int(indx[0])

    return matchscores
```

This function uses the angle between descriptor vectors as distance measure. This makes sense only after we have normalized the vectors to unit length.[2] Since the matching is one-sided, meaning that we are matching each feature to all features in the other image, we can pre-compute the transpose of the matrix containing the descriptor vectors containing the points in the second image, so that we don't have to repeat this exact same operation for each feature.

To further increase the robustness of the matches, we can reverse the procedure and match the other way (from the features in the second image to features in the first) and only keep the correspondences that satisfy the matching criteria both ways (same as we did for the Harris points). The function match_twosided() does just this:

```
def match_twosided(desc1,desc2):
    """ Two-sided symmetric version of match(). """

    matches_12 = match(desc1,desc2)
    matches_21 = match(desc2,desc1)

    ndx_12 = matches_12.nonzero()[0]

    # remove matches that are not symmetric
    for n in ndx_12:
        if matches_21[int(matches_12[n])] != n:
            matches_12[n] = 0

    return matches_12
```

To plot the matches, we can use the same functions used in *harris.py*. Just copy the functions appendimages() and plot_matches() and add them to *sift.py* for convenience. You could also import *harris.py* and use them from there if you like.

Figures 2-5 and 2-6 show some examples of SIFT feature points detected in image pairs together with pair-wise matches returned from the function match_twosided().

Figure 2-7 shows another example of matching features found in two images using match() and match_twosided(). As you can see, using the symmetric (two-sided) matching condition removes the incorrect matches and keeps the good ones (some correct matches are also removed).

With detection and matching of feature points, we have everything needed to apply these local descriptors to a number of applications. The coming two chapters will add geometric constraints on correspondences in order to robustly filter out the incorrect ones and apply local descriptors to examples such as automatic panorama creation, camera pose estimation, and 3D structure computation.

---

[2] In the case of unit length vectors, the scalar product (without the arccos()) is equivalent to the standard Euclidean distance.

Figure 2-5. An example of detecting and matching SIFT features between two images.

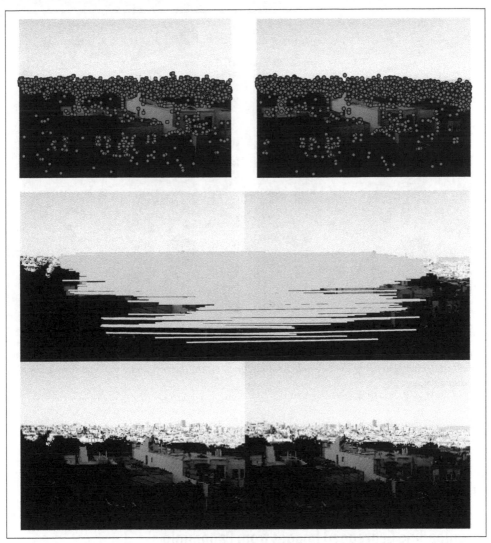

Figure 2-6. An example of detecting and matching SIFT features between two images.

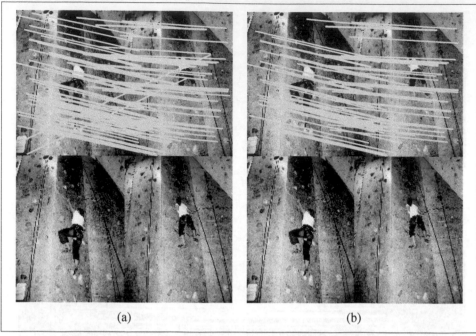

Figure 2-7. *An example of matching SIFT features between two images: (a) matches from features in the left image without using the two-sided match function; (b) the remaining matches after using the two-sided version.*

2.3   Matching Geotagged Images

Let's end this chapter by looking at an example application of using local descriptors for matching images with geotags.

Downloading Geotagged Images from Panoramio

One source of geotagged images is the photo-sharing service Panoramio (*http://www .panoramio.com/*), owned by Google. Like many web services, Panoramio has an API to access content programmatically. Their API is simple and straightforward and is described at *http://www.panoramio.com/api/*. By making an HTTP GET call to a url like this:

```
http://www.panoramio.com/map/get_panoramas.php?order=popularity&set=public&
from=0&to=20&minx=-180&miny=-90&maxx=180&maxy=90&size=medium
```

where *minx, miny, maxx, maxy* define the geographic area from which to select photos, (minimum longitude, latitude, maximum longitude and latitude, respectively), you will get the response in easy-to-parse JSON format. JSON is a common format for data transfer between web services and is more lightweight than XML and other alternatives. You can read more about JSON at *http://en.wikipedia.org/wiki/JSON*.

An interesting location with two distinct views is the White House in Washington, D.C., which is usually photographed from Pennsylvania Avenue from the south side or from the north. The coordinates (latitude, longitude) are:

```
lt=38.897661
ln=-77.036564
```

To convert to the format needed for the API call, subtract and add a number from these coordinates to get all images within a square centered around the White house. The call:

```
http://www.panoramio.com/map/get_panoramas.php?order=popularity&set=public&
from=0&to=20&minx=-77.037564&miny=38.896662&maxx=-77.035564&maxy=38.898662&
size=medium
```

returns the first 20 images within the coordinate bounds (±0.001), ordered according to popularity. The response looks something like this:

```
{ "count": 349,
"photos": [{"photo_id": 7715073, "photo_title": "White House", "photo_url":
"http://www.panoramio.com/photo/7715073", "photo_file_url":
"http://mw2.google.com/mw-panoramio/photos/medium/7715073.jpg", "longitude":
-77.036583, "latitude": 38.897488, "width": 500, "height": 375, "upload_date":
"10 February 2008", "owner_id": 1213603, "owner_name": "***", "owner_url":
"http://www.panoramio.com/user/1213603"}
,
{"photo_id": 1303971, "photo_title": "White House balcony", "photo_url":
"http://www.panoramio.com/photo/1303971", "photo_file_url":
"http://mw2.google.com/mw-panoramio/photos/medium/1303971.jpg", "longitude":
-77.036353, "latitude": 38.897471, "width": 500, "height": 336, "upload_date":
"13 March 2007", "owner_id": 195000, "owner_name": "***", "owner_url":
"http://www.panoramio.com/user/195000"}
.
.
.
]}
```

To parse this JSON response, we can use the `simplejson` package, which is available at *http://github.com/simplejson/simplejson*. There is online documentation available on the project page.

If you are running Python 2.6 or later, there is no need to use `simplejson` as there is a JSON library included with these later versions of Python. To use the built-in one, just import like this:

```
import json
```

If you want to use `simplejson` where available (it is faster and could contain newer features than the built-in one), a good idea is to import with a fallback, like this:

```
try: import simplejson as json
except ImportError: import json
```

The following code will use the `urllib` package that comes with Python to handle the requests and then parse the result using `simplejson`:

```
import os
import urllib, urlparse
import simplejson as json

# query for images
url = 'http://www.panoramio.com/map/get_panoramas.php?order=popularity&\
    set=public&from=0&to=20&minx=-77.037564&miny=38.896662&\
    maxx=-77.035564&maxy=38.898662&size=medium'
c = urllib.urlopen(url)

# get the urls of individual images from JSON
j = json.loads(c.read())
imurls = []
for im in j['photos']:
  imurls.append(im['photo_file_url'])

# download images
for url in imurls:
  image = urllib.URLopener()
  image.retrieve(url, os.path.basename(urlparse.urlparse(url).path))
  print 'downloading:', url
```

As you can easily see by looking at the JSON output, it is the "photo_file_url" field we are after. Running the code above, you should see something like this in your console:

```
downloading: http://mw2.google.com/mw-panoramio/photos/medium/7715073.jpg
downloading: http://mw2.google.com/mw-panoramio/photos/medium/1303971.jpg
downloading: http://mw2.google.com/mw-panoramio/photos/medium/270077.jpg
downloading: http://mw2.google.com/mw-panoramio/photos/medium/15502.jpg
  .
  .
  .
```

Figure 2-8 shows the 20 images returned for this example. Now we just need to find and match features between pairs of images.

Matching Using Local Descriptors

Having downloaded the images, we now need to extract local descriptors. In this case, we will use SIFT descriptors as described in the previous section. Let's assume that the images have been processed with the SIFT extraction code and the features are stored in files with the same name as the images (but with file ending ".sift" instead of ".jpg"). The lists *imlist* and *featlist* are assumed to contain the filenames. We can do a pairwise matching between all combinations as follows:

```
import sift

nbr_images = len(imlist)

matchscores = zeros((nbr_images,nbr_images))
```

```
for i in range(nbr_images):
  for j in range(i,nbr_images): # only compute upper triangle
    print 'comparing ', imlist[i], imlist[j]

    l1,d1 = sift.read_features_from_file(featlist[i])
    l2,d2 = sift.read_features_from_file(featlist[j])

    matches = sift.match_twosided(d1,d2)

    nbr_matches = sum(matches > 0)
    print 'number of matches = ', nbr_matches
    matchscores[i,j] = nbr_matches

# copy values
for i in range(nbr_images):
  for j in range(i+1,nbr_images): # no need to copy diagonal
    matchscores[j,i] = matchscores[i,j]
```

We store the number of matching features between each pair in *matchscores*. The last
part of copying the values to fill the matrix completely is not necessary, since this
"distance measure" is symmetric; it just looks better that way. The *matchscores* matrix
for these particular images looks like this:

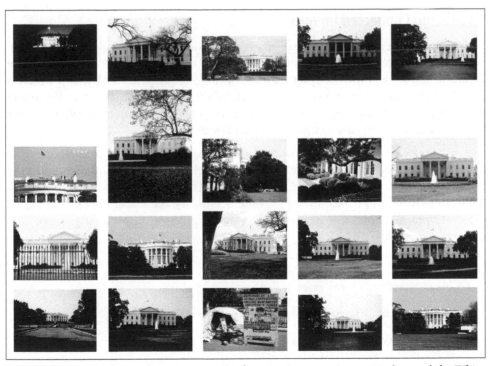

*Figure 2-8. Images taken at the same geographic location (square region centered around the White
house) downloaded from panoramio.com.*

```
662 0 0 2 0 0 0 0 1 0 0 1 2 0 3 0 19 1 0 2
0 901 0 1 0 0 0 1 1 0 0 1 0 0 0 0 0 0 1 2
0 0 266 0 0 0 0 0 0 0 0 0 0 1 0 0 0 0 0 0
2 1 0 1481 0 0 2 2 0 0 0 2 2 0 0 0 2 3 2 0
0 0 0 0 1748 0 0 1 0 0 0 0 2 0 0 0 0 0 0 1
0 0 0 0 0 1747 0 0 1 0 0 0 0 0 0 0 0 1 1 0
0 0 0 2 0 0 555 0 0 0 1 4 4 0 2 0 0 5 1 0
0 1 0 2 1 0 0 2206 0 0 0 1 0 0 1 0 2 0 1 1
1 1 0 0 0 1 0 0 629 0 0 0 0 0 0 0 1 0 0 20
0 0 0 0 0 0 0 0 0 829 0 0 1 0 0 0 0 0 0 2
0 0 0 0 0 0 1 0 0 0 1025 0 0 0 0 0 1 1 1 0
1 1 0 2 0 0 4 1 0 0 0 528 5 2 15 0 3 6 0 0
2 0 0 2 0 0 4 0 0 1 0 5 736 1 4 0 3 37 1 0
0 0 1 0 2 0 0 0 0 0 0 2 1 620 1 0 0 1 0 0
3 0 0 0 0 0 2 1 0 0 0 15 4 1 553 0 6 9 1 0
0 0 0 0 0 0 0 0 0 0 0 0 0 0 0 2273 0 1 0 0
19 0 0 2 0 0 0 2 1 0 1 3 3 0 6 0 542 0 0 0
1 0 0 3 0 1 5 0 0 0 1 6 37 1 9 1 0 527 3 0
0 1 0 2 0 1 1 1 0 0 1 0 1 0 1 0 0 3 1139 0
2 2 0 0 1 0 0 1 20 2 0 0 0 0 0 0 0 0 0 499
```

Using this as a simple distance measure between images (images with similar content have higher number of matching features), we can now connect images with similar visual content.

Visualizing Connected Images

Let's visualize the connections between images defined by them having matching local descriptors. To do this, we can show the images in a graph with edges indicating connections. We will use the pydot package (*http://code.google.com/p/pydot/*), which is a Python interface to the powerful GraphViz graphing library. Pydot uses Pyparsing (*http://pyparsing.wikispaces.com/*) and GraphViz (*http://www.graphviz.org/*), but don't worry; all of them are easy to install in just a few minutes.

Pydot is very easy to use. The following code snippet illustrates this nicely by creating a graph illustrating a tree with depth two and branching factor five adding numbering to the nodes. The graph is shown in Figure 2-9. There are many ways to customize the graph layout and appearance. For more details, see the Pydot documentation or the description of the DOT language used by GraphViz at *http://www.graphviz.org/Documentation.php*.

```python
import pydot

g = pydot.Dot(graph_type='graph')

g.add_node(pydot.Node(str(0),fontcolor='transparent'))
for i in range(5):
  g.add_node(pydot.Node(str(i+1)))
  g.add_edge(pydot.Edge(str(0),str(i+1)))
  for j in range(5):
    g.add_node(pydot.Node(str(j+1)+'-'+str(i+1)))
    g.add_edge(pydot.Edge(str(j+1)+'-'+str(i+1),str(j+1)))
g.write_png('graph.jpg',prog='neato')
```

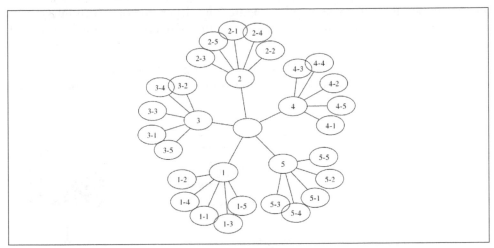

Figure 2-9. An example of using pydot to create graphs.

Let's get back to our example with the geotagged images. To create a graph showing potential groups of images, we create an edge between nodes if the number of matches is above a threshold. To get the images in the graph, you need to use the full path of each image (represented by the variable *path* in the example below). To make it look nice, we also scale each image to a thumbnail with largest side 100 pixels. Here's how to do it:

```
import pydot

threshold = 2 # min number of matches needed to create link

g = pydot.Dot(graph_type='graph') # don't want the default directed graph
for i in range(nbr_images):
  for j in range(i+1,nbr_images):
    if matchscores[i,j] > threshold:
      # first image in pair
      im = Image.open(imlist[i])
      im.thumbnail((100,100))
      filename = str(i)+'.png'
      im.save(filename) # need temporary files of the right size
      g.add_node(pydot.Node(str(i),fontcolor='transparent',
          shape='rectangle',image=path+filename))

      # second image in pair
      im = Image.open(imlist[j])
      im.thumbnail((100,100))
      filename = str(j)+'.png'
      im.save(filename) # need temporary files of the right size
      g.add_node(pydot.Node(str(j),fontcolor='transparent',
          shape='rectangle',image=path+filename))

      g.add_edge(pydot.Edge(str(i),str(j)))

g.write_png('whitehouse.png')
```

The result should look something like Figure 2-10, depending on which images you download. For this particular set, we see two groups of images, one from each side of the White House.

This application was a very simple example of using local descriptors for matching regions between images. For example, we did not use any verification on the matches.

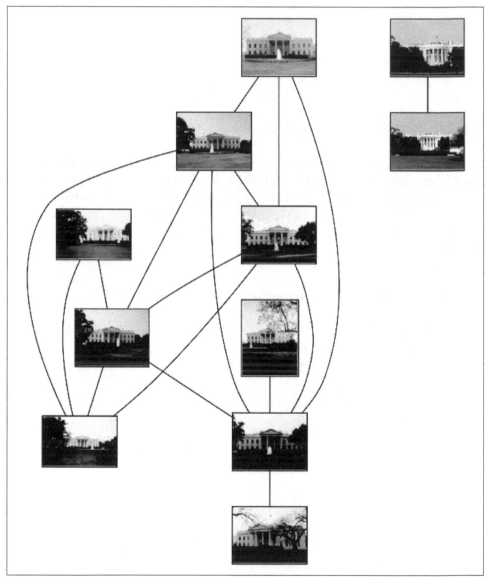

Figure 2-10. An example of grouping images taken at the same geographic location using local descriptors.

This can be done (in a very robust way) using concepts that we will define in the coming two chapters.

Exercises

1. Modify the function for matching Harris corner points to also take a maximum pixel distance between points for them to be considered as correspondences, in order to make matching more robust.

2. Incrementally apply stronger blur (or ROF de-noising) to an image and extract Harris corners. What happens?

3. An alternative corner detector to Harris is the FAST corner detector. There are a number of implementations, including a pure Python version available at *http:// www.edwardrosten.com/work/fast.html*. Try this detector, play with the sensitivity threshold, and compare the corners with the ones from our Harris implementation.

4. Create copies of an image with different resolutions (for example, by halving the size a few times). Extract SIFT features for each image. Plot and match features to get a feel for how and when the scale independence breaks down.

5. The VLFeat command line tools also contain an implementation of Maximally Stable Extremal Regions (MSER) (*http://en.wikipedia.org/wiki/Maximally_stable_ extremal_regions*) a region detector that finds blob-like regions. Create a function for extracting MSER regions and pass them to the descriptor part of SIFT using the `--read-frames` option and one function for plotting the ellipse regions.

6. Write a function that matches features between a pair of images and estimates the scale difference and in-plane rotation of the scene, based on the correspondences.

7. Download images for a location of your choice and match them as in the White House example. Can you find a better criteria for linking images? How could you use the graph to choose representative images for geographic locations?

## CHAPTER 3

Image to Image Mappings

This chapter describes transformations between images and some practical methods for computing them. These transformations are used for warping and image registration. Finally, we look at an example of automatically creating panoramas.

3.1 Homographies

A *homography* is a 2D projective transformation that maps points in one plane to another. In our case, the planes are images or planar surfaces in 3D. Homographies have many practical uses, such as registering images, rectifying images, texture warping, and creating panoramas. We will make frequent use of them. In essence, a homography H maps 2D points (in homogeneous coordinates) according to

$$\begin{bmatrix} x' \\ y' \\ w' \end{bmatrix} = \begin{bmatrix} h_1 & h_2 & h_3 \\ h_4 & h_5 & h_6 \\ h_7 & h_8 & h_9 \end{bmatrix} \begin{bmatrix} x \\ y \\ w \end{bmatrix} \quad \text{or} \quad \mathbf{x}' = H\mathbf{x}.$$

Homogeneous coordinates are a useful representation for points in image planes (and in 3D, as we will see later). Points in homogeneous coordinates are only defined up to scale so that $\mathbf{x} = [x, y, w] = [\alpha x, \alpha y, \alpha w] = [x/w, y/w, 1]$ all refer to the same 2D point. As a consequence, the homography H is also only defined up to scale and has eight independent degrees of freedom. Often points are normalized with $w = 1$ to have a unique identification of the image coordinates x, y. The extra coordinate makes it easy to represent transformations with a single matrix.

Create a file *homography.py* and add the following functions to normalize and convert to homogeneous coordinates:

```
def normalize(points):
    """ Normalize a collection of points in
        homogeneous coordinates so that last row = 1. """
```

```
    for row in points:
        row /= points[-1]
    return points


def make_homog(points):
    """ Convert a set of points (dim*n array) to
        homogeneous coordinates. """

    return vstack((points,ones((1,points.shape[1]))))
```

When working with points and transformations, we will store the points column-wise so that a set of n points in two dimensions will be a $3 \times n$ array in homogeneous coordinates. This format makes matrix multiplications and point transforms easier. For all other cases, we will typically use rows to store data, for example features for clustering and classification.

There are some important special cases of these projective transformations. An *affine transformation*

$$\begin{bmatrix} x' \\ y' \\ 1 \end{bmatrix} = \begin{bmatrix} a_1 & a_2 & t_x \\ a_3 & a_4 & t_y \\ 0 & 0 & 1 \end{bmatrix} \begin{bmatrix} x \\ y \\ 1 \end{bmatrix} \quad \text{or} \quad \mathbf{x}' = \begin{bmatrix} A & \mathbf{t} \\ \mathbf{0} & 1 \end{bmatrix} \mathbf{x},$$

preserves $w = 1$ and cannot represent as strong deformations as a full projective transformation. The affine transformation contains an invertible matrix A and a translation vector $\mathbf{t} = [t_x, t_y]$. Affine transformations are used, for example, in warping.

A *similarity transformation*

$$\begin{bmatrix} x' \\ y' \\ 1 \end{bmatrix} = \begin{bmatrix} s \, \cos(\theta) & -s \, \sin(\theta) & t_x \\ s \, \sin(\theta) & s \, \cos(\theta) & t_y \\ 0 & 0 & 1 \end{bmatrix} \begin{bmatrix} x \\ y \\ 1 \end{bmatrix} \quad \text{or} \quad \mathbf{x}' = \begin{bmatrix} sR & \mathbf{t} \\ \mathbf{0} & 1 \end{bmatrix} \mathbf{x},$$

is a rigid 2D transformation that also includes scale changes. The scalar s specifies scaling, R is a rotation of an angle θ, and $\mathbf{t} = [t_x, t_y]$ is again a translation. With $s = 1$ distances are preserved and it is then a *rigid transformation*. Similarity transformations are used, for example, in image registration.

Let's look at algorithms for estimating homographies and then go into examples of using affine transformations for warping, similarity transformations for registration, and finally full projective transformations for creating panoramas.

The Direct Linear Transformation Algorithm

Homographies can be computed directly from corresponding points in two images (or planes). As mentioned earlier, a full projective transformation has eight degrees of freedom. Each point correspondence gives two equations, one each for the x and y coordinates, and therefore four point correspondences are needed to compute H.

The *direct linear transformation* (DLT) is an algorithm for computing H given four or more correspondences. By rewriting the equation for mapping points using H for several correspondences, we get an equation like

$$
\begin{bmatrix}
-x_1 & -y_1 & -1 & 0 & 0 & 0 & x_1 x_1' & y_1 x_1' & x_1' \\
0 & 0 & 0 & -x_1 & -y_1 & -1 & x_1 y_1' & y_1 y_1' & y_1' \\
-x_2 & -y_2 & -1 & 0 & 0 & 0 & x_2 x_2' & y_2 x_2' & x_2' \\
0 & 0 & 0 & -x_2 & -y_2 & -1 & x_2 y_2' & y_2 y_2' & y_2' \\
& \vdots & & & \vdots & & & \vdots &
\end{bmatrix}
\begin{bmatrix}
h_1 \\ h_2 \\ h_3 \\ h_4 \\ h_5 \\ h_6 \\ h_7 \\ h_8 \\ h_9
\end{bmatrix}
= \mathbf{0},
$$

or $A\mathbf{h} = \mathbf{0}$ where A is a matrix with twice as many rows as correspondences. By stacking all corresponding points, a least squares solution for H can be found using singular value decomposition (SVD). Here's what it looks like in code. Add the function below to *homography.py*:

```python
def H_from_points(fp,tp):
    """ Find homography H, such that fp is mapped to tp
        using the linear DLT method. Points are conditioned
        automatically. """

    if fp.shape != tp.shape:
        raise RuntimeError('number of points do not match')

    # condition points (important for numerical reasons)
    # --from points--
    m = mean(fp[:2], axis=1)
    maxstd = max(std(fp[:2], axis=1)) + 1e-9
    C1 = diag([1/maxstd, 1/maxstd, 1])
    C1[0][2] = -m[0]/maxstd
    C1[1][2] = -m[1]/maxstd
    fp = dot(C1,fp)

    # --to points--
    m = mean(tp[:2], axis=1)
    maxstd = max(std(tp[:2], axis=1)) + 1e-9
    C2 = diag([1/maxstd, 1/maxstd, 1])
    C2[0][2] = -m[0]/maxstd
    C2[1][2] = -m[1]/maxstd
    tp = dot(C2,tp)

    # create matrix for linear method, 2 rows for each correspondence pair
    nbr_correspondences = fp.shape[1]
    A = zeros((2*nbr_correspondences,9))
    for i in range(nbr_correspondences):
        A[2*i] = [-fp[0][i],-fp[1][i],-1,0,0,0,
                    tp[0][i]*fp[0][i],tp[0][i]*fp[1][i],tp[0][i]]
        A[2*i+1] = [0,0,0,-fp[0][i],-fp[1][i],-1,
                    tp[1][i]*fp[0][i],tp[1][i]*fp[1][i],tp[1][i]]

    U,S,V = linalg.svd(A)
    H = V[8].reshape((3,3))
```

```
# decondition
H = dot(linalg.inv(C2),dot(H,C1))

# normalize and return
return H / H[2,2]
```

The first thing that happens in this function is a check that the number of points are equal. If not, an exception is thrown. This is useful for writing robust code, but we will only use exceptions in very few cases in this book to make the code samples simpler and easier to follow. You can read more about exception types at *http://docs.python.org/library/exceptions.html* and how to use them at *http://docs.python.org/tutorial/errors.html*.

The points are conditioned by normalizing so that they have zero mean and unit standard deviation. This is very important for numerical reasons, since the stability of the algorithm is dependent on the coordinate representation. Then the matrix A is created using the point correspondences. The least squares solution is found as the last row of the matrix V of the SVD. The row is reshaped to create H. This matrix is then de-conditioned and normalized before being returned.

Affine Transformations

An affine transformation has six degrees of freedom and therefore three point correspondences are needed to estimate H. Affine transforms can be estimated using the DLT algorithm above by setting the last two elements equal to zero, $h_7 = h_8 = 0$.

Here we will use a different approach, described in detail in [13] (page 130). Add the following function to *homography.py*, which computes the affine transformation matrix from point correspondences:

```
def Haffine_from_points(fp,tp):
  """ Find H, affine transformation, such that
    tp is affine transf of fp. """

  if fp.shape != tp.shape:
    raise RuntimeError('number of points do not match')

  # condition points
  # --from points--
  m = mean(fp[:2], axis=1)
  maxstd = max(std(fp[:2], axis=1)) + 1e-9
  C1 = diag([1/maxstd, 1/maxstd, 1])
  C1[0][2] = -m[0]/maxstd
  C1[1][2] = -m[1]/maxstd
  fp_cond = dot(C1,fp)

  # --to points--
  m = mean(tp[:2], axis=1)
  C2 = C1.copy() # must use same scaling for both point sets
  C2[0][2] = -m[0]/maxstd
  C2[1][2] = -m[1]/maxstd
  tp_cond = dot(C2,tp)
```

```
# conditioned points have mean zero, so translation is zero
A = concatenate((fp_cond[:2],tp_cond[:2]), axis=0)
U,S,V = linalg.svd(A.T)

# create B and C matrices as Hartley-Zisserman (2:nd ed) p 130.
tmp = V[:2].T
B = tmp[:2]
C = tmp[2:4]

tmp2 = concatenate((dot(C,linalg.pinv(B)),zeros((2,1))), axis=1)
H = vstack((tmp2,[0,0,1]))

# decondition
H = dot(linalg.inv(C2),dot(H,C1))

return H / H[2,2]
```

Again, the points are conditioned and de-conditioned as in the DLT algorithm. Let's see what these affine transformations can do with images in the next section.

3.2 Warping Images

Applying an affine transformation matrix *H* on image patches is called *warping* (or *affine warping*) and is frequently used in computer graphics but also in several computer vision algorithms. A warp can easily be performed with SciPy using the ndimage package. The command

```
transformed_im = ndimage.affine_transform(im,A,b,size)
```

transforms the image patch *im* with *A* a linear transformation and **b** a translation vector as above. The optional argument *size* can be used to specify the size of the output image. The default is an image with the same size as the original. To see how this works, try running the following commands:

```
from scipy import ndimage

im = array(Image.open('empire.jpg').convert('L'))
H = array([[1.4,0.05,-100],[0.05,1.5,-100],[0,0,1]])
im2 = ndimage.affine_transform(im,H[:2,:2],(H[0,2],H[1,2]))

figure()
gray()
imshow(im2)
show()
```

This gives a result like the image to the right in Figure 3-1. As you can see, missing pixel values in the result image are filled with zeros.

Image in Image

A simple example of affine warping is to place images, or parts of images, inside another image so that they line up with specific areas or landmarks.

Figure 3-1. An example of warping an image using an affine transform: original (left), image after warping with ndimage.affine_transform() *(right).*

Add the function image_in_image() to *warp.py*. This function takes two images and the corner coordinates of where to put the first image in the second:

```
def image_in_image(im1,im2,tp):
    """ Put im1 in im2 with an affine transformation
        such that corners are as close to tp as possible.
        tp are homogeneous and counterclockwise from top left. """

    # points to warp from
    m,n = im1.shape[:2]
    fp = array([[0,m,m,0],[0,0,n,n],[1,1,1,1]])

    # compute affine transform and apply
    H = homography.Haffine_from_points(tp,fp)
    im1_t = ndimage.affine_transform(im1,H[:2,:2],
            (H[0,2],H[1,2]),im2.shape[:2])
    alpha = (im1_t > 0)

    return (1-alpha)*im2 + alpha*im1_t
```

As you can see, there is not much needed to do this. When blending together the warped image and the second image, we create an *alpha map* that defines how much of each pixel to take from each image. Here we use the fact that the warped image is filled with zeros outside the borders of the warped area to create a binary alpha map. To be really strict, we could have added a small number to the potential zero pixels of the first image, or done it properly (see exercises at the end of the chapter). Note that the image coordinates are in homogeneous form.

To try this function, let's insert an image on a billboard in another image. The following lines of code will put the leftmost image of Figure 3-2 into the second image. The coordinates were determined manually by looking at a plot of the image (in PyLab

Figure 3-2. An example of placing an image inside another image using an affine transformation.

figures, the mouse coordinates are shown near the bottom). PyLab's `ginput()` could, of course, also have been used.

```
import warp

# example of affine warp of im1 onto im2
im1 = array(Image.open('beatles.jpg').convert('L'))
im2 = array(Image.open('billboard_for_rent.jpg').convert('L'))

# set to points
tp = array([[264,538,540,264],[40,36,605,605],[1,1,1,1]])

im3 = warp.image_in_image(im1,im2,tp)

figure()
gray()
imshow(im3)
axis('equal')
axis('off')
show()
```

This puts the image on the upper part of the billboard. Note again that the landmark coordinates *tp* are in homogeneous coordinates. Changing the coordinates to

```
tp = array([[675,826,826,677],[55,52,281,277],[1,1,1,1]])
```

will put the image on the lower-left "for rent" part.

The function `Haffine_from_points()` gives the best affine transform for the given point correspondences. In the example above, those were the image corners and the corners of the billboard. If the perspective effects are small, this will give good results. The top row of Figure 3-3 shows what happens if we try to use an affine transformation to a billboard image with more perspective. It is not possible to transform all four corner points to their target locations with the same affine transform (a full projective transform would have been able to do this, though). If you want to use an affine warp so that all corner points match, there is a useful trick.

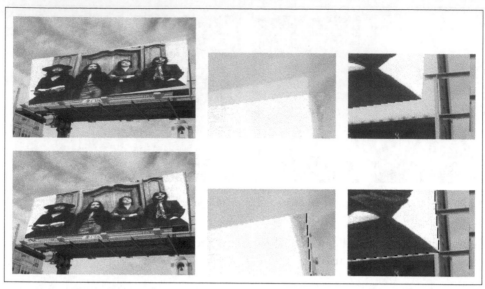

Figure 3-3. Comparing an affine warp of the full image with an affine warp using two triangles. The image is placed on a billboard with some perspective effects. Using an affine transform for the whole image results in a bad fit. The two right-hand corners are enlarged for clarity (top). Using an affine warp consisting of two triangles gives an exact fit (bottom).

For three points, an affine transform can warp an image so that the three correspondences match perfectly. This is because an affine transform has six degrees of freedom and three correspondences give exactly six constraints (*x* and *y* coordinates must match for all three). So if you really want the image to fit the billboard using affine transforms, you can divide the image into two triangles and warp them separately. Here's how to do it:

```
# set from points to corners of im1
m,n = im1.shape[:2]
fp = array([[0,m,m,0],[0,0,n,n],[1,1,1,1]])

# first triangle
tp2 = tp[:,:3]
fp2 = fp[:,:3]

# compute H
H = homography.Haffine_from_points(tp2,fp2)
im1_t = ndimage.affine_transform(im1,H[:2,:2],
        (H[0,2],H[1,2]),im2.shape[:2])

# alpha for triangle
alpha = warp.alpha_for_triangle(tp2,im2.shape[0],im2.shape[1])
im3 = (1-alpha)*im2 + alpha*im1_t

# second triangle
tp2 = tp[:,[0,2,3]]
fp2 = fp[:,[0,2,3]]
```

```
# compute H
H = homography.Haffine_from_points(tp2,fp2)
im1_t = ndimage.affine_transform(im1,H[:2,:2],
        (H[0,2],H[1,2]),im2.shape[:2])

# alpha for triangle
alpha = warp.alpha_for_triangle(tp2,im2.shape[0],im2.shape[1])
im4 = (1-alpha)*im3 + alpha*im1_t

figure()
gray()
imshow(im4)
axis('equal')
axis('off')
show()
```

Here we simply create the alpha map for each triangle and then merge all images together. The alpha map for a triangle can be computed simply by checking if a pixel's coordinates can be written as a convex combination of the triangle's corner points.[1] If the coordinates can be expressed this way, that means the pixel is inside the triangle. Add the following function alpha_for_triangle(), which was used in the example above, to *warp.py*:

```
def alpha_for_triangle(points,m,n):
    """ Creates alpha map of size (m,n)
    for a triangle with corners defined by points
    (given in normalized homogeneous coordinates). """

    alpha = zeros((m,n))
    for i in range(min(points[0]),max(points[0])):
        for j in range(min(points[1]),max(points[1])):
            x = linalg.solve(points,[i,j,1])
            if min(x) > 0: #all coefficients positive
                alpha[i,j] = 1
    return alpha
```

This is an operation your graphics card can do extremely fast. Python is a lot slower than your graphics card (or a C/C++ implementation for that matter) but it works just fine for our purposes. As you can see at the bottom of Figure 3-3, the corners now match.

Piecewise Affine Warping

As we saw in the example above, affine warping of triangle patches can be done to exactly match the corner points. Let's look at the most common form of warping between a set of corresponding points, *piecewise affine warping*. Given any image with landmark points, we can warp that image to corresponding landmarks in another image by triangulating the points into a triangle mesh and then warping each triangle with an

---

[1] A *convex combination* is a linear combination $\sum_j \alpha_j \mathbf{x}_i$ (in this case of the triangle points) such that all coefficients α_j are non-negative and sum to 1.

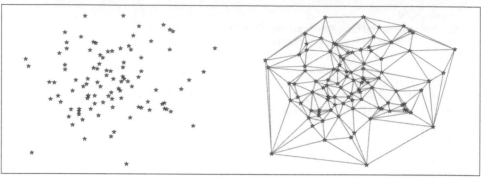

Figure 3-4. An example of Delaunay triangulation of a set of random 2D points.

affine transform. These are standard operations for any graphics and image processing library. Here we show how to do this using Matplotlib and SciPy.

To triangulate points, *Delaunay triangulation* is often used. An implementation of Delaunay triangulation comes included in Matplotlib (but outside the PyLab part) and can be used like this:

```
import matplotlib.delaunay as md

x,y = array(random.standard_normal((2,100)))
centers,edges,tri,neighbors = md.delaunay(x,y)

figure()
for t in tri:
    t_ext = [t[0], t[1], t[2], t[0]] # add first point to end
    plot(x[t_ext],y[t_ext],'r')

plot(x,y,'*')
axis('off')
show()
```

Figure 3-4 shows some example points and the resulting triangulation. Delaunay triangulation chooses the triangles so that the minimum angle of all the angles of the triangles in the triangulation is maximized.[2] There are four outputs of delaunay(), of which we only need the list of triangles (the third of the outputs). Create a function in *warp.py* for the triangulation:

```
import matplotlib.delaunay as md

def triangulate_points(x,y):
    """ Delaunay triangulation of 2D points. """

    centers,edges,tri,neighbors = md.delaunay(x,y)
    return tri
```

---

[2] The edges are actually the dual graph of a Voronoi diagram. See *http://en.wikipedia.org/wiki/Delaunay_triangulation*.

The output is an array with each row containing the indices in the arrays x and y for the three points of each triangle.

Let's now apply this to an example of warping an image to a non-flat object in another image using 30 control points in a 5 × 6 grid. Figure 3-5b shows an image to be warped to the facade of the "turning torso." The target points were manually selected using ginput() and stored in the file *turningtorso_points.txt*.

First, we need a general warp function for piecewise affine image warping. The code below does the trick, where we also take the opportunity to show how to warp color images (you simply warp each color channel):

```python
def pw_affine(fromim,toim,fp,tp,tri):
  """ Warp triangular patches from an image.
    fromim = image to warp
    toim = destination image
    fp = from points in hom. coordinates
    tp = to points in hom.  coordinates
    tri = triangulation. """

  im = toim.copy()

  # check if image is grayscale or color
  is_color = len(fromim.shape) == 3

  # create image to warp to (needed if iterate colors)
  im_t = zeros(im.shape, 'uint8')

  for t in tri:
    # compute affine transformation
    H = homography.Haffine_from_points(tp[:,t],fp[:,t])

    if is_color:
      for col in range(fromim.shape[2]):
        im_t[:,:,col] = ndimage.affine_transform(
          fromim[:,:,col],H[:2,:2],(H[0,2],H[1,2]),im.shape[:2])
    else:
      im_t = ndimage.affine_transform(
          fromim,H[:2,:2],(H[0,2],H[1,2]),im.shape[:2])

    # alpha for triangle
    alpha = alpha_for_triangle(tp[:,t],im.shape[0],im.shape[1])

    # add triangle to image
    im[alpha>0] = im_t[alpha>0]

  return im
```

Here we first check if the image is grayscale or color and in the case of colors, we warp each color channel. The affine transform for each triangle is uniquely determined, so we use Haffine_from_points(). Add this function to the file *warp.py*.

To use this function on the current example, the following short script puts it all together:

```
import homography
import warp

# open image to warp
fromim = array(Image.open('sunset_tree.jpg'))
x,y = meshgrid(range(5),range(6))
x = (fromim.shape[1]/4) * x.flatten()
y = (fromim.shape[0]/5) * y.flatten()

# triangulate
tri = warp.triangulate_points(x,y)

# open image and destination points
im = array(Image.open('turningtorso1.jpg'))
tp = loadtxt('turningtorso1_points.txt') # destination points

# convert points to hom. coordinates
fp = vstack((y,x,ones((1,len(x)))))
tp = vstack((tp[:,1],tp[:,0],ones((1,len(tp)))))

# warp triangles
im = warp.pw_affine(fromim,im,fp,tp,tri)

# plot
figure()
imshow(im)
warp.plot_mesh(tp[1],tp[0],tri)
axis('off')
show()
```

The resulting image is shown in Figure 3-5c. The triangles are plotted with the following helper function (add this to *warp.py*):

```
def plot_mesh(x,y,tri):
    """ Plot triangles. """

    for t in tri:
        t_ext = [t[0], t[1], t[2], t[0]] # add first point to end
        plot(x[t_ext],y[t_ext],'r')
```

This example should give you all you need to apply piecewise affine warping of images to your own applications. There are many improvements that can be made to the functions used. Let's leave some to the exercises and the rest to you.

Registering Images

Image registration is the process of transferring images so that they are aligned in a common coordinate frame. Registration can be rigid or non-rigid and is an important step in order to be able to do image comparisons and more sophisticated analysis.

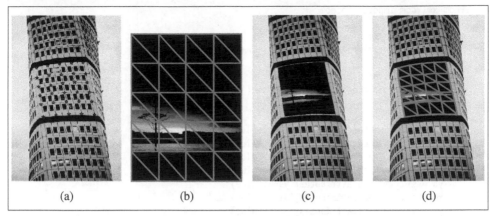

Figure 3-5. An example of piecewise affine warping using Delaunay triangulated landmark points: (a) the target image with landmarks; (b) image with triangulation; (c) with warped image; (d) with warped image and triangulation.

Let's look at an example of rigidly registering a set of face images so that we can compute the mean face and face appearance variations in a meaningful way. In this type of registration we are actually looking for a similarity transform (rigid with scale) to map correspondences. This is because the faces are not all at the same size, position, and rotation in the images.

In the file *jkfaces.zip* are 366 images of a single person (one for each day in 2008).[3] The images are annotated with eye and mouth coordinates in the file *jkfaces.xml*. Using the points, a similarity transformation can be computed and the images warped to a normalized coordinate frame using this transformation (which, as mentioned, includes scaling). To read XML files, we will use `minidom` that comes with Python's built-in `xml.dom` module.

The XML file looks like this:

```
<?xml version="1.0" encoding="utf-8"?>
<faces>
        <face file="jk-002.jpg" xf="46" xm="56" xs="67" yf="38" ym="65" ys="39"/>
        <face file="jk-006.jpg" xf="38" xm="48" xs="59" yf="38" ym="65" ys="38"/>
        <face file="jk-004.jpg" xf="40" xm="50" xs="61" yf="38" ym="66" ys="39"/>
        <face file="jk-010.jpg" xf="33" xm="44" xs="55" yf="38" ym="65" ys="38"/>
    .
    .
    .
</faces>
```

To read the coordinates from the file, add the following function that uses `minidom` to a new file *imregistration.py*:

---

[3] Images are courtesy of J. K. Keller (with permission). See *http://jk-keller.com/daily-photo/* for more details.

```
from xml.dom import minidom

def read_points_from_xml(xmlFileName):
    """ Reads control points for face alignment. """

    xmldoc = minidom.parse(xmlFileName)
    facelist = xmldoc.getElementsByTagName('face')
    faces = {}
    for xmlFace in facelist:
        fileName = xmlFace.attributes['file'].value
        xf = int(xmlFace.attributes['xf'].value)
        yf = int(xmlFace.attributes['yf'].value)
        xs = int(xmlFace.attributes['xs'].value)
        ys = int(xmlFace.attributes['ys'].value)
        xm = int(xmlFace.attributes['xm'].value)
        ym = int(xmlFace.attributes['ym'].value)
        faces[fileName] = array([xf, yf, xs, ys, xm, ym])
    return faces
```

The landmark points are returned in a Python dictionary with the filename of the image as key. The format is: *xf,yf* coordinates of the leftmost eye in the image (the person's right), *xs,ys* coordinates of the rightmost eye, and *xm,ym* mouth coordinates. To compute the parameters of the similarity transformation, we can use a least squares solution. For each point $\mathbf{x}_i = [x_i, y_i]$ (in this case there are three of them), the point should be mapped to the target location $[\hat{x}_i, \hat{y}_i]$ as

$$
\begin{bmatrix} \hat{x}_i \\ \hat{y}_i \end{bmatrix} = \begin{bmatrix} a & -b \\ b & a \end{bmatrix} \begin{bmatrix} x_i \\ y_i \end{bmatrix} + \begin{bmatrix} t_x \\ t_y \end{bmatrix}.
$$

Taking all three points, we can rewrite this as a system of equations with the unknowns a, b, t_x, t_y like this:

$$
\begin{bmatrix} \hat{x}_1 \\ \hat{y}_1 \\ \hat{x}_2 \\ \hat{y}_2 \\ \hat{x}_3 \\ \hat{y}_3 \end{bmatrix} = \begin{bmatrix} x_1 & -y_1 & 1 & 0 \\ y_1 & x_1 & 0 & 1 \\ x_2 & -y_2 & 1 & 0 \\ y_2 & x_2 & 0 & 1 \\ x_3 & -y_3 & 1 & 0 \\ y_3 & x_3 & 0 & 1 \end{bmatrix} \begin{bmatrix} a \\ b \\ t_x \\ t_y \end{bmatrix}.
$$

Here we used the parameterization of similarity matrices

$$
\begin{bmatrix} a & -b \\ b & a \end{bmatrix} = s \begin{bmatrix} \cos(\theta) & -\sin(\theta) \\ \sin(\theta) & \cos(\theta) \end{bmatrix} = sR,
$$

with scale $s = \sqrt{a^2 + b^2}$ and rotation matrix R.

More point correspondences would work the same way and only add extra rows to the matrix. The least squares solution is found using `linalg.lstsq()`. This idea of using least squares solutions is a standard trick that will be used many times in this book. Actually this is the same as used in the DLT algorithm earlier.

The code looks like this (add to *imregistration.py*):

```
from scipy import linalg

def compute_rigid_transform(refpoints,points):
  """ Computes rotation, scale and translation for
    aligning points to refpoints. """

  A = array([ [points[0], -points[1], 1, 0],
              [points[1],  points[0], 0, 1],
              [points[2], -points[3], 1, 0],
              [points[3],  points[2], 0, 1],
              [points[4], -points[5], 1, 0],
              [points[5],  points[4], 0, 1]])

  y = array([ refpoints[0],
              refpoints[1],
              refpoints[2],
              refpoints[3],
              refpoints[4],
              refpoints[5]])

  # least sq solution to mimimize ||Ax - y||
  a,b,tx,ty = linalg.lstsq(A,y)[0]
  R = array([[a, -b], [b, a]]) # rotation matrix incl scale

  return R,tx,ty
```

The function returns a rotation matrix with scale as well as translation in the x and y directions. To warp the images and store new aligned, images we can apply `ndimage.affine_transform()` to each color channel (these are color images). As reference frame, any three point coordinates could be used. Here we will use the landmark locations in the first image for simplicity:

```
from scipy import ndimage
from scipy.misc import imsave
import os

def rigid_alignment(faces,path,plotflag=False):
  """ Align images rigidly and save as new images.
    path determines where the aligned images are saved
    set plotflag=True to plot the images. """

  # take the points in the first image as reference points
  refpoints = faces.values()[0]

  # warp each image using affine transform
  for face in faces:
    points = faces[face]
```

```
R,tx,ty = compute_rigid_transform(refpoints, points)
T = array([[R[1][1], R[1][0]], [R[0][1], R[0][0]]])

im = array(Image.open(os.path.join(path,face)))
im2 = zeros(im.shape, 'uint8')

# warp each color channel
for i in range(len(im.shape)):
  im2[:,:,i] = ndimage.affine_transform(im[:,:,i],linalg.inv(T),offset=[-ty,-tx])

if plotflag:
  imshow(im2)
  show()

# crop away border and save aligned images
h,w = im2.shape[:2]
border = (w+h)/20

# crop away border
imsave(os.path.join(path, 'aligned/'+face),im2[border:h-border,border:w-border,:])
```

Here we use the `imsave()` function to save the aligned images to a sub-directory "aligned".

The following short script will read the XML file containing filenames as keys and points as values and then register all the images to align them with the first one:

```
import imregistration

# load the location of control points
xmlFileName = 'jkfaces2008_small/jkfaces.xml'
points = imregistration.read_points_from_xml(xmlFileName)

# register
imregistration.rigid_alignment(points,'jkfaces2008_small/')
```

If you run this, you should get aligned face images in a sub-directory. Figure 3-6 shows six sample images before and after registration. The registered images are cropped slightly to remove the undesired black fill pixels that may appear at the borders of the images.

Now let's see how this affects the mean image. Figure 3-7 shows the mean image for the unaligned face images next to the mean image of the aligned images (note the size difference due to cropping the borders of the aligned images). Although the original images show very little variation in size of the face, rotation and position, the effects on the mean computation are drastic.

Not surprisingly, using badly registered images also has a drastic impact on the computation of principal components. Figure 3-8 shows the result of PCA on the first 150 images from this set without and with registration. Just as with the mean image, the

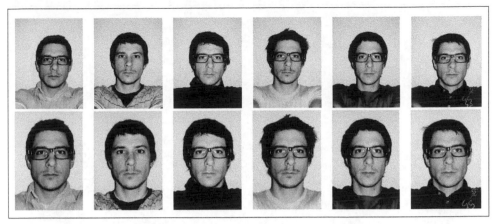

Figure 3-6. Sample images before (top) and after rigid registration (bottom).

PCA-modes are blurry. When computing the principal components, we used a mask consisting of an ellipse centered around the mean face position. By multiplying the images with this mask before stacking them, we can avoid bringing background variations into the PCA-modes. Just replace the line that creates the matrix in the PCA example in Section 1.3 (page 14) with

```
immatrix = array([mask*array(Image.open(imlist[i]).convert('L')).flatten()
        for i in range(150)],'f')
```

where *mask* is a binary image of the same size, already flattened.

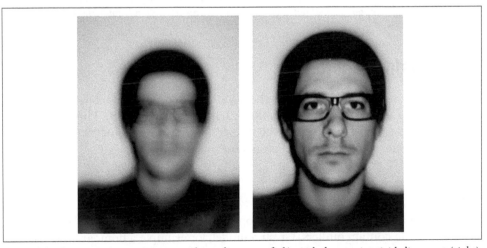

Figure 3-7. Comparing mean images: without alignment (left); with three-point rigid alignment (right).

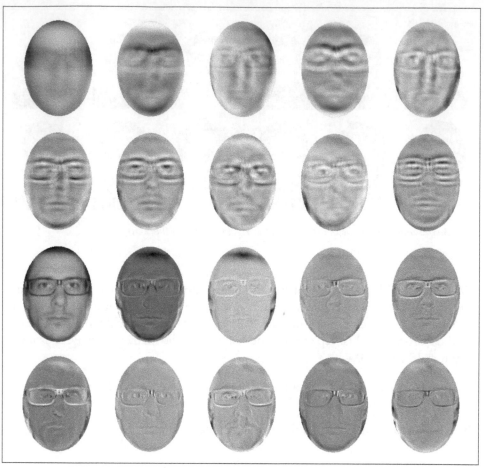

Figure 3-8. Comparing PCA-modes of unregistered and registered images: the mean image and the first nine principal components without registering the images beforehand (top); the same with the registered images (bottom).

3.3 Creating Panoramas

Two (or more) images that are taken at the same location (that is, the camera position is the same for the images) are homographically related (see Figure 3-9). This is frequently used for creating panoramic images where several images are stitched together into one big mosaic. In this section we will explore how this is done.

RANSAC

RANSAC, short for "RANdom SAmple Consensus," is an iterative method to fit models to data that can contain outliers. Given a model, for example a homography between sets of points, the basic idea is that the data contains *inliers*, the data points that can be described by the model, and *outliers*, those that do not fit the model.

Figure 3-9. Five images of the main university building in Lund, Sweden. The images are all taken from the same viewpoint.

The standard example is the case of fitting a line to a set of points that contains outliers. Simple least squares fitting will fail, but RANSAC can hopefully single out the inliers and obtain the correct fit. Let's look at using *ransac.py* from *http://www .scipy.org/Cookbook/RANSAC*, which contains this particular example as a test case. Figure 3-10 shows an example of running ransac.test(). As you can see, the algorithm selects only points consistent with a line model and correctly finds the right solution.

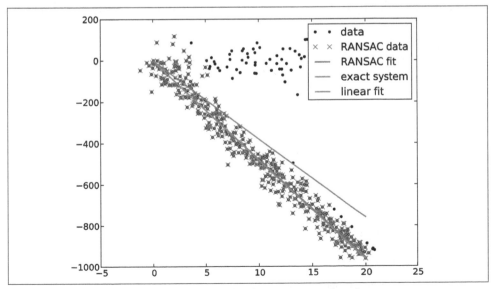

Figure 3-10. An example of using RANSAC to fit a line to points with outliers.

RANSAC is a very useful algorithm, which we will use in the next section for homography estimation and again for other examples. For more information, see the original paper by Fischler and Bolles [11], Wikipedia *http://en.wikipedia.org/wiki/RANSAC*, or the report [40].

Robust Homography Estimation

We can use this RANSAC module for any model. All that is needed is a Python class with fit() and get_error() methods, the rest is taken care of by *ransac.py*. Here we are interested in automatically finding a homography for the panorama images using a set of possible correspondences. Figure 3-11 shows the matching correspondences found automatically using SIFT features, by running the following commands:

```
import sift

featname = ['Univ'+str(i+1)+'.sift' for i in range(5)]
imname = ['Univ'+str(i+1)+'.jpg' for i in range(5)]
l = {}
d = {}
for i in range(5):
  sift.process_image(imname[i],featname[i])
  l[i],d[i] = sift.read_features_from_file(featname[i])

matches = {}
for i in range(4):
  matches[i] = sift.match(d[i+1],d[i])
```

It is clear from the images that not all correspondences are correct. SIFT is actually a very robust descriptor and gives fewer false matches than, for example, Harris points with patch correlation, but still it is far from perfect.

To fit a homography using RANSAC, we first need to add the following model class to *homography.py*:

```
class RansacModel(object):
    """ Class for testing homography fit with ransac.py from
        http://www.scipy.org/Cookbook/RANSAC"""

    def __init__(self,debug=False):
      self.debug = debug

    def fit(self, data):
      """ Fit homography to four selected correspondences. """

      # transpose to fit H_from_points()
      data = data.T

      # from points
      fp = data[:3,:4]
      # target points
      tp = data[3:,:4]

      # fit homography and return
      return H_from_points(fp,tp)
```

```
def get_error( self, data, H):
  """ Apply homography to all correspondences,
    return error for each transformed point. """

  data = data.T

  # from points
  fp = data[:3]
  # target points
  tp = data[3:]

  # transform fp
  fp_transformed = dot(H,fp)

  # normalize hom. coordinates
  for i in range(3):
    fp_transformed[i] /= fp_transformed[2]

  # return error per point
  return sqrt( sum((tp-fp_transformed)**2,axis=0) )
```

As you can see, this class contains a fit() method that just takes the four correspondences selected by *ransac.py* (they are the first four in *data*) and fits a homography. Remember, four points are the minimal number to compute a homography. The method

Figure 3-11. Matching correspondences found between consecutive image pairs using SIFT features.

get_error() applies the homography and returns the sum of squared distance for each correspondence pair, so that RANSAC can chose which points to keep as inliers and outliers. This is done with a threshold on this distance. For ease of use, add the following function to *homography.py*:

```
def H_from_ransac(fp,tp,model,maxiter=1000,match_theshold=10):
    """ Robust estimation of homography H from point
        correspondences using RANSAC (ransac.py from
        http://www.scipy.org/Cookbook/RANSAC).

        input: fp,tp (3*n arrays) points in hom. coordinates. """

    import ransac

    # group corresponding points
    data = vstack((fp,tp))

    # compute H and return
    H,ransac_data = ransac.ransac(data.T,model,4,maxiter,match_theshold,10,
                                    return_all=True)
    return H,ransac_data['inliers']
```

The function also lets you supply the threshold and the minimum number of points desired. The most important parameter is the maximum number of iterations: exiting too early might give a worse solution; too many iterations will take more time. The resulting homography is returned together with the inlier points.

Apply RANSAC to the correspondences like this:

```
# function to convert the matches to hom. points
def convert_points(j):
    ndx = matches[j].nonzero()[0]
    fp = homography.make_homog(l[j+1][ndx,:2].T)
    ndx2 = [int(matches[j][i]) for i in ndx]
    tp = homography.make_homog(l[j][ndx2,:2].T)
    return fp,tp

# estimate the homographies
model = homography.RansacModel()

fp,tp = convert_points(1)
H_12 = homography.H_from_ransac(fp,tp,model)[0] #im 1 to 2

fp,tp = convert_points(0)
H_01 = homography.H_from_ransac(fp,tp,model)[0] #im 0 to 1

tp,fp = convert_points(2) #NB: reverse order
H_32 = homography.H_from_ransac(fp,tp,model)[0] #im 3 to 2

tp,fp = convert_points(3) #NB: reverse order
H_43 = homography.H_from_ransac(fp,tp,model)[0] #im 4 to 3
```

In this example, image number 2 is the central image and the one we want to warp the others to. Image 0 and 1 should be warped from the right and image 3 and 4 from the left. The matches were computed from the rightmost image in each pair; therefore, we reverse the order of the correspondences for the images warped from the left. We also take only the first output (the homography), as we are not interested in the inlier points for this warping case.

Stitching the Images Together

With the homographies between the images estimated (using RANSAC), we now need to warp all images to a common image plane. It makes most sense to use the plane of the center image (otherwise the distortions will be huge). One way to do this is to create a very large image, for example filled with zeros, parallel to the central image and to warp all the images to it. Since all our images are taken with a horizontal rotation of the camera, we can use a simpler procedure: we just pad the central image with zeros to the left or right to make room for the warped images. Add the following function, which handles this to *warp.py*:

```
def panorama(H,fromim,toim,padding=2400,delta=2400):
    """ Create horizontal panorama by blending two images
        using a homography H (preferably estimated using RANSAC).
        The result is an image with the same height as toim. 'padding'
        specifies number of fill pixels and 'delta' additional translation. """

    # check if images are grayscale or color
    is_color = len(fromim.shape) == 3

    # homography transformation for geometric_transform()
    def transf(p):
        p2 = dot(H,[p[0],p[1],1])
        return (p2[0]/p2[2],p2[1]/p2[2])

    if H[1,2]<0: # fromim is to the right
        print 'warp - right'
        # transform fromim
        if is_color:
            # pad the destination image with zeros to the right
            toim_t = hstack((toim,zeros((toim.shape[0],padding,3))))
            fromim_t = zeros((toim.shape[0],toim.shape[1]+padding,toim.shape[2]))
            for col in range(3):
                fromim_t[:,:,col] = ndimage.geometric_transform(fromim[:,:,col],
                        transf,(toim.shape[0],toim.shape[1]+padding))
        else:
            # pad the destination image with zeros to the right
            toim_t = hstack((toim,zeros((toim.shape[0],padding))))
            fromim_t = ndimage.geometric_transform(fromim,transf,
                        (toim.shape[0],toim.shape[1]+padding))
    else:
        print 'warp - left'
        # add translation to compensate for padding to the left
        H_delta = array([[1,0,0],[0,1,-delta],[0,0,1]])
        H = dot(H,H_delta)
```

```
# transform fromim
if is_color:
  # pad the destination image with zeros to the left
  toim_t = hstack((zeros((toim.shape[0],padding,3)),toim))
  fromim_t = zeros((toim.shape[0],toim.shape[1]+padding,toim.shape[2]))
  for col in range(3):
    fromim_t[:,:,col] = ndimage.geometric_transform(fromim[:,:,col],
                  transf,(toim.shape[0],toim.shape[1]+padding))
else:
  # pad the destination image with zeros to the left
  toim_t = hstack((zeros((toim.shape[0],padding)),toim))
  fromim_t = ndimage.geometric_transform(fromim,
                transf,(toim.shape[0],toim.shape[1]+padding))

# blend and return (put fromim above toim)
if is_color:
  # all non black pixels
  alpha = ((fromim_t[:,:,0] * fromim_t[:,:,1] * fromim_t[:,:,2] ) > 0)
  for col in range(3):
    toim_t[:,:,col] = fromim_t[:,:,col]*alpha + toim_t[:,:,col]*(1-alpha)
else:
  alpha = (fromim_t > 0)
  toim_t = fromim_t*alpha + toim_t*(1-alpha)

return toim_t
```

For a general `geometric_transform()`, a function describing the pixel to pixel map needs to be specified. In this case, `transf()` does this by multiplying with H and normalizing the homogeneous coordinates. By checking the translation value in H we can decide if the image should be padded to the left or the right. When the image is padded to the left, the coordinates of the points in the target image changes so in the "left" case a translation is added to the homography. For simplicity, we also still use the trick of zero pixels for finding the alpha map.

Now use this function on the images as follows:

```
# warp the images
delta = 2000 # for padding and translation

im1 = array(Image.open(imname[1]))
im2 = array(Image.open(imname[2]))
im_12 = warp.panorama(H_12,im1,im2,delta,delta)

im1 = array(Image.open(imname[0]))
im_02 = warp.panorama(dot(H_12,H_01),im1,im_12,delta,delta)

im1 = array(Image.open(imname[3]))
im_32 = warp.panorama(H_32,im1,im_02,delta,delta)

im1 = array(Image.open(imname[j+1]))
im_42 = warp.panorama(dot(H_32,H_43),im1,im_32,delta,2*delta)
```

Note that, in the last line, *im_32* is already translated once. The resulting panorama image is shown in Figure 3-12. As you can see, there are effects of different exposure

Figure 3-12. Horizontal panorama automatically created from SIFT correspondences: the full panorama (top); a crop of the central part (bottom).

and edge effects at the boundaries between individual images. Commercial panorama software has extra processing to normalize intensity and smooth transitions to make the result look even better.

Exercises

1. Create a function that takes the image coordinates of a square (or rectangular) object (for example a book, a poster, or a 2D bar code) and estimates the transform that takes the rectangle to a full on frontal view in a normalized coordinate system. Use ginput() or the strongest Harris corners to find the points.

2. Write a function that correctly determines the alpha map for a warp like the one in Figure 3-1.

3. Find a data set of your own that contains three common landmark points (like those in the face example or using a famous object like the Eiffel tower). Create aligned images where the landmarks are in the same position. Compute mean and median images and visualize them.

4. Implement intensity normalization and a better way to blend the images in the panorama example to remove the edge effects in Figure 3-12.

5. Instead of warping to a central image, panoramas can be created by warping on to a cylinder. Try this for the example in Figure 3-12.

6. Use RANSAC to find several dominant homography inlier sets. An easy way to do this is to first make one run of RANSAC, find the homography with the largest consistent subset, then remove the inliers from the set of matches, then run RANSAC again to get the next biggest set, and so on.

7. Modify the homography RANSAC estimation to instead estimate affine transformations using three point correspondences. Use this to determine if a pair of images contains a planar scene, for example using the inlier count. A planar scene will have a high inlier count for an affine transformation.

8. Build a *panograph* (*http://en.wikipedia.org/wiki/Panography*) from a collection (for example from Flickr) by matching local features and using least-squares rigid registration.

## CHAPTER 4

Camera Models and Augmented Reality

In this chapter, we will look at modeling cameras and how to effectively use such models. In the previous chapter, we covered image to image mappings and transforms. To handle mappings between 3D and images, the projection properties of the camera generating the image needs to be part of the mapping. Here we show how to determine camera properties and how to use image projections for applications like augmented reality. In the next chapter, we will use the camera model to look at applications with multiple views and mappings between them.

4.1 The Pin-Hole Camera Model

The *pin-hole camera* model (or sometimes *projective camera* model) is a widely used camera model in computer vision. It is simple and accurate enough for most applications. The name comes from the type of camera, like a camera obscura, that collects light through a small hole to the inside of a dark box or room. In the pin-hole camera model, light passes through a single point, the *camera center*, **C**, before it is projected onto an *image plane*. Figure 4-1 shows an illustration where the image plane is drawn in front of the camera center. The image plane in an actual camera would be upside down behind the camera center, but the model is the same.

The projection properties of a pin-hole camera can be derived from this illustration and the assumption that the image axis is aligned with the x and y axis of a 3D coordinate system. The *optical axis* of the camera then coincides with the z axis and the projection follows from similar triangles. By adding rotation and translation to put a 3D point in this coordinate system before projecting, the complete projection transform follows. The interested reader can find the details in [13] and [25, 26].

With a pin-hole camera, a 3D point **X** is projected to an image point **x** (both expressed in homogeneous coordinates) as

$$\lambda \mathbf{x} = P\mathbf{X}. \tag{4.1}$$

Here, the 3×4 matrix P is called the *camera matrix* (or *projection matrix*). Note that the 3D point **X** has four elements in homogeneous coordinates, $\mathbf{X} = [X, Y, Z, W]$. The

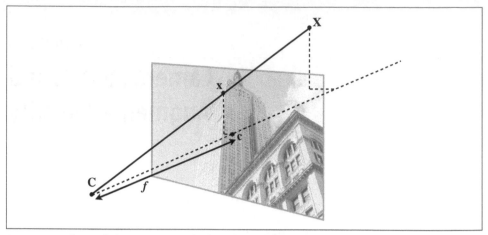

Figure 4-1. The pin-hole camera model. The image point **x** *is at the intersection of the image plane and the line joining the 3D point* **X** *and the camera center* **C**. *The dashed line is the optical axis of the camera.*

scalar λ is the *inverse depth* of the 3D point and is needed if we want all coordinates to be homogeneous with the last value normalized to one.

The Camera Matrix

The camera matrix can be decomposed as

$$P = K \ [R \mid \mathbf{t}], \tag{4.2}$$

where R is a rotation matrix describing the orientation of the camera, $\mathbf{t}$ a 3D translation vector describing the position of the camera center, and the intrinsic *calibration matrix* K describing the projection properties of the camera.

The calibration matrix depends only on the camera properties and is in a general form written as

$$K = \begin{bmatrix} \alpha f & s & c_x \\ 0 & f & c_y \\ 0 & 0 & 1 \end{bmatrix}.$$

The *focal length*, f, is the distance between the image plane and the camera center. The skew, s, is only used if the pixel array in the sensor is skewed and can in most cases safely be set to zero. This gives

$$K = \begin{bmatrix} f_x & 0 & c_x \\ 0 & f_y & c_y \\ 0 & 0 & 1 \end{bmatrix}, \tag{4.3}$$

where we used the alternative notation f_x and f_y, with $f_x = \alpha f_y$.

The *aspect ratio*, α is used for non-square pixel elements. It is often safe to assume $\alpha = 1$. With this assumption, the matrix becomes

$$K = \begin{bmatrix} f & 0 & c_x \\ 0 & f & c_y \\ 0 & 0 & 1 \end{bmatrix}.$$

Besides the focal length, the only remaining parameters are the coordinates of the *optical center* (sometimes called the *principal point*), the image point $\mathbf{c} = [c_x, c_y]$ where the optical axis intersects the image plane. Since this is usually in the center of the image and image coordinates are measured from the top-left corner, these values are often well approximated with half the width and height of the image. It is worth noting that in this last case the only unknown variable is the focal length f.

Projecting 3D Points

Let's create a camera class to handle all the operations we need for modeling cameras and projections:

```python
from scipy import linalg

class Camera(object):
    """ Class for representing pin-hole cameras. """

    def __init__(self,P):
        """ Initialize P = K[R|t] camera model. """
        self.P = P
        self.K = None # calibration matrix
        self.R = None # rotation
        self.t = None # translation
        self.c = None # camera center


    def project(self,X):
        """ Project points in X (4*n array) and normalize coordinates. """

        x = dot(self.P,X)
        for i in range(3):
            x[i] /= x[2]
        return x
```

The example below shows how to project 3D points into an image view. In this example, we will use one of the Oxford multi-view datasets, the "Model House" data set, available at *http://www.robots.ox.ac.uk/~vgg/data/data-mview.html*. Download the 3D geometry file and copy the *house.p3d* file to your working directory:

```python
import camera

# load points
points = loadtxt('house.p3d').T
points = vstack((points,ones(points.shape[1])))

# setup camera
P = hstack((eye(3),array([[0],[0],[-10]])))
cam = camera.Camera(P)
x = cam.project(points)
```

```
# plot projection
figure()
plot(x[0],x[1],'k.')
show()
```

First, we make the points into homogeneous coordinates and create a `Camera` object with a projection matrix before projection the 3D points and plotting them. The result looks like the middle plot in Figure 4-2.

To see how moving the camera changes the projection, try the following piece of code that incrementally rotates the camera around a random 3D axis:

```
# create transformation
r = 0.05*random.rand(3)
rot = camera.rotation_matrix(r)

# rotate camera and project
figure()
for t in range(20):
  cam.P = dot(cam.P,rot)
  x = cam.project(points)
  plot(x[0],x[1],'k.')
show()
```

Here we used the helper function `rotation_matrix()`, which creates a rotation matrix for 3D rotations around a vector (add this to *camera.py*):

```
def rotation_matrix(a):
    """ Creates a 3D rotation matrix for rotation
      around the axis of the vector a. """
    R = eye(4)
    R[:3,:3] = linalg.expm([[0,-a[2],a[1]],[a[2],0,-a[0]],[-a[1],a[0],0]])
    return R
```

Figure 4-2 shows one of the images from the sequence, a projection of the 3D points and the projected 3D point tracks after the points have been rotated around a random vector. Try this example a few times with different random rotations and you will get a feel for how the points rotate from the projections.

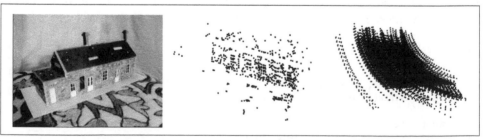

Figure 4-2. An example of projecting 3D points: sample image (left); projected points into a view (middle); trajectory of projected points under camera rotation (right). Data from the Oxford "Model House" dataset.

Factoring the Camera Matrix

If we are given a camera matrix P of the form in equation (4.2), we need to be able to recover the internal parameters K and the camera position and pose $\mathbf{t}$ and R. Partitioning the matrix is called *factorization*. In this case, we will use a type of matrix factorization called *RQ-factorization*.

Add the following method to the *Camera* class:

```
def factor(self):
    """ Factorize the camera matrix into K,R,t as P = K[R|t]. """

    # factor first 3*3 part
    K,R = linalg.rq(self.P[:,:3])

    # make diagonal of K positive
    T = diag(sign(diag(K)))
    if linalg.det(T) < 0:
        T[1,1] *= -1

    self.K = dot(K,T)
    self.R = dot(T,R) # T is its own inverse
    self.t = dot(linalg.inv(self.K),self.P[:,3])

    return self.K, self.R, self.t
```

RQ-factorization is not unique, there is a sign ambiguity in the factorization. Since we need the rotation matrix R to have positive determinant (otherwise the coordinate axis can get flipped), we can add a transform T to change the sign when needed.

Try this on a sample camera to see that it works:

```
import camera

K = array([[1000,0,500],[0,1000,300],[0,0,1]])
tmp = camera.rotation_matrix([0,0,1])[:3,:3]
Rt = hstack((tmp,array([[50],[40],[30]])))
cam = camera.Camera(dot(K,Rt))

print K,Rt
print cam.factor()
```

You should get the same printout in the console.

Computing the Camera Center

Given a camera projection matrix, P, it is useful to be able to compute the camera's position in space. The camera center, $\mathbf{C}$, is a 3D point with the property $P\mathbf{C} = 0$. For a camera with $P = K [R \mid \mathbf{t}]$, this gives

$$K[R \mid \mathbf{t}]\mathbf{C} = KR\mathbf{C} + K\mathbf{t} = 0,$$

and the camera center can be computed as

$$\mathbf{C} = -R^T\mathbf{t}.$$

Note that the camera center is independent of the intrinsic calibration K, as expected.

Add the following method for computing the camera center according to the formula above and/or returning the camera center to the `Camera` class:

```
def center(self):
    """ Compute and return the camera center. """

    if self.c is not None:
        return self.c
    else:
        # compute c by factoring
        self.factor()
        self.c = -dot(self.R.T,self.t)
        return self.c
```

This concludes the basic functions of our `Camera` class. Now, let's see how to work with this pin-hole camera model.

4.2 Camera Calibration

Calibrating a camera means determining the internal camera parameters, in our case the matrix K. It is possible to extend this camera model to include radial distortion and other artifacts if your application needs precise measurements. For most applications, however, the simple model in equation (4.3) is good enough. The standard way to calibrate cameras is to take lots of pictures of a flat checkerboard pattern. For example, the calibration tools in OpenCV use this approach (see [3] for details).

A Simple Calibration Method

Here we will look at a simple calibration method. Since most of the parameters can be set using basic assumptions (square straight pixels, optical center at the center of the image), the tricky part is getting the focal length right. For this calibration method, you need a flat rectangular calibration object (a book will do), measuring tape or a ruler, and a flat surface. Here's what to do:

- Measure the sides of your rectangular calibration object. Let's call these dX and dY.

- Place the camera and the calibration object on a flat surface so that the camera back and calibration object are parallel and the object is roughly in the center of the camera's view. You might have to raise the camera or object to get a nice alignment.

- Measure the distance from the camera to the calibration object. Let's call this dZ.

- Take a picture and check that the setup is straight, meaning that the sides of the calibration object align with the rows and columns of the image.

- Measure the width and height of the object in pixels. Let's call these dx and dy.

See Figure 4-3 for an example of a setup. Now, using similar triangles (look at Figure 4-1 to convince yourself of that), the following relation gives the focal lengths:

$$f_x = \frac{dx}{dX}dZ, \qquad f_y = \frac{dy}{dY}dZ.$$

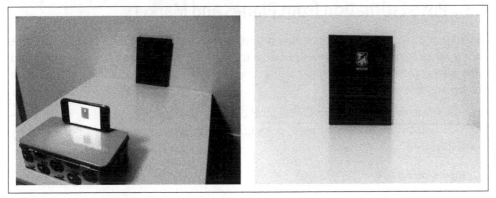

Figure 4-3. A simple camera calibration setup: an image of the setup used (left); the image used for the calibration (right). Measuring the width and height of the calibration object in the image and the physical dimensions of the setup is enough to determine the focal length.

For the particular setup in Figure 4-3, the object was measured to be 130 by 185 mm, so $dX = 130$ and $dY = 185$. The distance from camera to object was 460 mm, so $dZ = 460$. You can use any unit of measurement; only the ratios of the measurements matter. Using ginput() to select four points in the image, the width and height in pixels was 722 and 1040. This means that $dx = 722$ and $dy = 1040$. Putting these values in the relationship above gives

$$f_x = 2555, \qquad f_y = 2586.$$

Now, it is important to note that *this is for a particular image resolution*. In this case, the image was 2592×1936 pixels. Remember that the focal length and the optical center are measured in pixels and scale with the image resolution. If you take other image resolutions (for example a thumbnail image), the values will change. It is convenient to add the constants of your camera to a helper function like this:

```
def my_calibration(sz):
    row,col = sz
    fx = 2555*col/2592
    fy = 2586*row/1936
    K = diag([fx,fy,1])
    K[0,2] = 0.5*col
    K[1,2] = 0.5*row
    return K
```

This function then takes a size tuple and returns the calibration matrix. Here we assume the optical center to be the center of the image. Go ahead and replace the focal lengths with their mean if you like; for most consumer type cameras this is fine. Note that the calibration is for images in landscape orientation. For portrait orientation, you need to interchange the constants. Let's keep this function and make use of it in the next section.

4.3 Pose Estimation from Planes and Markers

In Chapter 3, we saw how to estimate homographies between planes. Combining this with a calibrated camera makes it possible to compute the camera's pose (rotation and translation) if the image contains a planar marker object. This marker object can be almost any flat object.

Let's illustrate with an example. Consider the two top images in Figure 4-4. The following code will extract SIFT features in both images and robustly estimate a homography using RANSAC:

```
import homography
import camera
import sift

# compute features
sift.process_image('book_frontal.JPG','im0.sift')
l0,d0 = sift.read_features_from_file('im0.sift')

sift.process_image('book_perspective.JPG','im1.sift')
l1,d1 = sift.read_features_from_file('im1.sift')
```

Figure 4-4. Example of computing the projection matrix for a new view using a planar object as marker. Matching image features to an aligned marker gives a homography that can be used to compute the pose of the camera. Template image with a gray square (top left); an image taken from an unknown viewpoint with the same square transformed with the estimated homography (top right); a cube transformed using the estimated camera matrix (bottom).

```
# match features and estimate homography
matches = sift.match_twosided(d0,d1)
ndx = matches.nonzero()[0]
fp = homography.make_homog(l0[ndx,:2].T)
ndx2 = [int(matches[i]) for i in ndx]
tp = homography.make_homog(l1[ndx2,:2].T)

model = homography.RansacModel()
H = homography.H_from_ransac(fp,tp,model)
```

Now we have a homography that maps points on the marker (in this case the book) in one image to their corresponding locations in the other image. Let's define our 3D coordinate system so that the marker lies in the X-Y plane ($Z = 0$) with the origin somewhere on the marker.

To check our results, we will need some simple 3D object placed on the marker. Here we will use a cube and generate the cube points using the function:

```
def cube_points(c,wid):
    """ Creates a list of points for plotting
        a cube with plot. (the first 5 points are
        the bottom square, some sides repeated). """
    p = []
    # bottom
    p.append([c[0]-wid,c[1]-wid,c[2]-wid])
    p.append([c[0]-wid,c[1]+wid,c[2]-wid])
    p.append([c[0]+wid,c[1]+wid,c[2]-wid])
    p.append([c[0]+wid,c[1]-wid,c[2]-wid])
    p.append([c[0]-wid,c[1]-wid,c[2]-wid]) # same as first to close plot

    # top
    p.append([c[0]-wid,c[1]-wid,c[2]+wid])
    p.append([c[0]-wid,c[1]+wid,c[2]+wid])
    p.append([c[0]+wid,c[1]+wid,c[2]+wid])
    p.append([c[0]+wid,c[1]-wid,c[2]+wid])
    p.append([c[0]-wid,c[1]-wid,c[2]+wid]) # same as first to close plot

    # vertical sides
    p.append([c[0]-wid,c[1]-wid,c[2]+wid])
    p.append([c[0]-wid,c[1]+wid,c[2]+wid])
    p.append([c[0]-wid,c[1]+wid,c[2]-wid])
    p.append([c[0]+wid,c[1]+wid,c[2]-wid])
    p.append([c[0]+wid,c[1]+wid,c[2]+wid])
    p.append([c[0]+wid,c[1]-wid,c[2]+wid])
    p.append([c[0]+wid,c[1]-wid,c[2]-wid])

    return array(p).T
```

Some points are reoccurring so that plot() will generate a nice-looking cube.

With a homography and a camera calibration matrix, we can now determine the relative transformation between the two views:

```
# camera calibration
K = my_calibration((747,1000))

# 3D points at plane z=0 with sides of length 0.2
box = cube_points([0,0,0.1],0.1)

# project bottom square in first image
cam1 = camera.Camera( hstack((K,dot(K,array([[0],[0],[-1]])) )) )
# first points are the bottom square
box_cam1 = cam1.project(homography.make_homog(box[:,:5]))

# use H to transfer points to the second image
box_trans = homography.normalize(dot(H,box_cam1))

# compute second camera matrix from cam1 and H
cam2 = camera.Camera(dot(H,cam1.P))
A = dot(linalg.inv(K),cam2.P[:,:3])
A = array([A[:,0],A[:,1],cross(A[:,0],A[:,1])]).T
cam2.P[:,:3] = dot(K,A)

# project with the second camera
box_cam2 = cam2.project(homography.make_homog(box))


# test: projecting point on z=0 should give the same
point = array([1,1,0,1]).T
print homography.normalize(dot(dot(H,cam1.P),point))
print cam2.project(point)
```

Here we use a version of the image with resolution 747×1000 and first generate the calibration matrix for that image size. Next, points for a cube at the origin are created. The first five points generated by cube_points() correspond to the bottom, which in this case will lie on the plane defined by $Z = 0$, the plane of the marker. The first image (top left in Figure 4-4) is roughly a straight frontal view of the book and will be used as our template image. Since the scale of the scene coordinates is arbitrary, we create a first camera with matrix

$$P_1 = K \begin{bmatrix} 1 & 0 & 0 & 0 \\ 0 & 1 & 0 & 0 \\ 0 & 0 & 1 & -1 \end{bmatrix},$$

which has coordinate axis aligned with the camera and placed above the marker. The first five 3D points are projected onto the image. With the estimated homography, we can transform these to the second image. Plotting them should show the corners at the same marker locations (see top right in Figure 4-4).

Now, composing P_1 with H as a camera matrix for the second image,

$$P_2 = HP_1,$$

will transform points on the marker plane $Z = 0$ correctly. This means that the first two columns and the fourth column of P_2 are correct. Since we know that the first 3×3 block should be KR and R is a rotation matrix, we can recover the third column by

---

multiplying P_2 with the inverse of the calibration matrix and replacing the third column with the cross product of the first two.

As a sanity check, we can project a point on the marker plane with the new matrix and check that it gives the same projection as the same point transformed with the first camera and the homography. You should get the same printout in your console.

Visualizing the projected points can be done like this:

```
im0 = array(Image.open('book_frontal.JPG'))
im1 = array(Image.open('book_perspective.JPG'))

# 2D projection of bottom square
figure()
imshow(im0)
plot(box_cam1[0,:],box_cam1[1,:],linewidth=3)

# 2D projection transferred with H
figure()
imshow(im1)
plot(box_trans[0,:],box_trans[1,:],linewidth=3)

# 3D cube
figure()
imshow(im1)
plot(box_cam2[0,:],box_cam2[1,:],linewidth=3)

show()
```

This should give three figures like the images in Figure 4-4. To be able to reuse these computations for future examples, we can save the camera matrices using Pickle:

```
import pickle

with open('ar_camera.pkl','w') as f:
    pickle.dump(K,f)
    pickle.dump(dot(linalg.inv(K),cam2.P),f)
```

Now we have seen how to compute the camera matrix given a planar scene object. We combined feature matching with homographies and camera calibration to produce a simple example of placing a cube in an image. With camera pose estimation, we now have the building blocks in place for creating simple augmented reality applications.

4.4 Augmented Reality

Augmented reality (AR) is a collective term for placing objects and information on top of image data. The classic example is placing a 3D computer graphics model so that it looks like it belongs in the scene, and moves naturally with the camera motion in the case of video. Given an image with a marker plane as in the section above, we can compute the camera's position and pose and use that to place computer graphics models so that they are rendered correctly. In this last section of our camera chapter we will show how to build a simple AR example. We will use two tools for this, PyGame and PyOpenGL.

PyGame and PyOpenGL

PyGame is a popular package for game development that easily handles display windows, input devices, events, and much more. PyGame is open source and available from *http://www.pygame.org/*. It is actually a Python binding for the SDL game engine. For installation instructions, see Appendix A. For more details on programming with PyGame, see, for example, [21].

PyOpenGL is the Python binding to the OpenGL graphics programming interface. OpenGL comes pre-installed on almost all systems and is a crucial part for graphics performance. OpenGL is cross platform and works the same across operating systems. Take a look at *http://www.opengl.org/* for more information on OpenGL. The getting started page (*http://www.opengl.org/wiki/Getting_started*) has resources for beginners. PyOpenGL is open source and easy to install; see Appendix A for details. More information can be found on the project website, *http://pyopengl.sourceforge.net/*.

There is no way we can cover any significant portion of OpenGL programming. We will instead just show the important parts, for example how to use camera matrices in OpenGL and setting up a basic 3D model. Some good examples and demos are available in the PyOpenGL-Demo package (*http://pypi.python.org/pypi/PyOpenGL-Demo*). This is a good place to start if you are new to PyOpenGL.

We want to place a 3D model in a scene using OpenGL. To use PyGame and PyOpenGL for this application, we need to import the following at the top of our scripts:

```
from OpenGL.GL import *
from OpenGL.GLU import *
import pygame, pygame.image
from pygame.locals import *
```

As you can see, we need two main parts from OpenGL. The GL part contains all functions stating with "gl", which, you will see, are most of the ones we need. The GLU part is the OpenGL Utility library and contains some higher-level functionality. We will mainly use it to set up the camera projection. The `pygame` part sets up the window and event controls, and `pygame.image` is used for loading image and creating OpenGL textures. The `pygame.locals` is needed for setting up the display area for OpenGL.

The two main components of setting up an OpenGL scene are the projection and model view matrices. Let's get started and see how to create these matrices from our pin-hole cameras.

From Camera Matrix to OpenGL Format

OpenGL uses 4×4 matrices to represent transforms (both 3D transforms and projections). This is only slightly different from our use of 3×4 camera matrices. However, the camera-scene transformations are separated in two matrices, the *GL_PROJECTION* matrix and the *GL_MODELVIEW* matrix. GL_PROJECTION handles the image formation properties and is the equivalent of our internal calibration matrix K. GL_MODELVIEW handles the 3D transformation of the relation between the objects and the camera. This corresponds roughly to the R and t part of our camera matrix. One difference is that the coordinate system is assumed to be centered at the camera so the

GL_MODELVIEW matrix actually contains the transformation that places the objects in front of the camera. There are many peculiarities with working in OpenGL; we will comment on them as they are encountered in the examples below.

Given that we have a camera calibrated so that the calibration matrix K is known, the following function translates the camera properties to an OpenGL projection matrix:

```
def set_projection_from_camera(K):
    """ Set view from a camera calibration matrix. """

    glMatrixMode(GL_PROJECTION)
    glLoadIdentity()

    fx = K[0,0]
    fy = K[1,1]
    fovy = 2*arctan(0.5*height/fy)*180/pi
    aspect = (width*fy)/(height*fx)

    # define the near and far clipping planes
    near = 0.1
    far = 100.0

    # set perspective
    gluPerspective(fovy,aspect,near,far)
    glViewport(0,0,width,height)
```

We assume the calibration to be of the simpler form in (4.3) with the optical center at the image center. The first function `glMatrixMode()` sets the working matrix to GL_PROJECTION and subsequent commands will modify this matrix.[1] Then `glLoadIdentity()` sets the matrix to the identity matrix, basically reseting any prior changes. We then calculate the vertical field of view in degrees with the help of the image height and the camera's focal length as well as the aspect ratio. An OpenGL projection also has a near and far clipping plane to limit the depth range of what is rendered. We just set the near depth to be small enough to contain the nearest object and the far depth to some large number. We use the GLU utility function `gluPerspective()` to set the projection matrix and define the whole image to be the view port (essentially what is to be shown). There is also an option to load a full projection matrix with `glLoadMatrixf()` similar to the model view function below. This is useful when the simple version of the calibration matrix is not good enough.

The model view matrix should encode the relative rotation and translation that brings the object in front of the camera (as if the camera was at the origin). It is a 4×4 matrix that typically looks like this:

$$\begin{bmatrix} R & \mathbf{t} \\ \mathbf{0} & 1 \end{bmatrix},$$

where R is a rotation matrix with columns equal to the direction of the three coordinate axis and $\mathbf{t}$ is a translation vector. When creating a model view matrix, the rotation part

---

[1] This is an odd way to handle things, but there are only two matrices to switch between, GL_PROJECTION and GL_MODELVIEW, so it is manageable.

will need to hold all rotations (object and coordinate system) by multiplying together the individual components.

The following function shows how to take a 3×4 pin-hole camera matrix with the calibration removed (multiply P with K^{-1}) and create a model view:

```
def set_modelview_from_camera(Rt):
    """ Set the model view matrix from camera pose. """

    glMatrixMode(GL_MODELVIEW)
    glLoadIdentity()

    # rotate teapot 90 deg around x-axis so that z-axis is up
    Rx = array([[1,0,0],[0,0,-1],[0,1,0]])

    # set rotation to best approximation
    R = Rt[:,:3]
    U,S,V = linalg.svd(R)
    R = dot(U,V)
    R[0,:] = -R[0,:] # change sign of x-axis

    # set translation
    t = Rt[:,3]

    # setup 4*4 model view matrix
    M = eye(4)
    M[:3,:3] = dot(R,Rx)
    M[:3,3] = t

    # transpose and flatten to get column order
    M = M.T
    m = M.flatten()

    # replace model view with the new matrix
    glLoadMatrixf(m)
```

First, we switch to work on the GL_MODELVIEW matrix and reset it. Then we create a 90-degree rotation matrix, since the object we want to place needs to be rotated (you will see below). Then we make sure that the rotation part of the camera matrix is indeed a rotation matrix, in case there are errors or noise when we estimated the camera matrix. This is done with SVD and the best rotation matrix approximation is given by $R = UV^T$. The OpenGL coordinate system is a little different, so we flip the x-axis around. Then we set the model view matrix M by multiplying the rotations. The function `glLoadMatrixf()` sets the model view matrix and takes an array of the 16 values of the matrix taken *column-wise*. Transposing and then flattening accomplishes this.

Placing Virtual Objects in the Image

The first thing we need to do is to add the image (the one we want to place virtual objects in) as a background. In OpenGL this is done by creating a quadrilateral, a *quad*, that fills the whole view. The easiest way to do this is to draw the quad with the projection and model view matrices reset so that the coordinates go from -1 to 1 in each dimension.

This function loads an image, converts it to an OpenGL texture, and places that texture on the quad:

```
def draw_background(imname):
    """ Draw background image using a quad. """

    # load background image (should be .bmp) to OpenGL texture
    bg_image = pygame.image.load(imname).convert()
    bg_data = pygame.image.tostring(bg_image,"RGBX",1)

    glMatrixMode(GL_MODELVIEW)
    glLoadIdentity()
    glClear(GL_COLOR_BUFFER_BIT | GL_DEPTH_BUFFER_BIT)

    # bind the texture
    glEnable(GL_TEXTURE_2D)
    glBindTexture(GL_TEXTURE_2D,glGenTextures(1))
    glTexImage2D(GL_TEXTURE_2D,0,GL_RGBA,width,height,0,GL_RGBA,GL_UNSIGNED_BYTE,bg_data)
    glTexParameterf(GL_TEXTURE_2D,GL_TEXTURE_MAG_FILTER,GL_NEAREST)
    glTexParameterf(GL_TEXTURE_2D,GL_TEXTURE_MIN_FILTER,GL_NEAREST)

    # create quad to fill the whole window
    glBegin(GL_QUADS)
    glTexCoord2f(0.0,0.0); glVertex3f(-1.0,-1.0,-1.0)
    glTexCoord2f(1.0,0.0); glVertex3f( 1.0,-1.0,-1.0)
    glTexCoord2f(1.0,1.0); glVertex3f( 1.0, 1.0,-1.0)
    glTexCoord2f(0.0,1.0); glVertex3f(-1.0, 1.0,-1.0)
    glEnd()

    # clear the texture
    glDeleteTextures(1)
```

This function first uses some PyGame functions to load an image and serialize it to a raw string representation that can be used by PyOpenGL. Then we reset the model view and clear the color and depth buffer. Next, we bind the texture so that we can use it for the quad and specify interpolation. The quad is defined with corners at −1 and 1 in both dimensions. Note that the coordinates in the texture image go from 0 to 1. Finally, we clear the texture so it doesn't interfere with what we want to draw later.

Now we are ready to place objects in the scene. We will use the "hello world" computer graphics example, the Utah teapot (*http://en.wikipedia.org/wiki/Utah_teapot*). This teapot has a rich history and is available as one of the standard shapes in GLUT:

```
from OpenGL.GLUT import *
glutSolidTeapot(size)
```

This generates a solid teapot model of relative size *size*.

The following function will set up the color and properties to make a pretty red teapot:

```
def draw_teapot(size):
    """ Draw a red teapot at the origin. """
    glEnable(GL_LIGHTING)
    glEnable(GL_LIGHT0)
    glEnable(GL_DEPTH_TEST)
    glClear(GL_DEPTH_BUFFER_BIT)
```

```
# draw red teapot
glMaterialfv(GL_FRONT,GL_AMBIENT,[0,0,0,0])
glMaterialfv(GL_FRONT,GL_DIFFUSE,[0.5,0.0,0.0,0.0])
glMaterialfv(GL_FRONT,GL_SPECULAR,[0.7,0.6,0.6,0.0])
glMaterialf(GL_FRONT,GL_SHININESS,0.25*128.0)
glutSolidTeapot(size)
```

The first two lines enable lighting and a light. Lights are numbered as GL_LIGHT0, GL_LIGHT1, etc. We will only use one light in this example. The `glEnable()` function is used to turn on OpenGL features. These are defined with uppercase constants. Turning off a feature is done with the corresponding function `glDisable()`. Next, depth testing is turned on so that objects are rendered according to their depth (so that far-away objects are not drawn in front of near objects) and the depth buffer is cleared. Next, the material properties of the object, such as the diffuse and specular colors, are specified. The last line adds a solid Utah teapot with the specified material properties.

Tying It All Together

The full script for generating an image like the one in Figure 4-5 looks like this (assuming that you also have the functions introduced above in the same file):

```
from OpenGL.GL import *
from OpenGL.GLU import *
from OpenGL.GLUT import *
import pygame, pygame.image
from pygame.locals import *
import pickle

width,height = 1000,747

def setup():
  """ Setup window and pygame environment. """
  pygame.init()
  pygame.display.set_mode((width,height),OPENGL | DOUBLEBUF)
  pygame.display.set_caption('OpenGL AR demo')

# load camera data
with open('ar_camera.pkl','r') as f:
  K = pickle.load(f)
  Rt = pickle.load(f)

setup()
draw_background('book_perspective.bmp')
set_projection_from_camera(K)
set_modelview_from_camera(Rt)
draw_teapot(0.02)

while True:
  event = pygame.event.poll()
  if event.type in (QUIT,KEYDOWN):
    break
  pygame.display.flip()
```

Figure 4-5. Augmented reality. Placing a computer graphics model on a book in a scene using camera parameters computed from feature matches: the Utah teapot rendered in place aligned with the coordinate axis (top); sanity check to see the position of the origin (bottom).

First, this script loads the camera calibration matrix and the rotation and translation part of the camera matrix using Pickle. This assumes that you saved them as described on page 89. The setup() function initializes PyGame, sets the window to the size of the image, and makes the drawing area a double buffer OpenGL window. Next, the background image is loaded and placed to fit the window. The camera and model view matrices are set and finally the teapot is drawn at the correct position.

Events in PyGame are handled using infinite loops with regular polling for any changes. These can be keyboard, mouse, or other events. In this case, we check if the application was quit or if a key was pressed and exit the loop. The command pygame.display.flip() draws the objects on the screen.

The result should look like Figure 4-5. As you can see, the orientation is correct (the teapot is aligned with the sides of the cube in Figure 4-4). To check that the placement is correct, you can try to make the teapot really small by passing a smaller value for the *size* variable. The teapot should be placed close to the [0, 0, 0] corner of the cube in Figure 4-4. An example is shown in Figure 4-5.

Loading Models

Before we end this chapter, we will touch upon one last detail: loading 3D models and displaying them. The PyGame cookbook has a script for loading models in .obj format available at *http://www.pygame.org/wiki/OBJFileLoader*. You can learn more about the .obj format and the corresponding material file format at *http://en.wikipedia.org/wiki/Wavefront_.obj_file*.

Let's see how to use that with a basic example. We will use a freely available toy plane model from *http://www.oyonale.com/modeles.php*.[2] Download the .obj version and save it as *toyplane.obj*. You can, of course, replace this model with any model of your choice; the code below will be the same.

Assuming that you downloaded the file as *objloader.py*, add the following function to the file you used for the teapot example above:

```
def load_and_draw_model(filename):
    """ Loads a model from an .obj file using objloader.py.
      Assumes there is a .mtl material file with the same name. """
    glEnable(GL_LIGHTING)
    glEnable(GL_LIGHT0)
    glEnable(GL_DEPTH_TEST)
    glClear(GL_DEPTH_BUFFER_BIT)

    # set model color
    glMaterialfv(GL_FRONT,GL_AMBIENT,[0,0,0,0])
    glMaterialfv(GL_FRONT,GL_DIFFUSE,[0.5,0.75,1.0,0.0])
    glMaterialf(GL_FRONT,GL_SHININESS,0.25*128.0)

    # load from a file
    import objloader
    obj = objloader.OBJ(filename,swapyz=True)
    glCallList(obj.gl_list)
```

Same as before, we set the lighting and the color properties of the model. Next, we load a model file into an OBJ object and execute the OpenGL calls from the file.

You can set the texture and material properties in a corresponding .mtl file. The objloader module actually requires a material file. Rather than modifying the loading script, we take the pragmatic approach of just creating a tiny material file. In this case, we'll just specify the color.

---

[2] Models courtesy of Gilles Tran (Creative Commons License By Attribution).

Create a file *toyplane.mtl* with the following lines:

```
newmtl lightblue
Kd  0.5  0.75  1.0
illum 1
```

This sets the diffuse color of the object to a light grayish blue. Now, make sure to replace the "usemtl" tag in your .obj file with

```
usemtl lightblue
```

Adding textures we leave to the exercises. Replacing the call to draw_teapot() in the example above with

```
load_and_draw_model('toyplane.obj')
```

should generate a window like the one shown in Figure 4-6.

This is as deep as we will go into augmented reality and OpenGL in this book. With the recipe for calibrating cameras, computing camera pose, translating the cameras into OpenGL format, and rendering models in the scene, the groundwork is laid for you to continue exploring augmented reality. In the next chapter, we will continue with the camera model and compute 3D structure and camera pose without the use of markers.

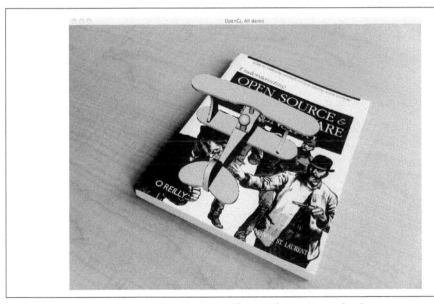

Figure 4-6. Loading a 3D model from an .obj file and placing it on a book in a scene using camera parameters computed from feature matches.

Exercises

1. Modify the example code for the motion in Figure 4-2 to transform the points instead of the camera. You should get the same plot. Experiment with different transformations and plot the results.

2. Some of the Oxford multi-view datasets have camera matrices given. Compute the camera positions for one of the sets an plot the camera path. Does it match with what you are seeing in the images?

3. Take some images of a scene with a planar marker or object. Match features to a full-frontal image to compute the pose of each image's camera location. Plot the camera trajectory and the plane of the marker. Add the feature points if you like.

4. In our augmented reality example, we assumed the object to be placed at the origin and applied only the camera's position to the model view matrix. Modify the example to place several objects at different locations by adding the object transformation to the matrix. For example, place a grid of teapots on the marker.

5. Take a look at the online documentation for .obj model files and see how to use textured models. Find a model (or create your own) and add it to the scene.

## CHAPTER 5

Multiple View Geometry

This chapter will show you how to handle multiple views and how to use the geometric relationships between them to recover camera positions and 3D structure. With images taken at different view points, it is possible to compute 3D scene points as well as camera locations from feature matches. We introduce the necessary tools and show a complete 3D reconstruction example. The last part of the chapter shows how to compute dense depth reconstructions from stereo images.

5.1 Epipolar Geometry

Multiple view geometry is the field studying the relationship between cameras and features when there are correspondences between many images that are taken from varying viewpoints. The image features are usually interest points, and we will focus on that case throughout this chapter. The most important constellation is two-view geometry.

With two views of a scene and corresponding points in these views, there are geometric constraints on the image points as a result of the relative orientation of the cameras, the properties of the cameras, and the position of the 3D points. These geometric relationships are described by what is called *epipolar geometry*. This section will give a very short description of the basic components we need. For more details on the subject, see [13].

Without any prior knowledge of the cameras, there is an inherent ambiguity in that a 3D point, $\mathbf{X}$, transformed with an arbitrary (4×4) homography H as $H\mathbf{X}$ will have the same image point in a camera PH^{-1} as the original point in the camera P. Expressed with the camera equation, this is

$$\lambda \mathbf{x} = P\mathbf{X} = PH^{-1}H\mathbf{X} = \hat{P}\hat{\mathbf{X}}.$$

Because of this ambiguity, when analyzing two view geometry we can always transform the cameras with a homography to simplify matters. Often this homography is just a rigid transformation to change the coordinate system. A good choice is to set the origin and coordinate axis to align with the first camera so that

$$P_1 = K_1[I \mid 0] \quad \text{and} \quad P_2 = K_2[R \mid \mathbf{t}].$$

Here we use the same notation as in Chapter 4; K_1 and K_2 are the calibration matrices, R is the rotation of the second camera, and $\mathbf{t}$ is the translation of the second camera. Using these camera matrices, one can derive a condition for the projection of a point $\mathbf{X}$ to image points $\mathbf{x}_1$ and $\mathbf{x}_2$ (with P_1 and P_2, respectively). This condition is what makes it possible to recover the camera matrices from corresponding image points.

The following equation must be satisfied:

$$\mathbf{x}_2^T F \, \mathbf{x}_1 = 0, \tag{5.1}$$

where

$$F = K_2^{-T} S_t R \, K_1^{-1},$$

and the matrix S_t is the skew symmetric matrix

$$S_t = \begin{bmatrix} 0 & -t_3 & t_2 \\ t_3 & 0 & -t_1 \\ -t_2 & t_1 & 0 \end{bmatrix}. \tag{5.2}$$

Equation (5.1) is called the *epipolar constraint*. The matrix F in the epipolar constraint is called the *fundamental matrix* and as you can see, it is expressed in components of the two camera matrices (their relative rotation R and translation $\mathbf{t}$). The fundamental matrix has rank 2 and $\det(F) = 0$. This will be used in algorithms for estimating F.

The equations above mean that the camera matrices can be recovered from F, which in turn can be computed from point correspondences, as we will see later. Without knowing the internal calibration (K_1 and K_2), the camera matrices are only recoverable up to a projective transformation. With known calibration, the reconstruction will be metric. A *metric reconstruction* is a 3D reconstruction that correctly represents distances and angles.[1]

There is one final piece of geometry needed before we can proceed to actually using this theory on some image data. Given a point in one of the images, for example $\mathbf{x}_2$ in the second view, equation (5.1) defines a line in the first image since

$$\mathbf{x}_2^T F \, \mathbf{x}_1 = \mathbf{l}_1^T \mathbf{x}_1 = 0.$$

The equation $\mathbf{l}_1^T \mathbf{x}_1 = 0$ determines a line with all points $\mathbf{x}_1$ in the first image satisfying the equation belonging to the line. This line is called an *epipolar line* corresponding to the point $\mathbf{x}_2$. This means that a corresponding point to $\mathbf{x}_2$ must lie on this line. The fundamental matrix can therefore help the search for correspondences by restricting the search to this line.

---

[1] The absolute scale of the reconstruction cannot be recovered, but that is rarely a problem.

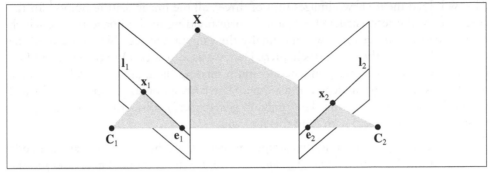

Figure 5-1. An illustration of epipolar geometry. A 3D point $\mathbf{X}$ is projected to $\mathbf{x}_1$ and $\mathbf{x}_2$, in the two views, respectively. The baseline between the two camera centers, $\mathbf{C}_1$ and $\mathbf{C}_2$, intersect the image planes in the epipoles, $\mathbf{e}_1$ and $\mathbf{e}_2$. The lines $\mathbf{l}_1$ and $\mathbf{l}_2$ are called epipolar lines.

The epipolar lines all meet in a point, $\mathbf{e}$, called the *epipole*. The epipole is actually the image point corresponding to the projection of the other camera center. This point can be outside the actual image, depending on the relative orientation of the cameras. Since the epipole lies on all epipolar lines, it must satisfy $F\mathbf{e}_1 = 0$. It can, therefore, be computed as the null vector of F, as we will see later. The other epipole can be computed from the relation $\mathbf{e}_2^T F = 0$. The epipoles and the epipolar lines are illustrated in Figure 5-1.

A Sample Data Set

In the coming sections, we will need a data set with image points, 3D points, and camera matrices to experiment with and illustrate the algorithms. We will use one of the sets from the Oxford multi-view datasets available at *http://www.robots.ox.ac.uk/~vgg/data/ data-mview.html*. Download the zipped file for the Merton1 data. The following script will load all the data for you:

```
import camera

# load some images
im1 = array(Image.open('images/001.jpg'))
im2 = array(Image.open('images/002.jpg'))

# load 2D points for each view to a list
points2D = [loadtxt('2D/00'+str(i+1)+'.corners').T for i in range(3)]

# load 3D points
points3D = loadtxt('3D/p3d').T

# load correspondences
corr = genfromtxt('2D/nview-corners',dtype='int',missing='*')

# load cameras to a list of Camera objects
P = [camera.Camera(loadtxt('2D/00'+str(i+1)+'.P')) for i in range(3)]
```

This will load the first two images (out of three), all the image feature points[2] for the three views, the reconstructed 3D points corresponding to the image points, which points correspond across views, and finally the camera matrices (where we used the Camera class from the previous chapter). Here we used `loadtxt()` to read the text files to NumPy arrays. The correspondences contain missing data, since not all points are visible or successfully matched in all views. The correspondences need to be loaded with this taken into account. The function `genfromtxt()` solves this by replacing the missing values (denoted with '*' in this file) with -1.

A convenient way of running this script and getting all the data is to save the code above in a file, for example *load_vggdata.py*, and use the command `execfile()` at the beginning of your scripts or experiments:

```
execfile('load_vggdata.py')
```

Let's see what this data looks like. Try to project the 3D points into one view and compare the results with the observed image points:

```
# make 3D points homogeneous and project
X = vstack( (points3D,ones(points3D.shape[1])) )
x = P[0].project(X)

# plotting the points in view 1
figure()
imshow(im1)
plot(points2D[0][0],points2D[0][1],'*')
axis('off')

figure()
imshow(im1)
plot(x[0],x[1],'r.')
axis('off')

show()
```

This creates a plot with the first view and image points in that view; for comparison, the projected points are shown in a separate figure. Figure 5-2 shows the resulting plots. If you look closely, you will see that the second plot with the projected 3D points contains more points than the first. These are image feature points reconstructed from view 2 and 3 but not detected in view 1.

Plotting 3D Data with Matplotlib

To visualize our 3D reconstructions, we need to be able to plot in 3D. The `mplot3d` toolkit in `Matplotlib` provides 3D plotting of points, lines, contours, surfaces and most other basic plotting components as well as 3D rotation and scaling from the controls of the figure window.

---

[2] Actually Harris corner points; see Section 2.1.

Figure 5-2. The Merton1 data set from the Oxford multi-view datasets: view 1 with image points shown (left); view 1 with projected 3D points (right).

Making a plot in 3D is done by adding the `projection="3d"` keyword to the axes object like this:

```
from mpl_toolkits.mplot3d import axes3d

fig = figure()
ax = fig.gca(projection="3d")

# generate 3D sample data
X,Y,Z = axes3d.get_test_data(0.25)

# plot the points in 3D
ax.plot(X.flatten(),Y.flatten(),Z.flatten(),'o')

show()
```

The function `get_test_data()` generates sample points on a regular x, y grid with the parameter determining the spacing. Flattening these grids gives three lists of points that can be sent to `plot()`. This should plot 3D points on what looks like a surface. Try it out and see for yourself.

Now we can plot the Merton sample data to see what the 3D points look like:

```
# plotting 3D points
from mpl_toolkits.mplot3d import axes3d
fig = figure()
ax = fig.gca(projection='3d')
ax.plot(points3D[0],points3D[1],points3D[2],'k.')
```

Figure 5-3 shows the 3D points from three different views. The figure window and controls look like the standard plot windows for images and 2D data with an additional 3D rotation tool.

Computing F—The Eight Point Algorithm

The *eight point algorithm* is an algorithm for computing the fundamental matrix from point correspondences. Here's a brief description; the details can be found in [14] and [13].

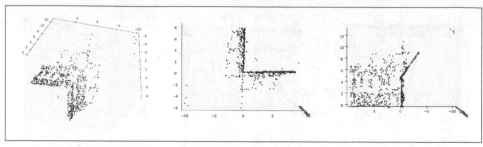

Figure 5-3. The 3D points of the Merton1 data set from the Oxford multi-view datasets shown using `Matplotlib`: *view from above and to the side (left); view from the top, showing the building walls and points on the roof (middle); side view showing the profile of one of the walls and a frontal view of points on the other wall (right).*

The epipolar constraint (5.1) can be written as a linear system like

$$
\begin{bmatrix}
x_2^1 x_1^1 & x_2^1 y_1^1 & x_2^1 w_1^1 & \cdots & w_2^1 w_1^1 \\
x_2^2 x_1^2 & x_2^2 y_1^2 & x_2^2 w_1^2 & \cdots & w_2^2 w_1^2 \\
\vdots & \vdots & \vdots & \ddots & \vdots \\
x_2^n x_1^n & x_2^n y_1^n & x_2^n w_1^n & \cdots & w_2^n w_1^n
\end{bmatrix}
\begin{bmatrix}
F_{11} \\
F_{12} \\
F_{13} \\
\vdots \\
F_{33}
\end{bmatrix}
= \mathbf{A}\mathbf{f} = 0,
$$

where $\mathbf{f}$ contains the elements of F, $\mathbf{x}_1^i = [x_1^i, y_1^i, w_1^i]$ and $\mathbf{x}_2^i = [x_2^i, y_2^i, w_2^i]$ is a correspondence pair, and there are n point correspondences in total. The fundamental matrix has nine elements, but since the scale is arbitrary, only eight equations are needed. Eight point correspondences are therefore needed to compute F; hence the name of the algorithm.

Create a file *sfm.py*, and add the following function for the eight point algorithm that minimizes $||Af||$:

```
def compute_fundamental(x1,x2):
    """ Computes the fundamental matrix from corresponding points
        (x1,x2 3*n arrays) using the normalized 8 point algorithm.
        each row is constructed as
        [x'*x, x'*y, x', y'*x, y'*y, y', x, y, 1] """

    n = x1.shape[1]
    if x2.shape[1] != n:
        raise ValueError("Number of points don't match.")

    # build matrix for equations
    A = zeros((n,9))
    for i in range(n):
        A[i] = [x1[0,i]*x2[0,i], x1[0,i]*x2[1,i], x1[0,i]*x2[2,i],
                x1[1,i]*x2[0,i], x1[1,i]*x2[1,i], x1[1,i]*x2[2,i],
                x1[2,i]*x2[0,i], x1[2,i]*x2[1,i], x1[2,i]*x2[2,i] ]

    # compute linear least square solution
    U,S,V = linalg.svd(A)
    F = V[-1].reshape(3,3)
```

```
# constrain F
# make rank 2 by zeroing out last singular value
U,S,V = linalg.svd(F)
S[2] = 0
F = dot(U,dot(diag(S),V))

return F
```

As usual, we compute the least squares solution using SVD. Since the resulting solution might not have rank 2 as a proper fundamental matrix should, we replace the result with the closest rank 2 approximation by zeroing out the last singular value. This is a standard trick and a useful one to know. The function ignores the important step of normalizing the image coordinates. Ignoring normalization could give numerical problems. Let's leave that for later.

The Epipole and Epipolar Lines

As mentioned at the start of this section, the epipole satisfies $F\mathbf{e}_1 = 0$ and can be computed from the null space of F. Add this function to *sfm.py*:

```
def compute_epipole(F):
    """ Computes the (right) epipole from a
        fundamental matrix F.
        (Use with F.T for left epipole.) """

    # return null space of F (Fx=0)
    U,S,V = linalg.svd(F)
    e = V[-1]
    return e/e[2]
```

If you want the epipole corresponding to the left null vector (corresponding to the epipole in the other image), just transpose F before passing it as input.

We can try these two functions on the first two views of our sample data set like this:

```
import sfm

# index for points in first two views
ndx = (corr[:,0]>=0) & (corr[:,1]>=0)

# get coordinates and make homogeneous
x1 = points2D[0][:,corr[ndx,0]]
x1 = vstack( (x1,ones(x1.shape[1])) )
x2 = points2D[1][:,corr[ndx,1]]
x2 = vstack( (x2,ones(x2.shape[1])) )

# compute F
F = sfm.compute_fundamental(x1,x2)

# compute the epipole
e = sfm.compute_epipole(F)

# plotting
figure()
imshow(im1)
```

```
# plot each line individually, this gives nice colors
for i in range(5):
    sfm.plot_epipolar_line(im1,F,x2[:,i],e,False)
axis('off')

figure()
imshow(im2)
# plot each point individually, this gives same colors as the lines
for i in range(5):
    plot(x2[0,i],x2[1,i],'o')
axis('off')

show()
```

First, the points that are in correspondence between the two images are selected and made into homogeneous coordinates. Here we just read them from a text file; in reality these would be the result of extracting features and matching them as we did in Chapter 2. The missing values in the correspondence list *corr* are -1, so picking indices greater or equal to zero gives the points visible in each view. The two conditions are combined with the array operator &.

Finally, the first five of the epipolar lines are shown in the first view and the corresponding matching points in view 2. Here we used the helper plot function:

```
def plot_epipolar_line(im,F,x,epipole=None,show_epipole=True):
    """ Plot the epipole and epipolar line F*x=0
        in an image. F is the fundamental matrix
        and x a point in the other image."""

    m,n = im.shape[:2]
    line = dot(F,x)

    # epipolar line parameter and values
    t = linspace(0,n,100)
    lt = array([(line[2]+line[0]*tt)/(-line[1]) for tt in t])

    # take only line points inside the image
    ndx = (lt>=0) & (lt<m)
    plot(t[ndx],lt[ndx],linewidth=2)

    if show_epipole:
        if epipole is None:
            epipole = compute_epipole(F)
        plot(epipole[0]/epipole[2],epipole[1]/epipole[2],'r*')
```

This function parameterizes the line with the range of the *x* axis and removes parts of lines above and below the image border. If the last parameter *show_epipole* is true, the epipole will be plotted as well (and computed if not passed as input). The plots are shown in Figure 5-4. The color coding matches between the plots so you can see that the corresponding point in one image lies somewhere along the same-color line as a point in the other image.

Figure 5-4. Epipolar lines in view 1 shown for five points in view 2 of the Merton1 data. The bottom row shows a closeup of the area around the points. The lines can be seen to converge on a point outside the image to the left. The lines show where point correspondences can be found in the other image (the color coding matches between lines and points).

5.2 Computing with Cameras and 3D Structure

The previous section covered relationships between views and how to compute the fundamental matrix and epipolar lines. Here we briefly explain the tools we need for computing with cameras and 3D structure.

Triangulation

Given known camera matrices, a set of point correspondences can be triangulated to recover the 3D positions of these points. The basic algorithm is fairly simple.

For two views with camera matrices P_1 and P_2, each with a projection $\mathbf{x}_1$ and $\mathbf{x}_2$ of the same 3D point $\mathbf{X}$ (all in homogeneous coordinates), the camera equation (4.1) gives the relation

$$\begin{bmatrix} P_1 & -\mathbf{x}_1 & 0 \\ P_2 & 0 & -\mathbf{x}_2 \end{bmatrix} \begin{bmatrix} \mathbf{X} \\ \lambda_1 \\ \lambda_2 \end{bmatrix} = 0.$$

There might not be an exact solution to these equations due to image noise, errors in the camera matrices, or other sources of errors. Using SVD, we can get a least squares estimate of the 3D point.

Add the following function that computes the *least squares triangulation* of a point pair to *sfm.py*:

```
def triangulate_point(x1,x2,P1,P2):
    """ Point pair triangulation from
        least squares solution. """

    M = zeros((6,6))
    M[:3,:4] = P1
    M[3:,:4] = P2
    M[:3,4] = -x1
    M[3:,5] = -x2

    U,S,V = linalg.svd(M)
    X = V[-1,:4]

    return X / X[3]
```

The first four values in the last eigenvector are the 3D coordinates in homogeneous co-ordinates. To triangulate many points, we can add the following convenience function:

```
def triangulate(x1,x2,P1,P2):
    """ Two-view triangulation of points in
        x1,x2 (3*n homog. coordinates). """

    n = x1.shape[1]
    if x2.shape[1] != n:
        raise ValueError("Number of points don't match.")

    X = [ triangulate_point(x1[:,i],x2[:,i],P1,P2) for i in range(n)]
    return array(X).T
```

This function takes two arrays of points and returns an array of 3D coordinates.

Try the triangulation on the Merton1 data like this:

```
import sfm

# index for points in first two views
ndx = (corr[:,0]>=0) & (corr[:,1]>=0)

# get coordinates and make homogeneous
x1 = points2D[0][:,corr[ndx,0]]
x1 = vstack( (x1,ones(x1.shape[1])) )
x2 = points2D[1][:,corr[ndx,1]]
x2 = vstack( (x2,ones(x2.shape[1])) )

Xtrue = points3D[:,ndx]
Xtrue = vstack( (Xtrue,ones(Xtrue.shape[1])) )

# check first 3 points
Xest = sfm.triangulate(x1,x2,P[0].P,P[1].P)
print Xest[:,:3]
print Xtrue[:,:3]
```

```
# plotting
from mpl_toolkits.mplot3d import axes3d
fig = figure()
ax = fig.gca(projection='3d')
ax.plot(Xest[0],Xest[1],Xest[2],'ko')
ax.plot(Xtrue[0],Xtrue[1],Xtrue[2],'r.')
axis('equal')

show()
```

This will triangulate the points in correspondence from the first two views and print out the coordinates of the first three points to the console before plotting the recovered 3D points next to the true values. The printout looks like this:

```
[[ 1.03743725  1.56125273  1.40720017]
 [-0.57574987 -0.55504127 -0.46523952]
 [ 3.44173797  3.44249282  7.53176488]
 [ 1.          1.          1.        ]]
[[ 1.0378863   1.5606923   1.4071907 ]
 [-0.54627892 -0.5211711  -0.46371818]
 [ 3.4601538   3.4636809   7.5323397 ]
 [ 1.          1.          1.        ]]
```

The estimated points are close enough. The plot looks like Figure 5-5; as you can see, the points match fairly well.

Computing the Camera Matrix from 3D Points

With known 3D points and their image projections, the camera matrix, P, can be computed using a direct linear transform approach. This is essentially the inverse problem to triangulation and is sometimes called *camera resectioning*. This way to recover the camera matrix is again a least squares approach.

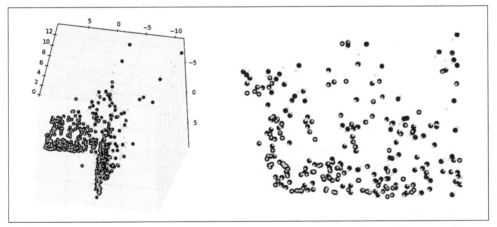

Figure 5-5. Triangulated points using camera matrices and point correspondences. The estimated points are shown with dark circles and the true points with light dots. View from above and to the side (left). Closeup of the points from one of the building walls (right).

From the camera equation (4.1), each visible 3D point $\mathbf{X}_i$ (in homogeneous coordinates) is projected to an image point $\mathbf{x}_i = [x_i, y_i, 1]$ as $\lambda_i\mathbf{x}_i = P\mathbf{X}_i$ and the corresponding points satisfy the relation

$$
\begin{bmatrix}
\mathbf{X}_1^T & 0 & 0 & -x_1 & 0 & 0 & \cdots \\
0 & \mathbf{X}_1^T & 0 & -y_1 & 0 & 0 & \cdots \\
0 & 0 & \mathbf{X}_1^T & -1 & 0 & 0 & \cdots \\
\mathbf{X}_2^T & 0 & 0 & 0 & -x_2 & 0 & \cdots \\
0 & \mathbf{X}_2^T & 0 & 0 & -y_2 & 0 & \cdots \\
0 & 0 & \mathbf{X}_2^T & 0 & -1 & 0 & \cdots \\
\vdots & \vdots & \vdots & \vdots & \vdots & \vdots &
\end{bmatrix}
\begin{bmatrix}
\mathbf{p}_1^T \\
\mathbf{p}_2^T \\
\mathbf{p}_3^T \\
\lambda_1 \\
\lambda_2 \\
\vdots
\end{bmatrix}
= 0,
$$

where $\mathbf{p}_1$, $\mathbf{p}_2$, and $\mathbf{p}_3$ are the three rows of P. This can be written more compactly as

$$M\mathbf{v} = 0.$$

The estimation of the camera matrix is then obtained using SVD. With the matrices described above, the code is straightforward. Add the function below to *sfm.py*:

```python
def compute_P(x,X):
  """ Compute camera matrix from pairs of
    2D-3D correspondences (in homog. coordinates). """

  n = x.shape[1]
  if X.shape[1] != n:
    raise ValueError("Number of points don't match.")

  # create matrix for DLT solution
  M = zeros((3*n,12+n))
  for i in range(n):
    M[3*i,0:4] = X[:,i]
    M[3*i+1,4:8] = X[:,i]
    M[3*i+2,8:12] = X[:,i]
    M[3*i:3*i+3,i+12] = -x[:,i]

  U,S,V = linalg.svd(M)

  return V[-1,:12].reshape((3,4))
```

This function takes the image points and 3D points and builds up the matrix M above. The first 12 values of the last eigenvector are the elements of the camera matrix and are returned after a reshaping operation.

Again, let's try this on our sample data set. The following script will pick out the points that are visible in the first view (using the missing values from the correspondence list), make them into homogeneous coordinates, and estimate the camera matrix:

```python
import sfm, camera

corr = corr[:,0] # view 1
ndx3D = where(corr>=0)[0] # missing values are -1
ndx2D = corr[ndx3D]
```

```
# select visible points and make homogeneous
x = points2D[0][:,ndx2D] # view 1
x = vstack( (x,ones(x.shape[1])) )
X = points3D[:,ndx3D]
X = vstack( (X,ones(X.shape[1])) )

# estimate P
Pest = camera.Camera(sfm.compute_P(x,X))

# compare!
print Pest.P / Pest.P[2,3]
print P[0].P / P[0].P[2,3]

xest = Pest.project(X)

# plotting
figure()
imshow(im1)
plot(x[0],x[1],'bo')
plot(xest[0],xest[1],'r.')
axis('off')

show()
```

To check the camera matrices, they are printed to the console in normalized form (by dividing with the last element). The printout looks like this:

```
[[  1.06520794e+00  -5.23431275e+01   2.06902749e+01   5.08729305e+02]
 [ -5.05773115e+01  -1.33243276e+01  -1.47388537e+01   4.79178838e+02]
 [  3.05121915e-03  -3.19264684e-02  -3.43703738e-02   1.00000000e+00]]
[[  1.06774679e+00  -5.23448212e+01   2.06926980e+01   5.08764487e+02]
 [ -5.05834364e+01  -1.33201976e+01  -1.47406641e+01   4.79228998e+02]
 [  3.06792659e-03  -3.19008054e-02  -3.43665129e-02   1.00000000e+00]]
```

The top is the estimated camera matrix, and below is the one computed by the creators of the data set. As you can see, they are almost identical. Last, the 3D points are projected using the estimated camera and plotted. The result looks like Figure 5-6 with the true points shown as circles and the estimated camera projection as dots.

Figure 5-6. Projected points in view 1 computed using an estimated camera matrix.

Computing the Camera Matrix from a Fundamental Matrix

In a two view scenario, the camera matrices can be recovered from the fundamental matrix. Assuming the first camera matrix is normalized to $P_1 = [I \mid 0]$, the problem is to find the second camera matrix P_2. There are two different cases, the uncalibrated case and the calibrated case.

The uncalibrated case—projective reconstruction

Without any knowledge of the camera's intrinsic parameters, the camera matrix can only be retrieved up to a projective transformation. This means that if the camera pair is used to reconstruct 3D points, the reconstruction is only accurate up to a projective transformation (you can get any solution out of the whole range of projective scene distortions). This means that angles and distances are not respected.

Therefore, in the uncalibrated case the second camera matrix can be chosen up to a (3×3) projective transformation. A simple choice is

$$P_2 = [S_e F \mid \mathbf{e}],$$

where $\mathbf{e}$ is the left epipole, $\mathbf{e}^T F = 0$ and S_e a skew matrix as in equation (5.2). Remember, a triangulation with this matrix will most likely give distortions, for example in the form of skewed reconstructions.

Here is what it looks like in code:

```
def compute_P_from_fundamental(F):
    """ Computes the second camera matrix (assuming P1 = [I 0])
        from a fundamental matrix. """

    e = compute_epipole(F.T) # left epipole
    Te = skew(e)
    return vstack((dot(Te,F.T).T,e)).T
```

We used the helper function skew() defined as:

```
def skew(a):
    """ Skew matrix A such that a x v = Av for any v. """

    return array([[0,-a[2],a[1]],[a[2],0,-a[0]],[-a[1],a[0],0]])
```

Add both these functions to the file *sfm.py*.

The calibrated case—metric reconstruction

With known calibration, the reconstruction will be metric and preserve properties of Euclidean space (except for a global scale parameter). In terms of reconstructing a 3D scene, this calibrated case is the interesting one.

With known calibration K, we can apply its inverse K^{-1} to the image points $\mathbf{x}_K = K^{-1}\mathbf{x}$ so that the camera equation becomes

$$\mathbf{x}_K = K^{-1}K[R \mid \mathbf{t}]\mathbf{X} = [R \mid \mathbf{t}]\mathbf{X},$$

in the new image coordinates. The points in these new image coordinates satisfy the same fundamental equation as before:

$$\mathbf{x}_{K_2}^T F \mathbf{x}_{K_1} = 0.$$

The fundamental matrix for calibration-normalized coordinates is called the *essential matrix* and is usually denoted E instead of F, to make it clear that this is the calibrated case and the image coordinates are normalized.

The camera matrices recovered from an essential matrix respect metric relationships but there are four possible solutions. Only one of them has the scene in front of both cameras, so it is easy to pick the right one.

Here is an algorithm for computing the four solutions (see [13] for the details). Add this function to *sfm.py*:

```python
def compute_P_from_essential(E):
    """ Computes the second camera matrix (assuming P1 = [I 0])
        from an essential matrix. Output is a list of four
        possible camera matrices. """

    # make sure E is rank 2
    U,S,V = svd(E)
    if det(dot(U,V))<0:
        V = -V
    E = dot(U,dot(diag([1,1,0]),V))

    # create matrices (Hartley p 258)
    Z = skew([0,0,-1])
    W = array([[0,-1,0],[1,0,0],[0,0,1]])

    # return all four solutions
    P2 = [vstack((dot(U,dot(W,V)).T,U[:,2])).T,
          vstack((dot(U,dot(W,V)).T,-U[:,2])).T,
          vstack((dot(U,dot(W.T,V)).T,U[:,2])).T,
          vstack((dot(U,dot(W.T,V)).T,-U[:,2])).T]

    return P2
```

First, this function makes sure the essential matrix is rank 2 (with two equal non-zero singular values), then the four solutions are created according to the recipe in [13]. A list with four camera matrices is returned. How to pick the right one, we leave to an example later.

This concludes all the theory needed to compute 3D reconstructions from a collection of images.

5.3 Multiple View Reconstruction

Let's look at how to use the concepts above to compute an actual 3D reconstruction from a pair of images. Computing a 3D reconstruction like this is usually referred to as *structure from motion* (*SfM*) since the motion of a camera (or cameras) gives you 3D structure.

Assuming the camera has been calibrated, the steps are as follows:

1. Detect feature points and match them between the two images.
2. Compute the fundamental matrix from the matches.

3. Compute the camera matrices from the fundamental matrix.

4. Triangulate the 3D points.

We have all the tools to do this, but we need a robust way to compute a fundamental matrix when the point correspondences between the images contain incorrect matches.

Robust Fundamental Matrix Estimation

Similar to when we needed a robust way to compute homographies (Section 3.3), we also need to be able to estimate a fundamental matrix when there is noise and incorrect matches. As before, we will use RANSAC, this time combined with the eight point algorithm. It should be mentioned that the eight point algorithm breaks down for planar scenes, so you cannot use it for scenes where the scene points are all on a plane.

Add this class to *sfm.py*:

```python
class RansacModel(object):
    """ Class for fundmental matrix fit with ransac.py from
        http://www.scipy.org/Cookbook/RANSAC"""

    def __init__(self,debug=False):
        self.debug = debug

    def fit(self,data):
        """ Estimate fundamental matrix using eight
            selected correspondences. """

        # transpose and split data into the two point sets
        data = data.T
        x1 = data[:3,:8]
        x2 = data[3:,:8]

        # estimate fundamental matrix and return
        F = compute_fundamental_normalized(x1,x2)
        return F

    def get_error(self,data,F):
        """ Compute x^T F x for all correspondences,
            return error for each transformed point. """

        # transpose and split data into the two point
        data = data.T
        x1 = data[:3]
        x2 = data[3:]

        # Sampson distance as error measure
        Fx1 = dot(F,x1)
        Fx2 = dot(F,x2)
        denom = Fx1[0]**2 + Fx1[1]**2 + Fx2[0]**2 + Fx2[1]**2
        err = ( diag(dot(x1.T,dot(F,x2))) )**2 / denom

        # return error per point
        return err
```

As before, we need `fit()` and `get_error()` methods. The error measure chosen here is the Sampson distance (see [13]). The `fit()` method now selects eight points and uses a normalized version of the eight point algorithm:

```
def compute_fundamental_normalized(x1,x2):
    """ Computes the fundamental matrix from corresponding points
        (x1,x2 3*n arrays) using the normalized 8 point algorithm. """

    n = x1.shape[1]
    if x2.shape[1] != n:
        raise ValueError("Number of points don't match.")

    # normalize image coordinates
    x1 = x1 / x1[2]
    mean_1 = mean(x1[:2],axis=1)
    S1 = sqrt(2) / std(x1[:2])
    T1 = array([[S1,0,-S1*mean_1[0]],[0,S1,-S1*mean_1[1]],[0,0,1]])
    x1 = dot(T1,x1)

    x2 = x2 / x2[2]
    mean_2 = mean(x2[:2],axis=1)
    S2 = sqrt(2) / std(x2[:2])
    T2 = array([[S2,0,-S2*mean_2[0]],[0,S2,-S2*mean_2[1]],[0,0,1]])
    x2 = dot(T2,x2)

    # compute F with the normalized coordinates
    F = compute_fundamental(x1,x2)

    # reverse normalization
    F = dot(T1.T,dot(F,T2))

    return F/F[2,2]
```

This function normalizes the image points to zero mean and fixed variance.

Now we can use this class in a function. Add the following function to *sfm.py*:

```
def F_from_ransac(x1,x2,model,maxiter=5000,match_theshold=1e-6):
    """ Robust estimation of a fundamental matrix F from point
        correspondences using RANSAC (ransac.py from
        http://www.scipy.org/Cookbook/RANSAC).

        input: x1,x2 (3*n arrays) points in hom. coordinates. """

    import ransac

    data = vstack((x1,x2))

    # compute F and return with inlier index
    F,ransac_data = ransac.ransac(data.T,model,8,maxiter,match_theshold,20,
                                    return_all=True)
    return F, ransac_data['inliers']
```

Here we return the best fundamental matrix F together with the inlier index so that we know what matches were consistent with F. Compared to the homography estimation, we increased the default max iterations and changed the matching threshold, which was in pixels before and is in Sampson distance now.

Figure 5-7. Example image pair of a scene where the images are taken at different viewpoints.

3D Reconstruction Example

In this section, we will see a complete example of reconstructing a 3D scene from start to finish. We will use two images taken with a camera with known calibration. The images are of the famous Alcatraz prison and are shown in Figure 5-7.[3]

Let's split up the code into a few chunks so that it is easier to follow. First, we extract features, match them, and estimate a fundamental matrix and camera matrices:

```
import homography
import sfm
import sift

# calibration
K = array([[2394,0,932],[0,2398,628],[0,0,1]])


# load images and compute features
im1 = array(Image.open('alcatraz1.jpg'))
sift.process_image('alcatraz1.jpg','im1.sift')
l1,d1 = sift.read_features_from_file('im1.sift')

im2 = array(Image.open('alcatraz2.jpg'))
sift.process_image('alcatraz2.jpg','im2.sift')
l2,d2 = sift.read_features_from_file('im2.sift')


# match features
matches = sift.match_twosided(d1,d2)
ndx = matches.nonzero()[0]

# make homogeneous and normalize with inv(K)
x1 = homography.make_homog(l1[ndx,:2].T)
ndx2 = [int(matches[i]) for i in ndx]
x2 = homography.make_homog(l2[ndx2,:2].T)

x1n = dot(inv(K),x1)
x2n = dot(inv(K),x2)
```

---

[3] Images courtesy of Carl Olsson (*http://www.maths.lth.se/matematiklth/personal/calle/*).

```
# estimate E with RANSAC
model = sfm.RansacModel()
E,inliers = sfm.F_from_ransac(x1n,x2n,model)

# compute camera matrices (P2 will be list of four solutions)
P1 = array([[1,0,0,0],[0,1,0,0],[0,0,1,0]])
P2 = sfm.compute_P_from_essential(E)
```

The calibration is known, so here we just hardcode the K matrix at the beginning. As in earlier examples, we pick out the points that belong to matches. After that, we normalize them with K^{-1} and run the RANSAC estimation with the normalized eight point algorithm. Since the points are normalized, this gives us an essential matrix. We make sure to keep the index of the inliers, as we will need them. From the essential matrix we compute the four possible solutions of the second camera matrix.

From the list of camera matrices, we pick the one that has the most scene points in front of both cameras after triangulation:

```
# pick the solution with points in front of cameras
ind = 0
maxres = 0
for i in range(4):
  # triangulate inliers and compute depth for each camera
  X = sfm.triangulate(x1n[:,inliers],x2n[:,inliers],P1,P2[i])
  d1 = dot(P1,X)[2]
  d2 = dot(P2[i],X)[2]
  if sum(d1>0)+sum(d2>0) > maxres:
    maxres = sum(d1>0)+sum(d2>0)
    ind = i
    infront = (d1>0) & (d2>0)


# triangulate inliers and remove points not in front of both cameras
X = sfm.triangulate(x1n[:,inliers],x2n[:,inliers],P1,P2[ind])
X = X[:,infront]
```

We loop through the four solutions and each time triangulate the 3D points corresponding to the inliers. The sign of the depth is given by the third value of each image point after projecting the triangulated X back to the images. We keep the index with the most positive depths and also store a boolean for each point in the best solution so that we can pick only the ones that actually are in front. Due to noise and errors in all of the estimations done, there is a risk that some points still are behind one camera, even with the correct camera matrices. Once we have the right solution, we triangulate the inliers and keep the points in front of the cameras.

Now we can plot the reconstruction:

```
# 3D plot
from mpl_toolkits.mplot3d import axes3d

fig = figure()
ax = fig.gca(projection='3d')
ax.plot(-X[0],X[1],X[2],'k.')
axis('off')
```

The 3D plots with `mplot3d` have the first axis reversed compared to our coordinate system, so we change the sign.

We can then plot the reprojection in each view:

```
# plot the projection of X
import camera

# project 3D points
cam1 = camera.Camera(P1)
cam2 = camera.Camera(P2[ind])
x1p = cam1.project(X)
x2p = cam2.project(X)

# reverse K normalization
x1p = dot(K,x1p)
x2p = dot(K,x2p)


figure()
imshow(im1)
gray()
plot(x1p[0],x1p[1],'o')
plot(x1[0],x1[1],'r.')
axis('off')

figure()
imshow(im2)
gray()
plot(x2p[0],x2p[1],'o')
plot(x2[0],x2[1],'r.')
axis('off')
show()
```

After projecting the 3D points, we need to reverse the initial normalization by multiplying with the calibration matrix.

The result looks like Figure 5-8. As you can see, the reprojected points don't exactly match the original feature locations, but they are reasonably close. It is possible to further refine the camera matrices to improve the reconstruction and reprojection, but that is outside the scope of this simple example.

Extensions and More Than Two Views

There are some steps and further extensions to multiple view reconstructions that we cannot cover in a book like this. Here are some of them with references for further reading.

More views

With more than two views of the same scene, the 3D reconstruction will usually be more accurate and more detailed. Since the fundamental matrix only relates a pair of views, the process is a little different with many images.

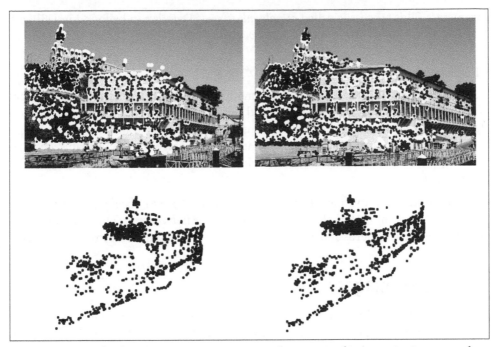

Figure 5-8. Example of computing a 3D reconstruction from a pair of images using image matches: the two images with feature points shown in black and reprojected reconstructed 3D points shown in white (top); the 3D reconstruction (bottom).

For video sequences, we can use the temporal aspect and match features in consecutive frame pairs. The relative orientation needs to be added incrementally from each pair to the next (similar to how we added homographies in the panorama example in Figure 3-12). This approach usually works well, and tracking can be used to effectively find correspondences (see Section 10.4 for more on tracking). One problem is that errors will accumulate the more views that are added. This can be fixed with a final optimization step; see below.

With still images, one approach is to find a central reference view and compute all the other camera matrices relative to that one. Another method is to compute camera matrices and a 3D reconstruction for one image pair and then incrementally add new images and 3D points; see for example [34]. As a side note, there are ways to compute 3D and camera positions from three views at the same time (see for example [13]), but beyond that an incremental approach is needed.

Bundle adjustment

From our simple 3D reconstruction example in Figure 5-8, it is clear that there will be errors in the position of the recovered points and in the camera matrices computed from the estimated fundamental matrix. With more views, the errors will accumulate. Therefore, a final step in multiple view reconstructions is often to try to minimize the reprojection errors by optimizing the position of the 3D points and the camera parameters. This process is called *bundle adustment*. Details can be found in [13] and [35] and a short overview at *http://en.wikipedia.org/wiki/Bundle_adjustment*.

Self-calibration

In the case of uncalibrated cameras, it is sometimes possible to compute the calibration from image features. This process is called *self-calibration*. There are many different algorithms, depending on what assumptions can be made on parameters of the camera calibration matrix and depending on what types of image data is available (feature matches, parallel lines, planes, etc.). The interested reader can take a look at [13] and [26, Chap. 6].

As a side note to calibration, there is a useful script, *extract_focal.pl*, as part of the Bundler SfM system (*http://phototour.cs.washington.edu/bundler/*). This uses a lookup table for common cameras and estimates the focal length based on the image EXIF data.

5.4   Stereo Images

A special case of multi-view imaging is *stereo vision* (or *stereo imaging*), where two cameras are observing the same scene with only a horizontal (sideways) displacement between the cameras. When the cameras are configured so that the two images have the same image plane with the image rows vertically aligned, the image pair is said to be *rectified*. This is common in robotics, and such a setup is often called a *stereo rig*.

Any stereo camera setup can be rectified by warping the images to a common plane so that the epipolar lines are image rows (a stereo rig is usually constructed to give such rectified image pairs). This is outside the scope of this section, but the interested reader can find the details in [13, p. 303] or [3, p. 430].

Assuming that the two images are rectified, finding correspondences is constrained to searching along image rows. Once a corresponding point is found, its depth (Z coordinate) can be computed directly from the horizontal displacement as it is inversely proportional to the displacement,

$$Z = \frac{fb}{x_l - x_r},$$

where f is the rectified image focal length, b the distance between the camera centers, and x_l and x_r the x-coordinate of the corresponding point in the left and right image. The distance separating the camera centers is called the *baseline*. Figure 5-9 illustrates a rectified stereo camera setup.

Stereo reconstruction (sometimes called *dense depth reconstruction*) is the problem of recovering a depth map (or, inversely, a disparity map) where the depth (or disparity) for each pixel in the image is estimated. This is a classic problem in computer vision and there are many algorithms for solving it. The Middlebury Stereo Vision Page (*http://vision.middlebury.edu/stereo/*) contains a constantly updated evaluation of the best algorithms with code and descriptions of many implementations. In the next

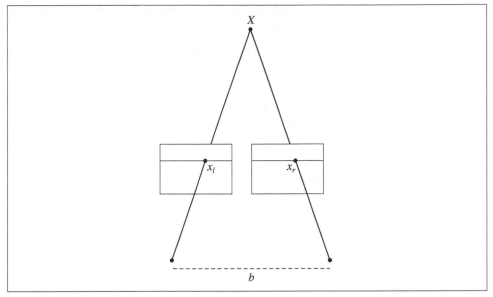

Figure 5-9. An illustration of a rectified stereo image setup where corresponding points are on the same row in both images.

section, we will implement a stereo reconstruction algorithm based on normalized cross-correlation.

Computing Disparity Maps

In this stereo reconstruction algorithm, we will try a range of displacements and record the best displacement for each pixel by selecting the one with the best score according to normalized cross-correlation of the local image neighborhood. This is sometimes called plane sweeping, since each displacement step corresponds to a plane at some depth. While not exactly state of the art in stereo reconstruction, this is a simple method that usually gives decent results.

Normalized cross-correlation can be efficiently computed when applied densely across images. This is different from when we applied it between sparse point correspondences in Chapter 2. We want to evaluate normalized cross-correlation on a patch (basically a local neighborhood) around each pixel. For this case, we can rewrite the NCC around a pixel, equation (2.3), as

$$\mathrm{ncc}(I_1, I_2) = \frac{\sum_{\mathbf{x}}(I_1(\mathbf{x}) - \mu_1)(I_2(\mathbf{x}) - \mu_2)}{\sqrt{\sum_{\mathbf{x}}(I_1(\mathbf{x}) - \mu_1)^2 \sum_{\mathbf{x}}(I_2(\mathbf{x}) - \mu_2)^2}},$$

where we skip the normalizing constant in front (it is not needed here) and the sums are taken over the pixels of a local patch around the pixel.

Now, we want this for every pixel in the image. The three sums are over a local patch region and can be computed efficiently using image filters, just as we did for blur and derivatives. The function `uniform_filter()` in the `ndimage.filters` module will compute the sums over a rectangular patch.

Here's the function that does the plane sweep and returns the best disparity for each pixel. Create a file *stereo.py* and add the following:

```python
def plane_sweep_ncc(im_l,im_r,start,steps,wid):
    """ Find disparity image using normalized cross-correlation. """

    m,n = im_l.shape

    # arrays to hold the different sums
    mean_l = zeros((m,n))
    mean_r = zeros((m,n))
    s = zeros((m,n))
    s_l = zeros((m,n))
    s_r = zeros((m,n))

    # array to hold depth planes
    dmaps = zeros((m,n,steps))

    # compute mean of patch
    filters.uniform_filter(im_l,wid,mean_l)
    filters.uniform_filter(im_r,wid,mean_r)

    # normalized images
    norm_l = im_l - mean_l
    norm_r = im_r - mean_r

    # try different disparities
    for displ in range(steps):
        # move left image to the right, compute sums
        filters.uniform_filter(roll(norm_l,-displ-start)*norm_r,wid,s) # sum nominator
        filters.uniform_filter(roll(norm_l,-displ-start)*roll(norm_l,-displ-start),wid,
            s_l)
        filters.uniform_filter(norm_r*norm_r,wid,s_r) # sum denominator

        # store ncc scores
        dmaps[:,:,displ] = s/sqrt(s_l*s_r)

    # pick best depth for each pixel
    return argmax(dmaps,axis=2)
```

First, we need to create some arrays to hold the filtering results as `uniform_filter()` takes them as input arguments. Then, we create an array to hold each of the planes so that we can apply `argmax()` along the last dimension to find the best depth for each pixel. The function iterates over all *steps* displacements from *start*. One image is shifted using the `roll()` function, and the three sums of the NCC are computed using filtering.

Here is a full example of loading images and computing the displacement map using this function:

```
import stereo

im_l = array(Image.open('scene1.row3.col3.ppm').convert('L'),'f')
im_r = array(Image.open('scene1.row3.col4.ppm').convert('L'),'f')

# starting displacement and steps
steps = 12
start = 4

# width for ncc
wid = 9

res = stereo.plane_sweep_ncc(im_l,im_r,start,steps,wid)

import scipy.misc
scipy.misc.imsave('depth.png',res)
```

Here we first load a pair of images from the classic "tsukuba" set and convert them to grayscale. Next, we set the parameters needed for the plane sweep function, the number of displacements to try, the starting value and the width of the NCC patch. You will notice that this method is fairly fast, at least compared to matching features with NCC. This is because everything is computed using filters.

This approach also works for other filters. The uniform filter gives all pixels in a square patch equal weight, but in some cases other filters for the NCC computation might be preferred. Here is one alternative using a Gaussian filter that produces smoother disparity maps. Add this to *stereo.py*:

```
def plane_sweep_gauss(im_l,im_r,start,steps,wid):
    """ Find disparity image using normalized cross-correlation
        with Gaussian weighted neigborhoods. """

    m,n = im_l.shape

    # arrays to hold the different sums
    mean_l = zeros((m,n))
    mean_r = zeros((m,n))
    s = zeros((m,n))
    s_l = zeros((m,n))
    s_r = zeros((m,n))

    # array to hold depth planes
    dmaps = zeros((m,n,steps))

    # compute mean
    filters.gaussian_filter(im_l,wid,0,mean_l)
    filters.gaussian_filter(im_r,wid,0,mean_r)

    # normalized images
    norm_l = im_l - mean_l
    norm_r = im_r - mean_r
```

```
# try different disparities
for displ in range(steps):
    # move left image to the right, compute sums
    filters.gaussian_filter(roll(norm_1,-displ-start)*norm_r,wid,0,s) # sum nominator
    filters.gaussian_filter(roll(norm_1,-displ-start)*roll(norm_1,-displ-start),wid,
                            0,s_1)
    filters.gaussian_filter(norm_r*norm_r,wid,0,s_r) # sum denominator

    # store ncc scores
    dmaps[:,:,displ] = s/sqrt(s_1*s_r)

# pick best depth for each pixel
return argmax(dmaps,axis=2)
```

The code is the same as for the uniform filter with the exception of the extra argument in the filtering. We need to pass a zero to `gaussian_filter()` to indicate that we want a standard Gaussian and not any derivatives (see page 18 for details).

Use this function the same way as the previous plane sweep function. Figures 5-10 and 5-11 show some results of these two plane sweep implementations on some standard stereo benchmark images. The images are from [29] and [30] and are available at *http://vision.middlebury.edu/stereo/data/*. Here we used the "tsukuba" and "cones" images and set *wid* to 9 in the standard version and 3 for the Gaussian version. The top row shows the image pair, bottom left is the standard NCC plane sweep, and bottom

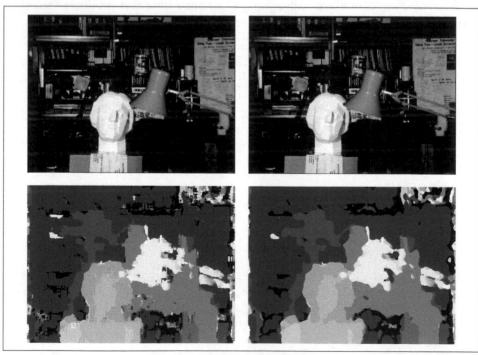

Figure 5-10. Example of computing disparity maps from a stereo image pair with normalized cross-correlation.

Figure 5-11. Example of computing disparity maps from a stereo image pair with normalized cross-correlation.

right is the Gaussian version. As you can see, the Gaussian version is less noisy but also has less detail than the standard version.

Exercises

1. Use the techniques introduced in this chapter to verify matches in the White House example on page 46 (or even better, an example of your own) and see if you can improve on the results.

2. Compute feature matches for an image pair and estimate the fundamental matrix. Use the epipolar lines to do a second pass to find more matches by searching for the best match along the epipolar line for each feature.

3. Take a set with three or more images. Pick one pair and compute 3D points and camera matrices. Match features to the remaining images to get correspondences. Then take the 3D points for the correspondences and compute camera matrices for the other images using resection. Plot the 3D points and the camera positions. Use a set of your own or one of the Oxford multi-view sets.

4. Implement a stereo version that uses sum of squared differences (SSD) instead of NCC using filtering the same way as in the NCC example.

5. Try smoothing the stereo depth maps using the ROF de-noising from Section 1.5. Experiment with the size of the cross-correlation patches to get sharp edges with noise levels that can be removed with smoothing.

6. One way to improve the quality of the disparity maps is to compare the disparities from moving the left image to the right and the right image to the left, and only keep the parts that are consistent. This will, for example, clean up the parts where there is occlusion. Implement this idea and compare the results to the one-directional plane sweeping.

7. The New York Public Library has many old historic stereo photographs. Browse the gallery at *http://stereo.nypl.org/gallery* and download some images you like (you can right click and save JPEGs). The images should be rectified already. Cut the image in two parts and try the dense depth reconstruction code.

## CHAPTER 6

Clustering Images

This chapter introduces several clustering methods and shows how to use them for clustering images for finding groups of similar images. Clustering can be used for recognition, for dividing data sets of images, and for organization and navigation. We also look at using clustering for visualizing similarity between images.

6.1 *K*-Means Clustering

K-means is a very simple clustering algorithm that tries to partition the input data in k clusters. *K*-means works by iteratively refining an initial estimate of *class centroids* as follows:

1. Initialize centroids $\boldsymbol{\mu}_i$, $i = 1 \ldots k$, randomly or with some guess.
2. Assign each data point to the class c_i of its nearest centroid.
3. Update the centroids as the average of all data points assigned to that class.
4. Repeat 2 and 3 until convergence.

K-means tries to minimize the *total within-class variance*

$$V = \sum_{i=1}^{k} \sum_{\mathbf{x}_j \in c_i} (\mathbf{x}_j - \boldsymbol{\mu}_i)^2,$$

where $\mathbf{x}_j$ are the data vectors. The algorithm above is a heuristic refinement algorithm that works fine for most cases, but it does not guarantee that the best solution is found. To avoid the effects of choosing a bad centroid initialization, the algorithm is often run several times with different initialization centroids. Then the solution with lowest variance V is selected.

The main drawback of this algorithm is that the number of clusters needs to be decided beforehand, and an inappropriate choice will give poor clustering results. The benefits are that it is simple to implement, it is parallelizable, and it works well for a large range of problems without any need for tuning.

The SciPy Clustering Package

Although simple to implement, there is no need to. The SciPy vector quantization package scipy.cluster.vq comes with a *k*-means implementation. Here's how to use it.

Let's start with creating some sample 2D data to illustrate:

```
from scipy.cluster.vq import *

class1 = 1.5 * randn(100,2)
class2 = randn(100,2) + array([5,5])
features = vstack((class1,class2))
```

This generates two normally distributed classes in two dimensions. To try to cluster the points, run *k*-means with $k = 2$ like this:

```
centroids,variance = kmeans(features,2)
```

The variance is returned but we don't really need it, since the SciPy implementation computes several runs (default is 20) and selects the one with smallest variance for us. Now you can check where each data point is assigned using the vector quantization function in the SciPy package:

```
code,distance = vq(features,centroids)
```

By checking the value of *code*, we can see if there are any incorrect assignments. To visualize, we can plot the points and the final centroids:

```
figure()
ndx = where(code==0)[0]
plot(features[ndx,0],features[ndx,1],'*')
ndx = where(code==1)[0]
plot(features[ndx,0],features[ndx,1],'r.')
plot(centroids[:,0],centroids[:,1],'go')
axis('off')
show()
```

Here the function where() gives the indices for each class. This should give a plot like the one in Figure 6-1.

Clustering Images

Let's try *k*-means on the font images described on page 14. The file *selectedfontimages.zip* contains 66 images from this font data set (these are selected for easy overview when illustrating the clusters). As descriptor vector for each image, we will use the projection coefficients after projecting on the 40 first principal components computed earlier. Loading the model file using pickle, projecting the images on the principal components, and clustering is then done like this:

```
import imtools
import pickle
from scipy.cluster.vq import *

# get list of images
imlist = imtools.get_imlist('selected_fontimages/')
imnbr = len(imlist)
```

```
# load model file
with open('a_pca_modes.pkl','rb') as f:
    immean = pickle.load(f)
    V = pickle.load(f)

# create matrix to store all flattened images
immatrix = array([array(Image.open(im)).flatten()
                        for im in imlist],'f')

# project on the 40 first PCs
immean = immean.flatten()
projected = array([dot(V[:40],immatrix[i]-immean) for i in range(imnbr)])

# k-means
projected = whiten(projected)
centroids,distortion = kmeans(projected,4)

code,distance = vq(projected,centroids)
```

Same as before, *code* contains the cluster assignment for each image. In this case, we tried $k = 4$. We also chose to "whiten" the data using SciPy's whiten(), normalizing so that each feature has unit variance. Try to vary parameters like the number of principal components used and the value of k to see how the clustering results change. The clusters can be visualized like this:

```
# plot clusters
for k in range(4):
    ind = where(code==k)[0]
    figure()
    gray()
    for i in range(minimum(len(ind),40)):
        subplot(4,10,i+1)
        imshow(immatrix[ind[i]].reshape((25,25)))
        axis('off')
show()
```

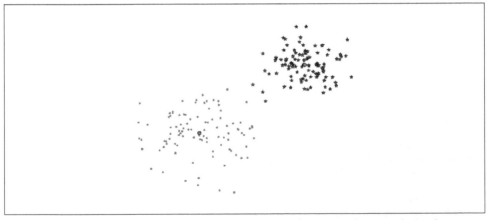

Figure 6-1. An example of k-means clustering of 2D points. Class centroids are marked as large rings and the predicted classes are stars and dots, respectively.

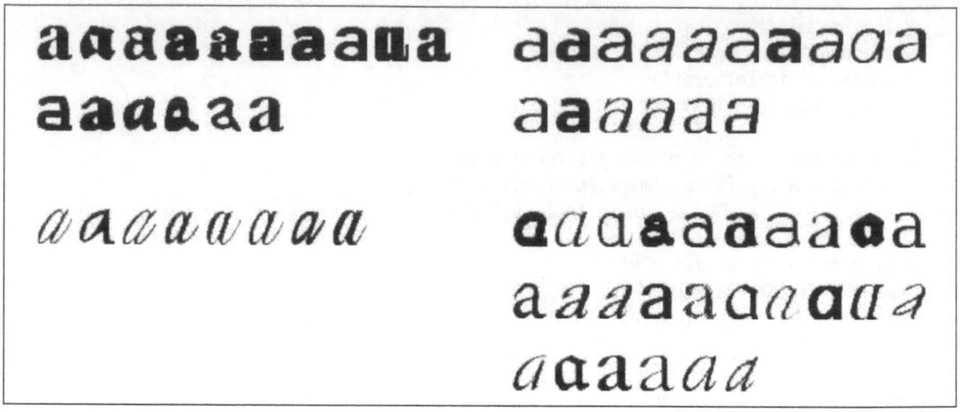

Figure 6-2. An example of k-means clustering with k = 4 of the font images using 40 principal components.

Here we show each cluster in a separate figure window in a grid with maximum 40 images from the cluster shown. We use the PyLab function subplot() to define the grid. A sample cluster result can look like the one in Figure 6-2.

For more details on the *k*-means SciPy implementation and the scipy.cluster.vq package, see the reference guide *http://docs.scipy.org/doc/scipy/reference/cluster.vq.html*.

Visualizing the Images on Principal Components

To see how the clustering using just a few principal components as above can work, we can visualize the images on their coordinates in a pair of principal component directions. One way is to project on two components by changing the projection to

```
projected = array([dot(V[[0,2]],immatrix[i]-immean) for i in range(imnbr)])
```

to get only the relevant coordinates (in this case $V[[0, 2]]$ gives the first and third). Alternatively, project on all components and afterward just pick out the columns you need.

For the visualization, we will use the ImageDraw module in PIL. Assuming that you have the projected images and image list as above, the following short script will generate a plot like the one in Figure 6-3:

```
from PIL import Image, ImageDraw

# height and width
h,w = 1200,1200

# create a new image with a white background
img = Image.new('RGB',(w,h),(255,255,255))
draw = ImageDraw.Draw(img)

# draw axis
draw.line((0,h/2,w,h/2),fill=(255,0,0))
draw.line((w/2,0,w/2,h),fill=(255,0,0))
```

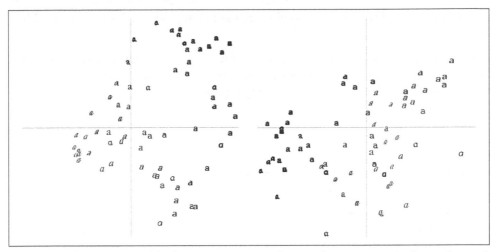

Figure 6-3. The projection of the font images on pairs of principal components: the first and second principal components (left); the second and third (right).

```
# scale coordinates to fit
scale = abs(projected).max(0)
scaled = floor(array([ (p / scale) * (w/2-20,h/2-20) +
                           (w/2,h/2) for p in projected]))

# paste thumbnail of each image
for i in range(imnbr):
    nodeim = Image.open(imlist[i])
    nodeim.thumbnail((25,25))
    ns = nodeim.size
    img.paste(nodeim,(scaled[i][0]-ns[0]//2,scaled[i][1]-
        ns[1]//2,scaled[i][0]+ns[0]//2+1,scaled[i][1]+ns[1]//2+1))

img.save('pca_font.jpg')
```

Here we used the integer or floor division operator //, which returns an integer pixel position by removing any values after the decimal point.

Plots like these illustrate how the images are distributed in the 40 dimensions and can be very useful for choosing a good descriptor. Already in just these two-dimensional projections the closeness of similar font images is clearly visible.

Clustering Pixels

Before closing this section, we will take a look at an example of clustering individual pixels instead of entire images. Grouping image regions and pixels into "meaningful" components is called *image segmentation* and will be the topic of Chapter 9. Naively applying *k*-means on the pixel values will not give anything meaningful except in very simple images. More sophisticated class models than average pixel color or spatial consistency is needed to produce useful results. For now, let's just apply *k*-means to the RGB values and worry about solving segmentation problems later (Section 9.2 has the details).

The following code sample takes an image, reduces it to a lower resolution version with pixels as mean values of the original image regions (taken over a square grid of size *steps* × *steps*), and clusters the regions using *k*-means:

```
from scipy.cluster.vq import *
from scipy.misc import imresize

steps = 50 # image is divided in steps*steps region
im = array(Image.open('empire.jpg'))

dx = im.shape[0] / steps
dy = im.shape[1] / steps

# compute color features for each region
features = []
for x in range(steps):
  for y in range(steps):
    R = mean(im[x*dx:(x+1)*dx,y*dy:(y+1)*dy,0])
    G = mean(im[x*dx:(x+1)*dx,y*dy:(y+1)*dy,1])
    B = mean(im[x*dx:(x+1)*dx,y*dy:(y+1)*dy,2])
    features.append([R,G,B])
features = array(features,'f') # make into array

# cluster
centroids,variance = kmeans(features,3)
code,distance = vq(features,centroids)

# create image with cluster labels
codeim = code.reshape(steps,steps)
codeim = imresize(codeim,im.shape[:2],interp='nearest')

figure()
imshow(codeim)
show()
```

The input to *k*-means is an array with *steps*steps* rows, each containing the R, G, and B mean values. To visualize the result, we use SciPy's imresize() function to show the *steps*steps* image at the original image coordinates. The parameter *interp* specifies what type of interpolation to use; here we use nearest neighbor so we don't introduce new pixel values at the transitions between classes.

Figure 6-4 shows results using 50 × 50 and 100 × 100 regions for two relatively simple example images. Note that the ordering of the *k*-means labels (in this case the colors in the result images) is arbitrary. As you can see, the result is noisy despite down-sampling to only use a few regions. There is no spatial consistency and it is hard to separate regions, like the boy and the grass in the lower example. Spatial consistency and better separation will be dealt with later, together with other image segmentation algorithms. Now let's move on to the next basic clustering algorithm.

Figure 6-4. Clustering of pixels based on their color value using k-means: original image (left); cluster result with k = 3 and 50 × 50 resolution (middle); cluster result with k = 3 and 100 × 100 resolution (right).

6.2 Hierarchical Clustering

Hierarchical clustering (or *agglomerative clustering*) is another simple but powerful clustering algorithm. The idea is to build a similarity tree based on pairwise distances. The algorithm starts with grouping the two closest objects (based on the distance between feature vectors) and creates an "average" node in a tree with the two objects as children. Then the next closest pair is found among the remaining objects but then also including any average nodes, and so on. At each node, the distance between the two children is also stored. Clusters can then be extracted by traversing this tree and stopping at nodes with distance smaller than some threshold that then determines the cluster size.

Hierarchical clustering has several benefits. For example, the tree structure can be used to visualize relationships and show how clusters are related. A good feature vector will give a nice separation in the tree. Another benefit is that the tree can be reused with different cluster thresholds without having to recompute the tree. The drawback is that one needs to choose a threshold if the actual clusters are needed.

Let's see what this looks like in code.[1] Create a file *hcluster.py* and add the following code (inspired by the hierarchical clustering example in [31]):

```python
from itertools import combinations

class ClusterNode(object):
    def __init__(self,vec,left,right,distance=0.0,count=1):
        self.left = left
        self.right = right
        self.vec = vec
        self.distance = distance
        self.count = count # only used for weighted average

    def extract_clusters(self,dist):
        """ Extract list of sub-tree clusters from
            hcluster tree with distance<dist. """
        if self.distance < dist:
            return [self]
        return self.left.extract_clusters(dist) + self.right.extract_clusters(dist)

    def get_cluster_elements(self):
        """ Return ids for elements in a cluster sub-tree. """
        return self.left.get_cluster_elements() + self.right.get_cluster_elements()

    def get_height(self):
        """ Return the height of a node,
            height is sum of each branch. """
        return self.left.get_height() + self.right.get_height()

    def get_depth(self):
        """ Return the depth of a node, depth is
            max of each child plus own distance. """
        return max(self.left.get_depth(), self.right.get_depth()) + self.distance


class ClusterLeafNode(object):
    def __init__(self,vec,id):
        self.vec = vec
        self.id = id

    def extract_clusters(self,dist):
        return [self]

    def get_cluster_elements(self):
        return [self.id]

    def get_height(self):
        return 1
```

---

[1] There is also a version of hierarchical clustering in the SciPy clustering package that you can look at if you like. We will not use that version here since we want a class that can draw dendrograms and visualize clusters using image thumbnails.

```
    def get_depth(self):
        return 0


def L2dist(v1,v2):
    return sqrt(sum((v1-v2)**2))


def L1dist(v1,v2):
    return sum(abs(v1-v2))


def hcluster(features,distfcn=L2dist):
    """ Cluster the rows of features using
        hierarchical clustering. """

    # cache of distance calculations
    distances = {}

    # initialize with each row as a cluster
    node = [ClusterLeafNode(array(f),id=i) for i,f in enumerate(features)]

    while len(node)>1:
        closest = float('Inf')

        # loop through every pair looking for the smallest distance
        for ni,nj in combinations(node,2):
            if (ni,nj) not in distances:
                distances[ni,nj] = distfcn(ni.vec,nj.vec)

            d = distances[ni,nj]
            if d<closest:
                closest = d
                lowestpair = (ni,nj)
        ni,nj = lowestpair

        # average the two clusters
        new_vec = (ni.vec + nj.vec) / 2.0

        # create new node
        new_node = ClusterNode(new_vec,left=ni,right=nj,distance=closest)
        node.remove(ni)
        node.remove(nj)
        node.append(new_node)

    return node[0]
```

We created two classes for tree nodes, ClusterNode and ClusterLeafNode, to be used to create the cluster tree. The function hcluster() builds the tree. First, a list of leaf nodes is created, then the closest pairs are iteratively grouped together based on the distance measure chosen. Returning the final node will give you the root of the tree. Running hcluster() on a matrix with feature vectors as rows will create and return the cluster tree.

The choice of distance measure depends on the actual feature vectors. Here, we used the Euclidean (L_2) distance (a function for L_1 distance is also provided), but you can create any function and use that as parameter to *hcluster()*. We also used the average feature vector of all nodes in a sub-tree as a new feature vector to represent the sub-tree and treat each sub-tree as objects. There are other choices for deciding which two nodes to merge next, such as using *single linking* (use the minimum distance between objects in two sub-trees) and *complete linking* (use the maximum distance between objects in two sub-trees). The choice of linking will affect the type of clusters produced.

To extract the clusters from the tree, you need to traverse the tree from the top until a node with distance value smaller than some threshold is found. This is easiest done recursively. The `ClusterNode` method `extract_clusters()` handles this by returning a list with the node itself if below the distance threshold, and otherwise calling the child nodes (leaf nodes always return themselves). Calling this function will return a list of sub-trees containing the clusters. To get the leaf nodes for each cluster sub-tree that contains the object ids, traverse each sub-tree and return a list of leaves using the method `get_cluster_elements()`.

Let's try this on a simple example to see it all in action. First create some 2D data points (same as for *k*-means above):

```
class1 = 1.5 * randn(100,2)
class2 = randn(100,2) + array([5,5])
features = vstack((class1,class2))
```

Cluster the points and extract the clusters from the list using some threshold (here we used 5) and print the clusters in the console:

```
import hcluster

tree = hcluster.hcluster(features)

clusters = tree.extract_clusters(5)

print 'number of clusters', len(clusters)
for c in clusters:
  print c.get_cluster_elements()
```

This should give a printout similar to this:

```
number of clusters 2

[184, 187, 196, 137, 174, 102, 147, 145, 185, 109, 166, 152, 173, 180, 128, 163, 141,
178, 151, 158, 108, 182, 112, 199, 100, 119, 132, 195, 105, 159, 140, 171, 191, 164,
130, 149, 150, 157, 176, 135, 123, 131, 118, 170, 143, 125, 127, 139, 179, 126, 160,
162, 114, 122, 103, 146, 115, 120, 142, 111, 154, 116, 129, 136, 144, 167, 106, 107,
198, 186, 153, 156, 134, 101, 110, 133, 189, 168, 183, 148, 165, 172, 188, 138, 192,
104, 124, 113, 194, 190, 161, 175, 121, 197, 177, 193, 169, 117, 155]

[56, 4, 47, 18, 51, 95, 29, 91, 23, 80, 83, 3, 54, 68, 69, 5, 21, 1, 44, 57, 17, 90,
30, 22, 63, 41, 7, 14, 59, 96, 20, 26, 71, 88, 86, 40, 27, 38, 50, 55, 67, 8, 28, 79,
64, 66, 94, 33, 53, 70, 31, 81, 9, 75, 15, 32, 89, 6, 11, 48, 58, 2, 39, 61, 45,
65, 82, 93, 97, 52, 62, 16, 43, 84, 24, 19, 74, 36, 37, 60, 87, 92, 181, 99, 10, 49,
12, 76, 98, 46, 72, 34, 35, 13, 73, 78, 25, 42, 77, 85]
```

Ideally, you should get two clusters, but depending on the actual data you might get three or even more. In this simple example of clustering 2D points, one cluster should contain values lower than 100 and the other values 100 and above.

Clustering Images

Let's look at an example of clustering images based on their color content. The file *sunsets.zip* contains 100 images downloaded from Flickr using the tag "sunset" or "sunsets." For this example, we will use a color histogram of each image as feature vector. This is a bit crude and simple but good enough for illustrating what hierarchical clustering does. Try running the following code in a folder containing the sunset images:

```
import os
import hcluster

# create a list of images
path = 'flickr-sunsets/'
imlist = [os.path.join(path,f) for f in os.listdir(path) if f.endswith('.jpg')]

# extract feature vector (8 bins per color channel)
features = zeros([len(imlist), 512])
for i,f in enumerate(imlist):
  im = array(Image.open(f))

  # multi-dimensional histogram
  h,edges = histogramdd(im.reshape(-1,3),8,normed=True,
                        range=[(0,255),(0,255),(0,255)])
  features[i] = h.flatten()

tree = hcluster.hcluster(features)
```

Here we take the R, G, and B color channels as vectors and feed them into NumPy's `histogramdd()`, which computes multi-dimensional histograms (in this case three dimensions). We chose 8 bins in each color dimension (8 × 8 × 8), which, after flattening, gives 512 bins in the feature vector. We use the "normed=True" option to normalize the histograms in case the images are of different size and set the range to 0 . . . 255 for each color channel. The use of `reshape()` with one dimension set to −1 will automatically determine the correct size, and thereby create an input array to the histogram computation consisting of the RGB color values as rows.

To visualize the cluster tree, we can draw a dendrogram. A *dendrogram* is a diagram that shows the tree layout. This often gives useful information on how good a given descriptor vector is and what is considered similar in a particular case. Add the following code to *hcluster.py*:

```
from PIL import Image,ImageDraw

def draw_dendrogram(node,imlist,filename='clusters.jpg'):
    """ Draw a cluster dendrogram and save to a file. """

  # height and width
  rows = node.get_height()*20
  cols = 1200

  # scale factor for distances to fit image width
  s = float(cols-150)/node.get_depth()

  # create image and draw object
  im = Image.new('RGB',(cols,rows),(255,255,255))
```

```
draw = ImageDraw.Draw(im)

# initial line for start of tree
draw.line((0,rows/2,20,rows/2),fill=(0,0,0))

# draw the nodes recursively
node.draw(draw,20,(rows/2),s,imlist,im)
im.save(filename)
im.show()
```

Here the dendrogram drawing uses a draw() method for each node. Add this method to the ClusterNode class:

```
def draw(self,draw,x,y,s,imlist,im):
    """ Draw nodes recursively with image
        thumbnails for leaf nodes. """

    h1 = int(self.left.get_height()*20 / 2)
    h2 = int(self.right.get_height()*20 /2)
    top = y-(h1+h2)
    bottom = y+(h1+h2)

    # vertical line to children
    draw.line((x,top+h1,x,bottom-h2),fill=(0,0,0))

    # horizontal lines
    ll = self.distance*s
    draw.line((x,top+h1,x+ll,top+h1),fill=(0,0,0))
    draw.line((x,bottom-h2,x+ll,bottom-h2),fill=(0,0,0))

    # draw left and right child nodes recursively
    self.left.draw(draw,x+ll,top+h1,s,imlist,im)
    self.right.draw(draw,x+ll,bottom-h2,s,imlist,im)
```

The leaf nodes have their own special method to draw thumbnails of the actual images. Add this to the ClusterLeafNode class:

```
def draw(self,draw,x,y,s,imlist,im):
    nodeim = Image.open(imlist[self.id])
    nodeim.thumbnail([20,20])
    ns = nodeim.size
    im.paste(nodeim,[int(x),int(y-ns[1]//2),int(x+ns[0]),int(y+ns[1]-ns[1]//2)])
```

The height of a dendrogram and the sub parts are determined by the distance values. These need to be scaled to fit inside the chosen image resolution. The nodes are drawn recursively with the coordinates passed down to the level below. Leaf nodes are drawn with small thumbnail images of 20×20 pixels. Two helper methods are used to get the height and width of the tree, get_height() and get_depth().

The dendrogram is drawn like this:

```
hcluster.draw_dendrogram(tree,imlist,filename='sunset.pdf')
```

The cluster dendrogram for the sunset images is shown in Figure 6-5. As can be seen, images with similar color are close in the tree. Three example clusters are shown in

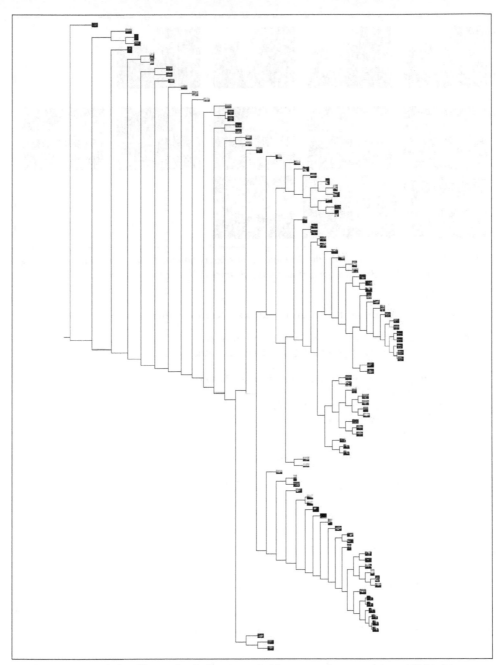

Figure 6-5. An example of hierarchical clustering of 100 images of sunsets using a 512 bin histogram in RGB coordinates as feature vector. Images close together in the tree have similar color distribution.

Figure 6-6. Example clusters from the 100 images of sunsets obtained with hierarchical clustering using a threshold set to 23% of the maximum node distance in the tree.

Figure 6-6. The clusters in this example are extracted as follows:

```
# visualize clusters with some (arbitrary) threshold
clusters = tree.extract_clusters(0.23*tree.distance)

# plot images for clusters with more than 3 elements
for c in clusters:
  elements = c.get_cluster_elements()
  nbr_elements = len(elements)
  if nbr_elements>3:
    figure()
    for p in range(minimum(nbr_elements,20)):
      subplot(4,5,p+1)
      im = array(Image.open(imlist[elements[p]]))
      imshow(im)
      axis('off')
show()
```

As a final example, we can create a dendrogram for the font images:

```
tree = hcluster.hcluster(projected)
hcluster.draw_dendrogram(tree,imlist,filename='fonts.jpg')
```

where *projected* and *imlist* refer to the variables used in the *k*-means example in Section 6.1. The resulting font images dendrogram is shown in Figure 6-7.

6.3 Spectral Clustering

Spectral clustering methods are an interesting type of clustering algorithm that have a different approach compared to *k*-means and hierarchical clustering.

A *similarity matrix* (or *affinity matrix*, or sometimes *distance matrix*) for *n* elements (for example images) is an *n* × *n* matrix with pair-wise similarity scores. Spectral clustering

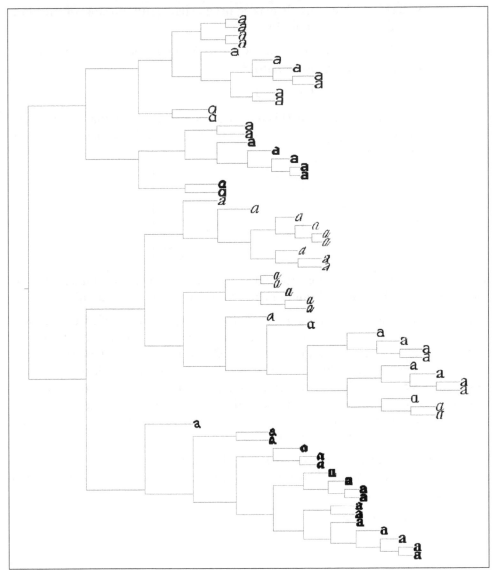

Figure 6-7. An example of hierarchical clustering of 66 selected font images using 40 principal components as feature vector.

gets its name from the use of the spectrum of a matrix constructed from a similarity matrix. The eigenvectors of this matrix are used for dimensionality reduction and then clustering.

One of the benefits of spectral clustering methods is that the only input needed is this matrix and it can be constructed from any measure of similarity you can think of. Methods like *k*-means and hierarchical clustering compute the mean of feature vectors, and this restricts the features (or descriptors) to vectors (in order to be able to compute the mean). With spectral methods, there is no need to have feature vectors of any kind, just a notion of "distance" or "similarity."

Here's how it works. Given a $n \times n$ similarity matrix S with similarity scores s_{ij}, we can create a matrix, called the *Laplacian matrix*[2],

$$L = I - D^{-1/2}SD^{-1/2},$$

where I is the identity matrix and D is the diagonal matrix containing the row sums of S, $D = \text{diag}(d_i)$, $d_i = \sum_j s_{ij}$. The matrix $D^{-1/2}$ used in the construction of the Laplacian matrix is then

$$D^{-1/2} = \begin{bmatrix} \frac{1}{\sqrt{d_1}} & & & \\ & \frac{1}{\sqrt{d_2}} & & \\ & & \ddots & \\ & & & \frac{1}{\sqrt{d_n}} \end{bmatrix}.$$

In order to make the presentation clearer, let's use low values of s_{ij} for similar elements and require $s_{ij} \geq 0$ (the term distance matrix is perhaps more fitting in this case).

The clusters are found by computing the eigenvectors of L and using the k eigenvectors corresponding to the k largest eigenvalues to construct a set of feature vectors (remember that we may not have had any to start with!). Create a matrix with the k eigenvectors as columns. The rows will then be treated as new feature vectors (of length k). These new feature vectors can then be clustered, using, for example, k-means to produce the final clusters. In essence, what the algorithm does is to transform the original data into new feature vectors that can be more easily clustered (and in some cases using cluster algorithms that could not be used in the first place).

Enough about the theory; let's see what it looks like in code when applied to a real example. Again, we take the font images used in the k-means example above (and introduced on page 14):

```
from scipy.cluster.vq import *

n = len(projected)

# compute distance matrix
S = array([[ sqrt(sum((projected[i]-projected[j])**2))
            for i in range(n) ] for j in range(n)], 'f')

# create Laplacian matrix
rowsum = sum(S,axis=0)
D = diag(1 / sqrt(rowsum))
I = identity(n)
L = I - dot(D,dot(S,D))
```

[2] Sometimes $L = D^{-1/2}SD^{-1/2}$ is used as the Laplacian matrix instead, but the choice doesn't really matter since it only changes the eigenvalues, not the eigenvectors.

```
# compute eigenvectors of L
U,sigma,V = linalg.svd(L)

k = 5
# create feature vector from k first eigenvectors
# by stacking eigenvectors as columns
features = array(V[:k]).T

# k-means
features = whiten(features)
centroids,distortion = kmeans(features,k)
code,distance = vq(features,centroids)

# plot clusters
for c in range(k):
    ind = where(code==c)[0]
    figure()
    for i in range(minimum(len(ind),39)):
        im = Image.open(path+imlist[ind[i]])
        subplot(4,10,i+1)
        imshow(array(im))
        axis('equal')
        axis('off')
show()
```

In this case, we just create S using pair-wise Euclidean distances and compute a standard k-means clustering on the k eigenvectors ($k = 5$ in this particular case). Remember that the matrix V contains the eigenvectors sorted with respect to the eigenvalues. Finally, the clusters are plotted. Figure 6-8 shows the clusters for an example run (remember that the k-means step might give different results each run).

We can also try this on an example where we don't have any feature vectors or any strict definition of similarity. The geotagged Panoramio images on page 44 were linked based on how many matching local descriptors were found between them. The matrix

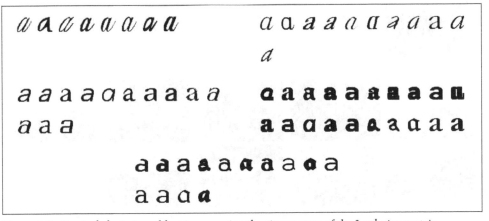

Figure 6-8. Spectral clustering of font images using the eigenvectors of the Laplacian matrix.

on page 48 is a similarity matrix with scores equal to the number of matching features (without any normalization). With *imlist* containing the filenames of the images and the similarity matrix saved to a file using NumPy's savetxt(), we only need to modify the first rows of the code above to

```
n = len(imlist)

# load the similarity matrix and reformat
S = loadtxt('panoramio_matches.txt')
S = 1 / (S + 1e-6)
```

where we invert the scores to have low values for similar images (so we don't have to modify the code above). We add a small number to avoid division with zero. The rest of the code you can leave as is.

Choosing *k* is a bit tricky in this case. Most people would consider there to be only two classes (the two sides of the White House) and then some junk images. With $k = 2$, you get something like Figure 6-9, with one large cluster of images of one side and the other cluster containing the other side plus all the junk images. Picking a larger value of *k*, like $k = 10$, gives several clusters with only one image (hopefully the junk images) and some real clusters. An example run is shown in Figure 6-10. In this case, there were only two actual clusters, each containing images of one side of the White House.

Figure 6-9. Spectral clustering of geotagged images of the White House with $k = 2$ and the similarity scores as the number of matching local descriptors.

Figure 6-10. Spectral clustering of geotagged images of the White House with $k = 10$ and the similarity scores as the number of matching local descriptors. Only the clusters with more than one image shown.

There are many different versions and alternatives to the algorithm presented here, each of them with its own idea of how to construct the matrix L and what to do with the eigenvectors. For further reading on spectral clustering and the details of some common algorithms, see for example the review paper [37].

Exercises

1. *Hierarchical k-means* is a clustering method that applies k-means recursively to the clusters to create a tree of incrementally refined clusters. In this case, each node in the tree will branch to k child nodes. Implement this and try it on the font images.

2. Using the hierarchical k-means from the previous exercise, make a tree visualization (similar to the dendrogram for hierarchical clustering) that shows the average image for each cluster node. Tip: You can take the average PCA coefficients feature vector and use the PCA basis to synthesize an image for each feature vector.

3. By modifying the class used for hierarchical clustering to include the number of images below the node, you have a simple and fast way of finding similar (tight) groups of a given size. Implement this small change and try it out on some real data. How does it perform?

4. Experiment with using single and complete linking for building the hierarchical cluster tree. How do the resulting clusters differ?

5. In some spectral clustering algorithms the matrix $D^{-1}S$ is used instead of L. Try replacing the Laplacian matrix with this and apply this on a few different data sets.

6. Download some image collections from Flickr searches with different tags. Extract the RGB histogram like you did for the sunset images. Cluster the images using one of the methods from this chapter. Can you separate the classes with the clusters?

## CHAPTER 7

Searching Images

This chapter shows how to use text mining techniques to search for images based on their visual content. The basic ideas of using visual words are presented and the details of a complete setup are explained and tested on an example image data set.

7.1 Content-Based Image Retrieval

Content-based image retrieval (CBIR) deals with the problem of retrieving visually similar images from a (large) database of images. This can be images with similar color, similar textures, or similar objects or scenes: basically any information contained in the images themselves.

For high-level queries, like finding similar objects, it is not feasible to do a full comparison (for example using feature matching) between a query image and all images in the database. It would simply take too much time to return any results if the database is large. In the last couple of years, researchers have successfully introduced techniques from the world of text mining for CBIR problems, making it possible to search millions of images for similar content.

Inspiration from Text Mining—The Vector Space Model

The *vector space model* is a model for representing and searching text documents. As we will see, it can be applied to essentially any kind of objects, including images. The name comes from the fact that text documents are represented with vectors that are histograms of the word frequencies in the text.[1] In other words, the vector will contain the number of occurrences of every word (at the position corresponding to that word) and zeros everywhere else. This model is also called a *bag-of-word representation*, since order and location of words is ignored.

---

[1] Often you see "term" used instead of "word"; the meaning is the same.

Documents are indexed by doing a word count to construct the document histogram vector **v**, usually with common words like "the," "and," "is," etc., ignored. These common words are called *stop words*. To compensate for document length, the vectors can be normalized to unit length by dividing with the total histogram sum. The individual components of the histogram vector are usually weighted according to the importance of each word. Usually, the importance of a word increases proportionally to how often it appears in the document, but decreases if the word is common in all documents in a data set (or "corpus").

The most common weighting is *tf-idf weighting* (*term frequency–inverse document frequency*) where the *term frequency* of a word w in document d is

$$\text{tf}_{w,d} = \frac{n_w}{\sum_j n_j},$$

where n_w is the number of occurrences of w in d. To normalize, this is divided by the total number of occurrences of all words in the document.

The *inverse document frequency* is

$$\text{idf}_{w,d} = \log \frac{|D|}{|\{d : w \in d\}|},$$

where $|D|$ is the number of documents in the corpus D and the denominator the number of documents d in D containing w. Multiplying the two gives the tf-idf weight, which becomes one of the elements in **v**. You can read more about tf-idf at *http://en .wikipedia.org/wiki/Tf-idf*.

This is really all we need at the moment. Let's see how to carry this model over to indexing and searching images based on their visual content.

7.2 Visual Words

To apply text mining techniques to images, we first need to create the visual equivalent of words. This is usually done using local descriptors like the SIFT descriptor in Section 2.2. The idea is to quantize the descriptor space into a number of typical examples and assign each descriptor in the image to one of those examples. These typical examples are determined by analyzing a training set of images and can be considered as *visual words*. The set of all words is then a *visual vocabulary* (sometimes called a *visual codebook*). This vocabulary can be created specifically for a given problem or type of image or just to try to represent visual content in general.

The visual words are constructed using some clustering algorithm applied to the feature descriptors extracted from a (large) training set of images. The most common choice is k-means,[2] which is what we will use here. Visual words are nothing but a collection of vectors in the given feature descriptor space; in the case of k-means, they are the cluster centroids. Representing an image with a histogram of visual words is then called a *bag-of-visual-words* model.

---

[2] Or in the more advanced cases, hierarchical k-means.

Let's introduce an example data set and use that to illustrate the concept. The file *first1000.zip* contains the first 1000 images from the University of Kentucky object recognition benchmark set (also known as "ukbench"). The full set, reported benchmarks, and some supporting code can be found at *http://www.vis.uky.edu/~stewe/ ukbench/*. The ukbench set contains many sets of four images, each of the same scene or object (stored consecutively so that 0 . . . 3, 4 . . . 7, etc., belong together). Figure 7-1 shows some examples from the data set. Appendix A has the details on the set and how to get the data.

Figure 7-1. Some examples of images from the ukbench (University of Kentucky object recognition benchmark) data set.

Creating a Vocabulary

To create a vocabulary of visual words we first need to extract descriptors. Here we will use the SIFT descriptor. Running the following lines of code, with *imlist*, as usual, containing the filenames of the images,

```
nbr_images = len(imlist)
featlist = [ imlist[i][:-3]+'sift' for i in range(nbr_images)]

for i in range(nbr_images):
  sift.process_image(imlist[i],featlist[i])
```

will give you descriptor files for each image. Create a file *vocabulary.py* and add the following code for a vocabulary class and a method for training a vocabulary on some training image data:

```
from scipy.cluster.vq import *
import vlfeat as sift


class Vocabulary(object):

  def __init__(self,name):
    self.name = name
    self.voc = []
    self.idf = []
    self.trainingdata = []
    self.nbr_words = 0

  def train(self,featurefiles,k=100,subsampling=10):
    """ Train a vocabulary from features in files listed
      in featurefiles using k-means with k number of words.
      Subsampling of training data can be used for speedup. """

    nbr_images = len(featurefiles)
    # read the features from file
    descr = []
    descr.append(sift.read_features_from_file(featurefiles[0])[1])
    descriptors = descr[0] #stack all features for k-means
    for i in arange(1,nbr_images):
      descr.append(sift.read_features_from_file(featurefiles[i])[1])
      descriptors = vstack((descriptors,descr[i]))

    # k-means: last number determines number of runs
    self.voc,distortion = kmeans(descriptors[::subsampling,:],k,1)
    self.nbr_words = self.voc.shape[0]

    # go through all training images and project on vocabulary
    imwords = zeros((nbr_images,self.nbr_words))
    for i in range( nbr_images ):
      imwords[i] = self.project(descr[i])

    nbr_occurences = sum( (imwords > 0)*1 ,axis=0)

    self.idf = log( (1.0*nbr_images) / (1.0*nbr_occurences+1) )
    self.trainingdata = featurefiles
```

```
def project(self,descriptors):
    """ Project descriptors on the vocabulary
        to create a histogram of words. """

    # histogram of image words
    imhist = zeros((self.nbr_words))
    words,distance = vq(descriptors,self.voc)
    for w in words:
        imhist[w] += 1

    return imhist
```

The class Vocabulary contains a vector of word cluster centers *voc* together with the idf values for each word. To train the vocabulary on some set of images, the method train() takes a list of .sift descriptor files and *k*, the desired number of words for the vocabulary. There is also an option of subsampling the training data for the *k*-means step, which will take a long time if too many features are used.

With the images and the feature files in a folder on your computer, the following code will create a vocabulary of length $k \approx 1000$ (again assuming that *imlist* contains a list of filenames for the images):

```
import pickle
import vocabulary

nbr_images = len(imlist)
featlist = [ imlist[i][:-3]+'sift' for i in range(nbr_images) ]

voc = vocabulary.Vocabulary('ukbenchtest')
voc.train(featlist,1000,10)

# saving vocabulary
with open('vocabulary.pkl', 'wb') as f:
    pickle.dump(voc,f)
print 'vocabulary is:', voc.name, voc.nbr_words
```

The last part also saves the entire vocabulary object for later use using the pickle module.

7.3 Indexing Images

Before we can start searching, we need to set up a database with the images and their visual word representations.

Setting Up the Database

To start indexing images, we first need to set up a database. Indexing images in this context means extracting descriptors from the images, converting them to visual words using a vocabulary, and storing the visual words and word histograms with information about which image they belong to. This will make it possible to query the database using an image and get the most similar images back as search result.

Table 7-1. A simple database schema for storing images and visual words.

imlist	imwords	imhistograms
rowid	imid	imid
filename	wordid	histogram
	vocname	vocname

Here we will use SQLite as database. SQLite is a database that stores everything in a single file and is very easy to set up and use. We are using it here since it is the easiest way to get started without having to go into database and server configurations and other details way outside the scope of this book. The Python version, pysqlite, is available from *http://code.google.com/p/pysqlite/* and also through many package repositories on Mac and Linux. SQLite uses the SQL query language so the transition should be easy if you want to use another database.

To get started, we need to create tables and indexes and an indexer class to write image data to the database. First, create a file *imagesearch.py* and add the following code:

```
import pickle
from pysqlite2 import dbapi2 as sqlite

class Indexer(object):

    def __init__(self,db,voc):
        """ Initialize with the name of the database
            and a vocabulary object. """

        self.con = sqlite.connect(db)
        self.voc = voc


    def __del__(self):
        self.con.close()


    def db_commit(self):
        self.con.commit()
```

First of all, we need Pickle for encoding and decoding these arrays to and from strings. SQLite is imported from the pysqlite2 module (see Appendix A for installation details). The Indexer class connects to a database and stores a vocabulary object upon creation (where the __init__() method is called). The __del__() method makes sure to close the database connection and db_commit() writes the changes to the database file.

We only need a very simple database schema of three tables. The table imlist contains the filenames of all indexed images, and imwords contains a *word index* of the words, which vocabulary was used, and which images the words appear in. Finally, imhistograms contains the full word histograms for each image. We need those to compare images according to our vector space model. The schema is shown in Table 7-1.

The following method for the Indexer class creates the tables and some useful indexes to make searching faster:

```
def create_tables(self):
    """ Create the database tables. """

    self.con.execute('create table imlist(filename)')
    self.con.execute('create table imwords(imid,wordid,vocname)')
    self.con.execute('create table imhistograms(imid,histogram,vocname)')
    self.con.execute('create index im_idx on imlist(filename)')
    self.con.execute('create index wordid_idx on imwords(wordid)')
    self.con.execute('create index imid_idx on imwords(imid)')
    self.con.execute('create index imidhist_idx on imhistograms(imid)')
    self.db_commit()
```

Adding Images

With the database tables in place, we can start adding images to the index. To do this, we need a method add_to_index() for our Indexer class. Add this method to *imagesearch.py*:

```
def add_to_index(self,imname,descr):
    """ Take an image with feature descriptors,
        project on vocabulary and add to database. """

    if self.is_indexed(imname): return
    print 'indexing', imname

    # get the imid
    imid = self.get_id(imname)

    # get the words
    imwords = self.voc.project(descr)
    nbr_words = imwords.shape[0]

    # link each word to image
    for i in range(nbr_words):
        word = imwords[i]
        # wordid is the word number itself
        self.con.execute("insert into imwords(imid,wordid,vocname)
                values (?,?,?)", (imid,word,self.voc.name))

    # store word histogram for image
    # use pickle to encode NumPy arrays as strings
    self.con.execute("insert into imhistograms(imid,histogram,vocname)
            values (?,?,?)", (imid,pickle.dumps(imwords),self.voc.name))
```

This method takes the image filename and a NumPy array with the descriptors found in the image. The descriptors are projected on the vocabulary and inserted in imwords (word by word) and imhistograms. We used two helper functions, is_indexed(), which checks if the image has been indexed already, and get_id(), which gives the image id for an image filename. Add these to *imagesearch.py*:

```
def is_indexed(self,imname):
    """ Returns True if imname has been indexed. """

    im = self.con.execute("select rowid from imlist where
            filename='%s'" % imname).fetchone()
    return im != None
```

```
def get_id(self,imname):
    """ Get an entry id and add if not present. """

    cur = self.con.execute(
    "select rowid from imlist where filename='%s'" % imname)
    res=cur.fetchone()
    if res==None:
        cur = self.con.execute(
        "insert into imlist(filename) values ('%s')" % imname)
        return cur.lastrowid
    else:
        return res[0]
```

Did you notice that we used Pickle in `add_to_index()`? Databases like SQLite do not have a standard type for storing objects or arrays. Instead, we can create a string representation using Pickle's `dumps()` function and write the string to the database. Consequently, we need to un-pickle the string when reading from the database. More on that in the next section.

The following code example will go through the ukbench sample images and add them to our index. Here we assume that the lists *imlist* and *featlist* contain the filenames of the images and the descriptor files and that the vocabulary you trained earlier was pickled to a file *vocabulary.pkl*:

```
import pickle
import sift
import imagesearch

nbr_images = len(imlist)

# load vocabulary
with open('vocabulary.pkl', 'rb') as f:
    voc = pickle.load(f)

# create indexer
indx = imagesearch.Indexer('test.db',voc)
indx.create_tables()

# go through all images, project features on vocabulary and insert
for i in range(nbr_images)[:100]:
    locs,descr = sift.read_features_from_file(featlist[i])
    indx.add_to_index(imlist[i],descr)

# commit to database
indx.db_commit()
```

We can now inspect the contents of our database:

```
from pysqlite2 import dbapi2 as sqlite
con = sqlite.connect('test.db')
print con.execute('select count (filename) from imlist').fetchone()
print con.execute('select * from imlist').fetchone()
```

This prints the following to your console:

```
(1000,)
(u'ukbench00000.jpg',)
```

If you try `fetchall()` instead of `fetchone()` in the last line, you will get a long list of all the filenames.

7.4 Searching the Database for Images

With a set of images indexed, we can search the database for similar images. Here we have used a bag-of-word representation for the whole image, but the procedure explained here is generic and can be used to find similar objects, similar faces, similar colors, etc. It all depends on the images and descriptors used.

To handle searches, we introduce a Searcher class to *imagesearch.py*:

```
class Searcher(object):

    def __init__(self,db,voc):
        """ Initialize with the name of the database. """
        self.con = sqlite.connect(db)
        self.voc = voc


    def __del__(self):
        self.con.close()
```

A new Searcher object connects to the database and closes the connection upon deletion, same as for the Indexer class before.

If the number of images is large, it is not feasible to do a full histogram comparison across all images in the database. We need a way to find a reasonably sized set of candidates (where "reasonable" can be determined by search response time, memory requirements, etc.). This is where the word index comes into play. Using the index, we can get a set of candidates and then do the full comparison against that set.

Using the Index to Get Candidates

We can use our index to find all images that contain a particular word. This is just a simple query to the database. Add `candidates_from_word()` as a method for the Searcher class:

```
def candidates_from_word(self,imword):
    """ Get list of images containing imword. """

    im_ids = self.con.execute(
        "select distinct imid from imwords where wordid=%d" % imword).fetchall()
    return [i[0] for i in im_ids]
```

This gives the image ids for all images containing the word. To get candidates for more than one word, for example all the nonzero entries in a word histogram, we can loop over each word, get images with that word, and aggregate the lists.[3] Here we should

---

[3] If you don't want to use all words, try ranking them according to their idf weight and use the ones with highest weights.

also keep track of how many times each image id appears in the aggregate list, since this shows how many words match the ones in the word histogram. This can be done with the following Searcher method:

```
def candidates_from_histogram(self,imwords):
  """ Get list of images with similar words. """

  # get the word ids
  words = imwords.nonzero()[0]

  # find candidates
  candidates = []
  for word in words:
    c = self.candidates_from_word(word)
    candidates+=c

  # take all unique words and reverse sort on occurrence
  tmp = [(w,candidates.count(w)) for w in set(candidates)]
  tmp.sort(cmp=lambda x,y:cmp(x[1],y[1]))
  tmp.reverse()

  # return sorted list, best matches first
  return [w[0] for w in tmp]
```

This method creates a list of word ids from the nonzero entries in a word histogram of an image. Candidates for each word are retrieved and aggregated in the list *candidates*. Then we create a list of tuples (word id, count) with the number of occurrences of each word in the candidate list and sort this list (in place for efficiency) using sort() with a custom comparison function that compares the second element in the tuple. The comparison function is declared inline using lambda functions, convenient one-line function declarations. The result is returned as a list of image ids with the best matching image first.

Consider the following example:

```
src = imagesearch.Searcher('test.db')
locs,descr = sift.read_features_from_file(featlist[0])
iw = voc.project(descr)

print 'ask using a histogram...'
print src.candidates_from_histogram(iw)[:10]
```

This prints the first 10 lookups from the index and gives the output (this will vary depending on your vocabulary):

```
ask using a histogram...
[655, 656, 654, 44, 9, 653, 42, 43, 41, 12]
```

None of the top 10 candidates are correct. Don't worry; we can now take any number of elements from this list and compare histograms. As you will see, this improves things considerably.

Querying with an Image

There is not much more needed to do a full search using an image as query. To do word histogram comparisons, a `Searcher` object needs to be able to read the image word histograms from the database. Add this method to the `Searcher` class:

```python
def get_imhistogram(self,imname):
    """ Return the word histogram for an image. """

    im_id = self.con.execute(
        "select rowid from imlist where filename='%s'" % imname).fetchone()
    s = self.con.execute(
        "select histogram from imhistograms where rowid='%d'" % im_id).fetchone()

    # use pickle to decode NumPy arrays from string
    return pickle.loads(str(s[0]))
```

Again we use Pickle to convert between string and NumPy arrays, this time with `loads()`.

Now we can combine everything into a query method:

```python
def query(self,imname):
    """ Find a list of matching images for imname"""

    h = self.get_imhistogram(imname)
    candidates = self.candidates_from_histogram(h)

    matchscores = []
    for imid in candidates:
        # get the name
        cand_name = self.con.execute(
            "select filename from imlist where rowid=%d" % imid).fetchone()
        cand_h = self.get_imhistogram(cand_name)
        cand_dist = sqrt( sum( (h-cand_h)**2 ) ) #use L2 distance
        matchscores.append( (cand_dist,imid) )

    # return a sorted list of distances and database ids
    matchscores.sort()
    return matchscores
```

This `Searcher` method takes the filename of an image and retrieves the word histogram and a list of candidates (which should be limited to some maximum number if you have a large data set). For each candidate, we compare histograms using standard Euclidean distance and return a sorted list of tuples containing distance and image id.

Let's try a query for the same image as in the previous section:

```python
src = imagesearch.Searcher('test.db')
print 'try a query...'
print src.query(imlist[0])[:10]
```

This will again print the top 10 results, including the distance, and should look something like this:

```
try a query...
[(0.0, 1), (100.03999200319841, 2), (105.45141061171255, 3), (129.47200469599596, 708),
(129.73819792181484, 707), (132.68006632497588, 4), (139.89639023220005, 10),
(142.31654858097141, 706), (148.1924424523734, 716), (148.22955170950223, 663)]
```

Much better. The image has distance zero to itself, and two out of the three images of the same scene are on the first two positions. The third image is coming in on position five.

Benchmarking and Plotting the Results

To get a feel for how good the search results are, we can compute the number of correct images on the top four positions. This is the measure used to report performance for the ukbench image set. Here's a function that computes this score. Add it to *imagesearch.py* and you can start optimizing your queries:

```python
def compute_ukbench_score(src,imlist):
    """ Returns the average number of correct
        images on the top four results of queries."""

    nbr_images = len(imlist)
    pos = zeros((nbr_images,4))
    # get first four results for each image
    for i in range(nbr_images):
        pos[i] = [w[1]-1 for w in src.query(imlist[i])[:4]]

    # compute score and return average
    score = array([ (pos[i]//4)==(i//4) for i in range(nbr_images)])*1.0
    return sum(score) / (nbr_images)
```

This function gets the top four results and subtracts one from the index returned by query() since the database index starts at one and the list of images at zero. Then we compute the score using integer division, using the fact that the correct images are consecutive in groups of four. A perfect result gives a score of 4, nothing right gives a score of 0, and only retrieving the identical images gives a score of 1. Finding the identical image together with two of the three other images gives a score of 3.

Try it out like this:

```python
imagesearch.compute_ukbench_score(src,imlist)
```

Or if you don't want to wait (it will take some time to do 1000 queries), just use a subset of the images:

```python
imagesearch.compute_ukbench_score(src,imlist[:100])
```

We can consider a score close to 3 as pretty good in this case. The state-of-the-art results reported on the ukbench website are just over 3 (note that they are using more images and your score will decrease with a larger set).

Finally, a function for showing the actual search results will be useful. Add this function,

```python
def plot_results(src,res):
    """ Show images in result list 'res'."""

    figure()
    nbr_results = len(res)
    for i in range(nbr_results):
        imname = src.get_filename(res[i])
        subplot(1,nbr_results,i+1)
```

```
        imshow(array(Image.open(imname)))
        axis('off')
    show()
```

which can be called with any number of search results in the list *res*. For example, like this:

```
nbr_results = 6
res = [w[1] for w in src.query(imlist[0])[:nbr_results]]
imagesearch.plot_results(src,res)
```

The helper function

```
def get_filename(self,imid):
    """ Return the filename for an image id"""

    s = self.con.execute(
        "select filename from imlist where rowid='%d'" % imid).fetchone()
    return s[0]
```

translates image id to filenames that we need for loading the images when plotting. Some example queries on our data set are shown using plot_results() in Figure 7-2.

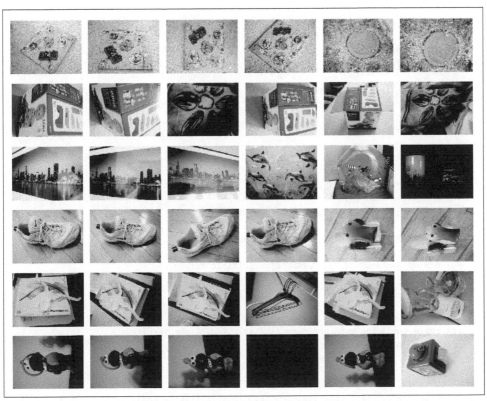

Figure 7-2. Some example search results on the ukbench data set. The query image is shown on the far left followed by the top five retrieved images.

7.5 Ranking Results Using Geometry

Let's briefly look at a common way of improving results obtained using a bag-of-visual-words model. One of the drawbacks of the model is that the visual words representation of an image does not contain the positions of the image features. This was the price paid to get speed and scalability.

One way to have the feature points improve results is to re-rank the top results using some criteria that takes the features' geometric relationships into account. The most common approach is to fit homographies between the feature locations in the query image and the top result images.

To make this efficient, the feature locations can be stored in the database and correspondences determined by the word id of the features (this only works if the vocabulary is large enough so that the word id matches contain mostly correct matches). This would require a major rewrite of our database and code above and complicate the presentation. To illustrate, we will just reload the features for the top images and match them.

Here is what a complete example of loading all the model files and re-ranking the top results using homographies looks like:

```
import pickle
import sift
import imagesearch
import homography

# load image list and vocabulary
with open('ukbench_imlist.pkl','rb') as f:
  imlist = pickle.load(f)
  featlist = pickle.load(f)

nbr_images = len(imlist)

with open('vocabulary.pkl', 'rb') as f:
  voc = pickle.load(f)


src = imagesearch.Searcher('test.db',voc)

# index of query image and number of results to return
q_ind = 50
nbr_results = 20

# regular query
res_reg = [w[1] for w in src.query(imlist[q_ind])[:nbr_results]]
print 'top matches (regular):', res_reg


# load image features for query image
q_locs,q_descr = sift.read_features_from_file(featlist[q_ind])
fp = homography.make_homog(q_locs[:,:2].T)
```

```
# RANSAC model for homography fitting
model = homography.RansacModel()

rank = {}
# load image features for result
for ndx in res_reg[1:]:
  locs,descr = sift.read_features_from_file(featlist[ndx])

  # get matches
  matches = sift.match(q_descr,descr)
  ind = matches.nonzero()[0]
  ind2 = matches[ind]
  tp = homography.make_homog(locs[:,:2].T)

  # compute homography, count inliers. if not enough matches return empty list
  try:
    H,inliers = homography.H_from_ransac(fp[:,ind],tp[:,ind2],model,match_theshold=4)
  except:
    inliers = []

  # store inlier count
  rank[ndx] = len(inliers)


# sort dictionary to get the most inliers first
sorted_rank = sorted(rank.items(), key=lambda t: t[1], reverse=True)
res_geom = [res_reg[0]]+[s[0] for s in sorted_rank]
print 'top matches (homography):', res_geom


# plot the top results
imagesearch.plot_results(src,res_reg[:8])
imagesearch.plot_results(src,res_geom[:8])
```

First, the image list, feature list (containing the filenames of the images and SIFT feature files, respectively), and the vocabulary is loaded. Then a Searcher object is created and a regular query is performed and stored in the list *res_reg*. The features for the query image are loaded. Then for each image in the result list, the features are loaded and matched against the query image. Homographies are computed from the matches and the number of inliers counted. If the homography fitting fails, we set the inlier list to an empty list. Finally, we sort the dictionary *rank* that contains image index and inlier count according to decreasing number of inliers. The result lists are printed to the console and the top images visualized.

The output looks like this:

```
top matches (regular): [39, 22, 74, 82, 50, 37, 38, 17, 29, 68, 52, 91, 15, 90, 31, ... ]
top matches (homography): [39, 38, 37, 45, 67, 68, 74, 82, 15, 17, 50, 52, 85, 22, 87, ... ]
```

Figure 7-3 shows some sample results with the regular and re-ranked top images.

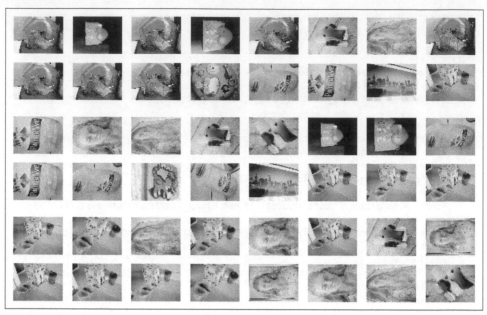

Figure 7-3. Some example search results with re-ranking based on geometric consistency using homographies. For each example, the top row is the regular result and the bottom row the re-ranked result.

7.6   Building Demos and Web Applications

In this last section on searching, we'll take a look at a simple way of building demos and web applications with Python. By making demos as web pages, you automatically get cross-platform support and an easy way to show and share your project with minimal requirements. In the sections below we will go through an example of a simple image search engine.

Creating Web Applications with CherryPy

To build these demos, we will use the CherryPy package, available at *http://www .cherrypy.org/*. CherryPy is a pure Python lightweight web server that uses an object oriented model. See Appendix A for more details on how to install and configure CherryPy. Assuming that you have studied the tutorial examples enough to have an initial idea of how CherryPy works, let's build an image search web demo on top of the image searcher you created earlier in this chapter.

Image Search Demo

First, we need to initialize with a few html tags and load the data using Pickle. We need the vocabulary for the Searcher object that interfaces with the database. Create a file *searchdemo.py* and add the following class with two methods:

```
import cherrypy, os, urllib, pickle
import imagesearch

class SearchDemo(object):

    def __init__(self):
        # load list of images
        with open('webimlist.txt') as f:
            self.imlist = f.readlines()

        self.nbr_images = len(self.imlist)
        self.ndx = range(self.nbr_images)

        # load vocabulary
        with open('vocabulary.pkl', 'rb') as f:
            self.voc = pickle.load(f)

        # set max number of results to show
        self.maxres = 15

        # header and footer html
        self.header = """
            <!doctype html>
            <head>
            <title>Image search example</title>
            </head>
            <body>
            """
        self.footer = """
            </body>
            </html>
            """

    def index(self,query=None):
        self.src = imagesearch.Searcher('web.db',self.voc)

        html = self.header
        html += """
            <br />
            Click an image to search. <a href='?query='>Random selection</a> of images.
            <br /><br />
            """
        if query:
            # query the database and get top images
            res = self.src.query(query)[:self.maxres]
            for dist,ndx in res:
                imname = self.src.get_filename(ndx)
                html += "<a href='?query="+imname+"'>"
                html += "<img src='"+imname+"' width='100' />"
                html += "</a>"
        else:
            # show random selection if no query
            random.shuffle(self.ndx)
            for i in self.ndx[:self.maxres]:
                imname = self.imlist[i]
                html += "<a href='?query="+imname+"'>"
```

```
        html += "<img src='"+imname+"' width='100' />"
        html += "</a>"

    html += self.footer
    return html

  index.exposed = True

cherrypy.quickstart(SearchDemo(), '/',
        config=os.path.join(os.path.dirname(__file__), 'service.conf'))
```

As you can see, this simple demo consists of a single class with one method for initialization and one for the "index" page (the only page in this case). Methods are automatically mapped to URLs, and arguments to the methods can be passed directly in the URL. The index method has a query parameter which, in this case, is the query image to sort the others against. If it is empty, a random selection of images is shown instead. The line

```
  index.exposed = True
```

makes the index URL accessible and the last line starts the CherryPy web server with configurations read from *service.conf*. Our configuration file for this example has the following lines:

```
[global]
server.socket_host = "127.0.0.1"
server.socket_port = 8080
server.thread_pool = 50
tools.sessions.on = True

[/]
tools.staticdir.root = "tmp/"
tools.staticdir.on = True
tools.staticdir.dir = ""
```

The first part specifies which IP address and port to use. The second part enables a local folder for reading (in this case "tmp/"). This should be set to the folder containing your images.

 Don't put anything secret in that folder if you plan to show this to people. The content of the folder will be accessible through CherryPy.

Start your web server with

```
$ python searchdemo.py
```

from the command line. Opening your browser and pointing it at the right URL (in this case *http://127.0.0.1:8080/*) should show the initial screen with a random selection of images. This should look like the top image in Figure 7-4. Clicking an image starts a query and shows the top results. Clicking an image in the results starts a new query with that image, and so on. There is a link to get back to the starting state of a random selection (by passing an empty query). Some examples are shown in Figure 7-4.

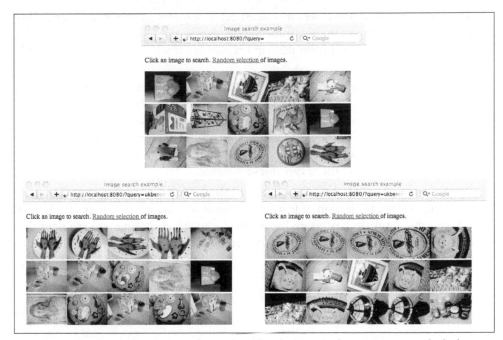

Figure 7-4. Some example search results on the ukbench data set: the starting page, which shows a random selection of the images (top); sample queries (bottom). The query image is shown on the top-left corner followed by the top image results shown row-wise.

This example shows a full integration from web page to database queries and presentation of results. Naturally, we kept the styling and options to a minimum and there are many possibilities for improvement. For example, you may add a stylesheet to make it prettier or upload files to use as queries.

Exercises

1. Try to speed up queries by only using part of the words in the query image to construct the list of candidates. Use the idf weight as a criteria for which words to use.

2. Implement a visual stop word list of the most common visual words in your vocabulary (say, the top 10%) and ignore these words. How does this change the search quality?

3. Visualize a visual word by saving all image features that are mapped to a given word id. Crop image patches around the feature locations (at the given scale) and plot them in a figure. Do the patches for a given word look the same?

4. Experiment with using different distance measures and weighting in the `query()` method. Use the score from `compute_ukbench_score()` to measure your progress.

5. Throughout this chapter, we only used SIFT features in our vocabulary. This completely disregards the color information, as you can see in the example results in Figure 7-2. Try to add color descriptors and see if you can improve the search results.

6. For large vocabularies, using arrays to represent the visual word frequencies is inefficient, since most of the entries will be zero (think of the case with a few hundred thousand words and images with typically a thousand features). One way to overcome this inefficiency is to use dictionaries as sparse array representations. Replace the arrays with a sparse class of your own and add the necessary methods. Alternatively, try to use the `scipy.sparse` module.

7. As you try to increase the size of the vocabulary, the clustering time will take too long and the projection of features to words also becomes slower. Implement a hierarchical vocabulary using hierarchical k-mean clustering and see how this improves scaling. See the paper [23] for details and inspiration.

## CHAPTER 8

Classifying Image Content

This chapter introduces algorithms for classifying images and image content. We look at some simple but effective methods as well as state-of-the-art classifiers and apply them to two-class and multi-class problems. We show examples with applications in gesture recognition and object recognition.

8.1 *K*-Nearest Neighbors

One of the simplest and most used methods for classification is the *k-nearest neighbor classifier (kNN)*. The algorithm simply compares an object (for example a feature vector) to be classified with all objects in a training set with known class labels and lets the *k* nearest vote for which class to assign. This method often performs well but has a number of drawbacks. Same as with the *k*-means clustering algorithm, the number *k* needs to be chosen and the value will affect performance. Furthermore, the method requires the entire training set to be stored, and if this set is large, it will be slow to search. For large training sets some form of binning is usually used to reduce the number of comparisons needed.[1] On the positive side, there are no restrictions on what distance measure to use; practically anything you can think of will work (which is not the same as saying that it will perform well). The algorithm is also trivially parallelizable.

Implementing kNN in a basic form is pretty straightforward. Given a set of training examples and a list of associated labels, the code below does the job. The training examples and labels can be rows in an array or just in a list. They can be numbers, strings, whatever you like. Add this class to a file called *knn.py*:

```
class KnnClassifier(object):

    def __init__(self,labels,samples):
        """ Initialize classifier with training data. """

        self.labels = labels
        self.samples = samples
```

---

[1] Another option is to only keep a selected subset of the training set. This can, however, impact accuracy.

```
def classify(self,point,k=3):
    """ Classify a point against k nearest
        in the training data, return label. """

    # compute distance to all training points
    dist = array([L2dist(point,s) for s in self.samples])

    # sort them
    ndx = dist.argsort()

    # use dictionary to store the k nearest
    votes = {}
    for i in range(k):
        label = self.labels[ndx[i]]
        votes.setdefault(label,0)
        votes[label] += 1

    return max(votes)

def L2dist(p1,p2):
    return sqrt( sum( (p1-p2)**2) )
```

It is easiest to define a class and initialize with the training data. That way, we don't have to store and pass the training data as arguments every time we want to classify something. Using a dictionary for storing the k nearest labels makes it possible to have labels as text strings or numbers. In this example, we used the Euclidean (L_2) distance measure. If you have other measures, just add them as functions.

A Simple 2D Example

Let's first create some simple 2D example data sets to illustrate and visualize how this classifier works. The following script will create two different 2D point sets, each with two classes, and save the data using Pickle:

```
from numpy.random import randn
import pickle

# create sample data of 2D points
n = 200

# two normal distributions
class_1 = 0.6 * randn(n,2)
class_2 = 1.2 * randn(n,2) + array([5,1])
labels = hstack((ones(n),-ones(n)))

# save with Pickle
with open('points_normal.pkl', 'w') as f:
    pickle.dump(class_1,f)
    pickle.dump(class_2,f)
    pickle.dump(labels,f)


# normal distribution and ring around it
class_1 = 0.6 * randn(n,2)
```

```
r = 0.8 * randn(n,1) + 5
angle = 2*pi * randn(n,1)
class_2 = hstack((r*cos(angle),r*sin(angle)))
labels = hstack((ones(n),-ones(n)))

# save with Pickle
with open('points_ring.pkl', 'w') as f:
  pickle.dump(class_1,f)
  pickle.dump(class_2,f)
  pickle.dump(labels,f)
```

Run the script twice with different filenames, for example *points_normal_test.pkl* first and *points_ring_test.pkl* the second time. You will now have four files with 2D data sets, two files for each of the distributions. We can use one for training and the other for testing.

Let's see how to do that with the kNN classifier. Create a script with the following commands:

```
import pickle
import knn
import imtools

# load 2D points using Pickle
with open('points_normal.pkl', 'r') as f:
  class_1 = pickle.load(f)
  class_2 = pickle.load(f)
  labels = pickle.load(f)

model = knn.KnnClassifier(labels,vstack((class_1,class_2)))
```

This will create a kNN classifier *model* using the data in the Pickle file. Now add the following:

```
# load test data using Pickle
with open('points_normal_test.pkl', 'r') as f:
  class_1 = pickle.load(f)
  class_2 = pickle.load(f)
  labels = pickle.load(f)

# test on the first point
print model.classify(class_1[0])
```

This loads the other data set (the test set) and prints the estimated class label of the first point to your console.

To visualize the classification of all the test points and show how well the classifier separates the two classes, we can add these lines:

```
# define function for plotting
def classify(x,y,model=model):
  return array([model.classify([xx,yy]) for (xx,yy) in zip(x,y)])

# plot the classification boundary
imtools.plot_2D_boundary([-6,6,-6,6],[class_1,class_2],classify,[1,-1])
show()
```

Here we created a small helper function that takes arrays of 2D coordinates x and y and the classifier and returns an array of estimated class labels. Now we can pass this function as an argument to the actual plotting function. Add the following function to your file *imtools*:

```
def plot_2D_boundary(plot_range,points,decisionfcn,labels,values=[0]):
    """ Plot_range is (xmin,xmax,ymin,ymax), points is a list
        of class points, decisionfcn is a funtion to evaluate,
        labels is a list of labels that decisionfcn returns for each class,
        values is a list of decision contours to show. """

    clist = ['b','r','g','k','m','y'] # colors for the classes

    # evaluate on a grid and plot contour of decision function
    x = arange(plot_range[0],plot_range[1],.1)
    y = arange(plot_range[2],plot_range[3],.1)
    xx,yy = meshgrid(x,y)
    xxx,yyy = xx.flatten(),yy.flatten() # lists of x,y in grid
    zz = array(decisionfcn(xxx,yyy))
    zz = zz.reshape(xx.shape)
    # plot contour(s) at values
    contour(xx,yy,zz,values)

    # for each class, plot the points with '*' for correct, 'o' for incorrect
    for i in range(len(points)):
        d = decisionfcn(points[i][:,0],points[i][:,1])
        correct_ndx = labels[i]==d
        incorrect_ndx = labels[i]!=d
        plot(points[i][correct_ndx,0],points[i][correct_ndx,1],'*',color=clist[i])
        plot(points[i][incorrect_ndx,0],points[i][incorrect_ndx,1],'o',color=clist[i])

    axis('equal')
```

This function takes a decision function (the classifier) and evaluates it on a grid using `meshgrid()`. The contours of the decision function can be plotted to show where the boundaries are. The default is the zero contour. The resulting plots look like the ones in Figure 8-1. As you can see, the kNN decision boundary can adapt to the distribution of the classes without any explicit modeling.

Dense SIFT as Image Feature

Let's look at classifying some images. To do so, we need a feature vector for the image. We saw feature vectors with average RGB and PCA coefficients as examples in the clustering chapter. Here we will introduce another representation, the *dense SIFT* feature vector.

A dense SIFT representation is created by applying the descriptor part of SIFT to a regular grid across the whole image.[2] We can use the same executables as in Section 2.2 and get dense SIFT features by adding some extra parameters. Create a file *dsift.py* as a placeholder for the dense SIFT computation and add the following function:

---

[2] Another common name is *Histogram of Oriented Gradients (HOG)*.

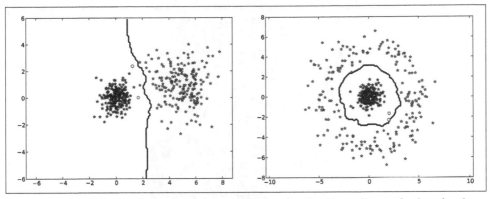

Figure 8-1. Classifying 2D data using a k-nearest neighbor classifier. For each example, the color shows the class label. Correctly classified points are shown with stars and misclassified points with circles. The curve is the classifier decision boundary.

```
import sift

def process_image_dsift(imagename,resultname,size=20,steps=10,
                        force_orientation=False,resize=None):
    """ Process an image with densely sampled SIFT descriptors
        and save the results in a file. Optional input: size of features,
        steps between locations, forcing computation of descriptor orientation
        (False means all are oriented upward), tuple for resizing the image."""

    im = Image.open(imagename).convert('L')
    if resize!=None:
        im = im.resize(resize)
    m,n = im.size

    if imagename[-3:] != 'pgm':
        # create a pgm file
        im.save('tmp.pgm')
        imagename = 'tmp.pgm'

    # create frames and save to temporary file
    scale = size/3.0
    x,y = meshgrid(range(steps,m,steps),range(steps,n,steps))
    xx,yy = x.flatten(),y.flatten()
    frame = array([xx,yy,scale*ones(xx.shape[0]),zeros(xx.shape[0])])
    savetxt('tmp.frame',frame.T,fmt='%03.3f')

    if force_orientation:
        cmmd = str("sift "+imagename+" --output="+resultname+
                " --read-frames=tmp.frame --orientations")
    else:
        cmmd = str("sift "+imagename+" --output="+resultname+
                " --read-frames=tmp.frame")
    os.system(cmmd)
    print 'processed', imagename, 'to', resultname
```

Figure 8-2. An example of applying dense SIFT descriptors over an image.

Compare this to the function process_image() in Section 2.2. We use the function savetxt() to store the *frame* array in a text file for command line processing. The last parameter of this function can be used to resize the image before extracting the descriptors. For example, passing *imsize*=(100, 100) will resize to square images 100 × 100 pixels. Last, if *force_orientation* is true the descriptors will be normalized based on the local dominant gradient direction. If it is false, all descriptors are simply oriented upward.

Use it like this to compute the dense SIFT descriptors and visualize the locations:

```
import dsift,sift

dsift.process_image_dsift('empire.jpg','empire.sift',90,40,True)
l,d = sift.read_features_from_file('empire.sift')

im = array(Image.open('empire.jpg'))
sift.plot_features(im,l,True)
show()
```

This will compute SIFT features densely across the image with the local gradient orientation used to orient the descriptors (by setting *force_orientation* to true). The locations are shown in Figure 8-2.

Classifying Images—Hand Gesture Recognition

In this application, we will look at applying the dense SIFT descriptor to images of hand gestures to build a simple hand gesture recognition system. We will use some images from the Static Hand Posture Database (available at *http://www.idiap.ch/resource/ gestures/*) to illustrate. Download the smaller test set ("test set 16.3Mb" on the web page)

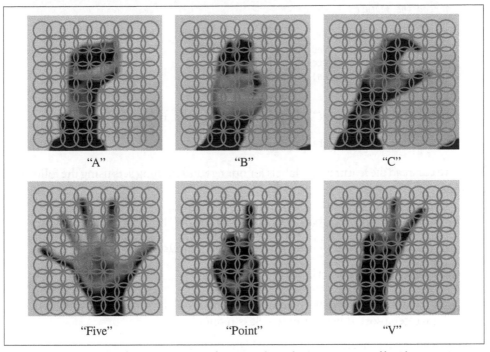

Figure 8-3. Dense SIFT descriptors on sample images from the six categories of hand gesture images. (images from the Static Hand Posture Database)

and take all the images in the "uniform" folders and split each class evenly into two folders called "train" and "test".

Process the images with the dense SIFT function above to get feature vectors for all images. Again, assuming the filenames are in a list *imlist*, this is done like this:

```
import dsift

# process images at fixed size (50,50)
for filename in imlist:
    featfile = filename[:-3]+'dsift'
    dsift.process_image_dsift(filename,featfile,10,5,resize=(50,50))
```

This creates feature files for each image with the extension ".dsift". *Note the resizing of the images to some common fixed size.* This is very important; otherwise your images will have varying number of descriptors, and therefore varying length of the feature vectors. This will cause errors when comparing them later. Plotting the images with the descriptors looks like Figure 8-3.

Define a helper function for reading the dense SIFT descriptor files like this:

```
import os, sift

def read_gesture_features_labels(path):
    # create list of all files ending in .dsift
    featlist = [os.path.join(path,f) for f in os.listdir(path) if f.endswith('.dsift')]
```

```
# read the features
features = []
for featfile in featlist:
    l,d = sift.read_features_from_file(featfile)
    features.append(d.flatten())
features = array(features)

# create labels
labels = [featfile.split('/')[-1][0] for featfile in featlist]

return features,array(labels)
```

Then we can read the features and labels for our test and training sets using the following commands:

```
features,labels = read_gesture_features_labels('train/')

test_features,test_labels = read_gesture_features_labels('test/')

classnames = unique(labels)
```

Here we used the first letter in the filename to create class labels. Using the NumPy function unique(), we get a sorted list of unique class names.

Now we can try our nearest neighbor code on this data:

```
# test kNN
k = 1
knn_classifier = knn.KnnClassifier(labels,features)
res = array([knn_classifier.classify(test_features[i],k) for i in
        range(len(test_labels))])

# accuracy
acc = sum(1.0*(res==test_labels)) / len(test_labels)
print 'Accuracy:', acc
```

First, the classifier object is created with the training data and labels as input. Then we iterate over the test set and classify each image using the classify() method. The accuracy is computed by multiplying the boolean array by one and summing. In this case, the true values are 1, so it is a simple thing to count the correct classifications. This gives a printout like:

```
Accuracy: 0.811518324607
```

which means that 81% were correctly classified in this case. The value will vary with the choice of k and the parameters for the dense SIFT image descriptor.

The accuracy above shows how many correct classifications there are for a given test set, but it does not tell us which signs are hard to classify or which mistakes are typically made. A *confusion matrix* is a matrix that shows how many samples of each class are classified as each of the classes. It shows how the errors are distributed and what classes are often "confused" for each other.

The following function will print the labels and the corresponding confusion matrix:

```
def print_confusion(res,labels,classnames):

  n = len(classnames)

  # confusion matrix
  class_ind = dict([(classnames[i],i) for i in range(n)])

  confuse = zeros((n,n))
  for i in range(len(test_labels)):
    confuse[class_ind[res[i]],class_ind[test_labels[i]]] += 1

  print 'Confusion matrix for'
  print classnames
  print confuse
```

The printout of running

```
print_confusion(res,test_labels,classnames)
```

looks like this:

```
Confusion matrix for
['A' 'B' 'C' 'F' 'P' 'V']
[[ 26.   0.   2.   0.   1.   1.]
 [  0.  26.   0.   1.   1.   1.]
 [  0.   0.  25.   0.   0.   1.]
 [  0.   3.   0.  37.   0.   0.]
 [  0.   1.   2.   0.  17.   1.]
 [  3.   1.   3.   0.  14.  24.]]
```

This shows that, for example, in this case "P" ("Point") is often misclassified as "V."

8.2 Bayes Classifier

Another simple but powerful classifier is the *Bayes classifier*[3] (or *naive Bayes classifier*). A Bayes classifier is a probabilistic classifier based on applying Bayes' theorem for conditional probabilities. The assumption is that all features are independent and unrelated to each other (this is the "naive" part). Bayes classifiers can be trained very efficiently, since the model chosen is applied to each feature independently. Despite their simplistic assumptions, Bayes classifiers have been very successful in practical applications, in particular for email spam filtering. Another benefit of this classifier is that once the model is learned, no training data needs to be stored. Only the model parameters are needed.

The classifier is constructed by multiplying the individual conditional probabilities from each feature to get the total probability of a class. Then the class with highest probability is selected.

[3] After Thomas Bayes, an 18th-century English mathematician and minister.

Let's look at a basic implementation of a Bayes classifier using Gaussian probability distribution models. This means that each feature is individually modeled using the feature mean and variance, computed from a set of training data. Add the following classifier class to a file called *bayes.py*:

```
class BayesClassifier(object):

    def __init__(self):
        """ Initialize classifier with training data. """

        self.labels = []   # class labels
        self.mean = []     # class mean
        self.var = []      # class variances
        self.n = 0         # nbr of classes

    def train(self,data,labels=None):
        """ Train on data (list of arrays n*dim).
            Labels are optional, default is 0...n-1. """

        if labels==None:
            labels = range(len(data))
        self.labels = labels
        self.n = len(labels)

        for c in data:
            self.mean.append(mean(c,axis=0))
            self.var.append(var(c,axis=0))

    def classify(self,points):
        """ Classify the points by computing probabilities
            for each class and return most probable label. """

        # compute probabilities for each class
        est_prob = array([gauss(m,v,points) for m,v in zip(self.mean,self.var)])

        # get index of highest probability, this gives class label
        ndx = est_prob.argmax(axis=0)
        est_labels = array([self.labels[n] for n in ndx])

        return est_labels, est_prob
```

The model has two variables per class, the class mean and covariance. The `train()` method takes a lists of feature arrays (one per class) and computes the mean and covariance for each. The method `classify()` computes the class probabilities for an array of data points and selects the class with highest probability. The estimated class labels and probabilities are returned. The helper function for the actual Gaussian function is also needed:

```
def gauss(m,v,x):
    """ Evaluate Gaussian in d-dimensions with independent
        mean m and variance v at the points in (the rows of) x. """

    if len(x.shape)==1:
        n,d = 1,x.shape[0]
    else:
        n,d = x.shape
```

```
# covariance matrix, subtract mean
S = diag(1/v)
x = x-m
# product of probabilities
y = exp(-0.5*diag(dot(x,dot(S,x.T))))

# normalize and return
return y * (2*pi)**(-d/2.0) / ( sqrt(prod(v)) + 1e-6)
```

This function computes the product of the individual Gaussian distributions and returns the probability for a given pair of model parameters m, v. For more details on this function, see for example *http://en.wikipedia.org/wiki/Multivariate_normal_distribution*.

Try this Bayes classifier on the 2D data from the previous section. This script will load the exact same point sets and train a classifier:

```
import pickle
import bayes
import imtools

# load 2D example points using Pickle
with open('points_normal.pkl', 'r') as f:
  class_1 = pickle.load(f)
  class_2 = pickle.load(f)
  labels = pickle.load(f)

# train Bayes classifier
bc = bayes.BayesClassifier()
bc.train([class_1,class_2],[1,-1])
```

Now, we can load the other one and test the classifier:

```
# load test data using Pickle
with open('points_normal_test.pkl', 'r') as f:
  class_1 = pickle.load(f)
  class_2 = pickle.load(f)
  labels = pickle.load(f)

# test on some points
print bc.classify(class_1[:10])[0]

# plot points and decision boundary
def classify(x,y,bc=bc):
  points = vstack((x,y))
  return bc.classify(points.T)[0]

imtools.plot_2D_boundary([-6,6,-6,6],[class_1,class_2],classify,[1,-1])
show()
```

This prints the classification result for the first 10 points to the console. It might look like this:

```
[1 1 1 1 1 1 1 1 1 1]
```

Again, we used a helper function `classify()` to pass to the plotting function for visualizing the classification results by evaluating the function on a grid. The plots for the

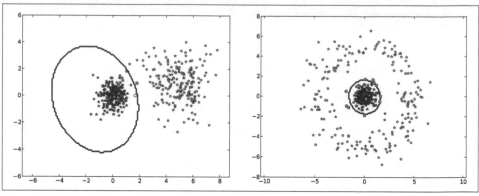

Figure 8-4. Classifying 2D data using a Bayes classifier. For each example, the color shows the class label. Correctly classified points are shown with stars and misclassified points with circles. The curve is the classifier decision boundary.

two sets look like Figure 8-4. The decision boundary, in this case, will be the ellipse-like level curves of a 2D Gaussian function.

Using PCA to Reduce Dimensions

Now, let's try the gesture recognition problem. Since the feature vectors are very large for the dense SIFT descriptor (more than 10,000 for the parameter choices in the example above), it is a good idea to do dimensionality reduction before fitting models to the data. Principal Component Analysis, PCA, (see Section 1.3) usually does a good job. Try the following script that uses PCA from the file *pca.py* (page 13):

```
import pca

V,S,m = pca.pca(features)

# keep most important dimensions
V = V[:50]
features = array([dot(V,f-m) for f in features])
test_features = array([dot(V,f-m) for f in test_features])
```

Here *features* and *test_features* are the same arrays that we loaded for the kNN example. In this case, we apply PCA on the training data and keep the 50 dimensions with most variance. This is done by subtracting the mean *m* (computed on the training data) and multiplying with the basis vectors *V*. The same transformation is applied to the test data.

Train and test the Bayes classifier like this:

```
# test Bayes
bc = bayes.BayesClassifier()
blist = [features[where(labels==c)[0]] for c in classnames]

bc.train(blist,classnames)
res = bc.classify(test_features)[0]
```

Since `BayesClassifier` takes a list of arrays (one array for each class), we transform the data before passing it to the `train()` method. Since we don't need the probabilities for now, we chose to return only the labels of the classification.

Checking the accuracy

```
acc = sum(1.0*(res==test_labels)) / len(test_labels)
print 'Accuracy:', acc
```

gives something like this:

```
Accuracy: 0.717277486911
```

Checking the confusion matrix

```
print_confusion(res,test_labels,classnames)
```

gives a print out like this:

```
Confusion matrix for
['A' 'B' 'C' 'F' 'P' 'V']
[[ 20.   0.   0.   4.   0.   0.]
 [  0.  26.   1.   7.   2.   2.]
 [  1.   0.  27.   5.   1.   0.]
 [  0.   2.   0.  17.   0.   0.]
 [  0.   1.   0.   4.  22.   1.]
 [  8.   2.   4.   1.   8.  25.]]
```

This is not as good as the kNN classifier, but with the Bayes classifier we don't need to keep any training data, just the model parameters for each of the classes. The result will vary greatly with the choice of dimensions after PCA.

8.3 Support Vector Machines

Support Vector Machines (SVM) are a powerful type of classifiers that often give state-of-the-art results for many classification problems. In its simplest form, an SVM finds a linear separating hyperplane (a plane in higher-dimensional spaces) with the best possible separation between two classes. The decision function for a feature vector $\mathbf{x}$ is

$$f(\mathbf{x}) = \mathbf{w} \cdot \mathbf{x} - b,$$

where $\mathbf{w}$ is the hyperplane normal and b an offset constant. The zero level of this function then ideally separates the two classes so that one class has positive values and the other negative. The parameters $\mathbf{w}$ and b are found by solving an optimization problem on a training set of labeled feature vectors $\mathbf{x}_i$ with labels $y_i \in \{-1, 1\}$ so that the hyperplane has maximal separation between the two classes. The normal is a linear combination of some of the training feature vectors

$$\mathbf{w} = \sum_i \alpha_i y_i \mathbf{x}_i,$$

so that the decision function can be written

$$f(\mathbf{x}) = \sum_i \alpha_i y_i \mathbf{x}_i \cdot \mathbf{x} - b.$$

Here i runs over a selection of the training vectors; the selected vectors $\mathbf{x}_i$ are called *support vectors* since they help define the classification boundary.

One of the strengths of SVM is that by using *kernel functions*, that is, functions that map the feature vectors to a different (higher) dimensional space, non-linear or very difficult classification problems can be effectively solved while still keeping some control over the decision function. Kernel functions replace the inner product of the classification function, $\mathbf{x}_i \cdot \mathbf{x}$, with a function $K(\mathbf{x}_i, \mathbf{x})$.

Some of the most common kernel functions are:

- *linear*, a hyperplane in feature space, the simplest case, $K(\mathbf{x}_i, \mathbf{x}) = \mathbf{x}_i \cdot \mathbf{x}$
- *polynomial*, features are mapped with polynomials of a defined degree d, $K(\mathbf{x}_i, \mathbf{x}) = (\gamma \mathbf{x}_i \cdot \mathbf{x} + r)^d, \gamma > 0$
- *radial basis functions*, exponential functions, usually a very effective choice, $K(\mathbf{x}_i, \mathbf{x}) = e^{(-\gamma \|\mathbf{x}_i - \mathbf{x}\|^2)}, \gamma > 0$
- *sigmoid*, a smoother alternative to hyperplane, $K(\mathbf{x}_i, \mathbf{x}) = \tanh(\gamma \mathbf{x}_i \cdot \mathbf{x} + r)$

The parameters of each kernel are also determined during training.

For multi-class problems, the usual procedure is to train multiple SVMs so that each separates one class from the rest (also known as "one-versus-all" classifiers). For more details on SVMs, see for example the book [9] and the online references at *http://www.support-vector.net/references.html*.

Using LibSVM

We will use one of the best and most commonly used implementations available, LibSVM [7]. LibSVM comes with a nice Python interface (there are also interfaces for many other programming languages). For installation instructions, see Section A.4.

Let's use LibSVM on the sample 2D point data to see how it works. This script will load the same points and train an SVM classifier using radial basis functions:

```
import pickle
from svmutil import *
import imtools

# load 2D example points using Pickle
with open('points_normal.pkl', 'r') as f:
  class_1 = pickle.load(f)
  class_2 = pickle.load(f)
  labels = pickle.load(f)

# convert to lists for libsvm
class_1 = map(list,class_1)
class_2 = map(list,class_2)
labels = list(labels)
samples = class_1+class_2 # concatenate the two lists

# create SVM
prob = svm_problem(labels,samples)
param = svm_parameter('-t 2')
```

```
# train SVM on data
m = svm_train(prob,param)

# how did the training do?
res = svm_predict(labels,samples,m)
```

Loading the data set is the same as before, but this time we have to convert the arrays to lists since LibSVM does not support array objects as input. Here we used Python's built-in map() function that applies the conversion function list() to each element. The next lines create a SVM problem object and sets some parameters. The svm_train() call solves the optimization problem for determining the model parameters. The model can then be used for predictions. The last call to svm_predict() will classify the training data with the model *m* and shows how successful the training was. The printout looks something like this:

```
Accuracy = 100% (400/400) (classification)
```

This means that the classifier completely separates the training data and correctly classifies all 400 data points.

Note that we added a string of parameter choices in the call to train the classifier. These parameters are used to control the kernel type, degree, and other choices for the classifier. Most of them are outside the scope of this book but the important ones to know are "t" and "k". The parameter "t" determines the type of kernel used. The options are:

"-t"	kernel
0	linear
1	polynomial
2	radial basis function (default)
3	sigmoid

The parameter "k" determines the degree of the polynomial (default is 3).

Now, load the other point set and test the classifier:

```
# load test data using Pickle
with open('points_normal_test.pkl', 'r') as f:
    class_1 = pickle.load(f)
    class_2 = pickle.load(f)
    labels = pickle.load(f)

# convert to lists for libsvm
class_1 = map(list,class_1)
class_2 = map(list,class_2)

# define function for plotting
def predict(x,y,model=m):
    return array(svm_predict([0]*len(x),zip(x,y),model)[0])

# plot the classification boundary
imtools.plot_2D_boundary([-6,6,-6,6],[array(class_1),array(class_2)],predict,[-1,1])
show()
```

Again we have to convert the data to lists for LibSVM. As before, we also define a helper function predict() for plotting the classification boundary. Note the use of a list of zeros

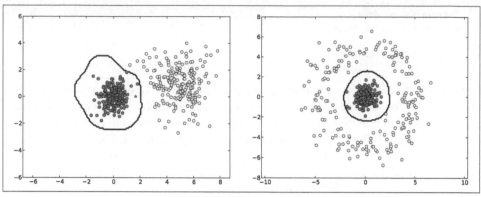

Figure 8-5. Classifying 2D data using a Support Vector Machine classifier. For each example, the color shows the class label. Correctly classified points are shown with stars and misclassified points with circles. The curve is the classifier decision boundary.

[0]*len(x) as a replacement for the label list if true labels are unavailable. You can use any list as long as it has the correct length. The 2D plots for the two different point data sets are shown in Figure 8-5.

Hand Gesture Recognition Again

Using LibSVM on our multi-class hand gesture recognition problem is fairly straight-forward. Multiple classes are automatically handled, so we only need to format the data so that the input and output matches the requirements of LibSVM.

With training and testing data in arrays named *features* and *test_features* as in the previous examples, the following will load the data and train a linear SVM classifier:

```
features = map(list,features)
test_features = map(list,test_features)

# create conversion function for the labels
transl = {}
for i,c in enumerate(classnames):
  transl[c],transl[i] = i,c

# create SVM
prob = svm_problem(convert_labels(labels,transl),features)
param = svm_parameter('-t 0')

# train SVM on data
m = svm_train(prob,param)

# how did the training do?
res = svm_predict(convert_labels(labels,transl),features,m)

# test the SVM
res = svm_predict(convert_labels(test_labels,transl),test_features,m)[0]
res = convert_labels(res,transl)
```

Same as before, we convert the data to lists using a map() call. Then the labels need to be converted since LibSVM does not handle string labels. The dictionary *transl* will contain a conversion between string and integer labels. Try to print it to your console to see what happens. The parameter "-t 0" makes it a linear classifier and the decision boundary will be a hyperplane in the original feature space of some 10,000 dimensions.

Now compare the labels, just like before:

```
acc = sum(1.0*(res==test_labels)) / len(test_labels)
print 'Accuracy:', acc

print_confusion(res,test_labels,classnames)
```

The output using this linear kernel should look like this:

```
Accuracy: 0.916230366492
Confusion matrix for
['A' 'B' 'C' 'F' 'P' 'V']
[[ 26.   0.   1.   0.   2.   0.]
 [  0.  28.   0.   0.   1.   0.]
 [  0.   0.  29.   0.   0.   0.]
 [  0.   2.   0.  38.   0.   0.]
 [  0.   1.   0.   0.  27.   1.]
 [  3.   0.   2.   0.   3.  27.]]
```

Now if we apply PCA to reduce the dimensions to 50, as we did in Section 8.2, this changes the accuracy to:

```
Accuracy: 0.890052356021
```

Not bad, seeing that the feature vectors are about 200 times smaller than the original data (and the space to store the support vectors then also 200 times less).

8.4 Optical Character Recognition

As an example of a multi-class problem, let's look at interpreting images of Sudokus. *Optical character recognition* (OCR) is the process of interpreting images of hand- or machine-written text. A common example is text extraction from scanned documents such as zip-codes on letters or book pages such as the library volumes in Google Books (*http://books.google.com/*). Here we will look at a simple OCR problem of recognizing numbers in images of printed Sudokus. Sudokus are a form of logic puzzles where the goal is to fill a 9×9 grid with the numbers $1 \ldots 9$ so that each column, each row, and each 3×3 sub-grid contains all nine digits.[4] In this example, we are just interested in reading the puzzle and interpreting it correctly. Actually solving the puzzle, we leave to you.

Training a Classifier

For this classification problem we have ten classes, the numbers $1 \ldots 9$, and the empty cells. Let's give the empty cells the label 0 so that our class labels are $0 \ldots 9$. To train

---

[4] See *http://en.wikipedia.org/wiki/Sudoku* for more details if you are unfamiliar with the concept.

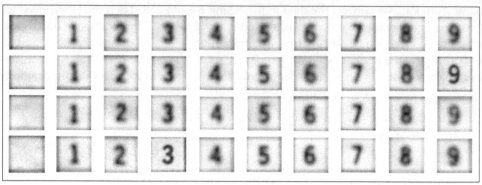

Figure 8-6. Sample training images for the 10 classes of the Sudoku OCR classifier.

this ten-class classifier, we will use a dataset of images of cropped Sudoku cells.[5] In the file *sudoku_images.zip* are two folders, "ocr_data" and "sudokus". The latter contains images of Sudokus under varying conditions. We will save those for later. For now, take a look at the folder "ocr_data". It contains two subfolders with images, one for training and one for testing. The images are named with the first character equal to the class (0 . . . 9). Figure 8-6 shows some samples from the training set. The images are grayscale and roughly 80 × 80 pixels (with some variation).

Selecting Features

We need to decide on what feature vector to use for representing each cell image. There are many good choices; here we'll try something simple but still effective. The following function takes an image and returns a feature vector of the flattened grayscale values:

```
def compute_feature(im):
    """ Returns a feature vector for an
        ocr image patch. """

    # resize and remove border
    norm_im = imresize(im,(30,30))
    norm_im = norm_im[3:-3,3:-3]

    return norm_im.flatten()
```

This function uses the resizing function `imresize()` from *imtools* to reduce the length of the feature vector. We also crop away about 10% border pixels since the crops often get parts of the grid lines on the edges, as you can see in Figure 8-6.

Now we can read the training data using a function like this:

```
def load_ocr_data(path):
    """ Return labels and ocr features for all images
        in path. """
```

---

[5] Images courtesy of Martin Byröd [4], *http://www.maths.lth.se/matematiklth/personal/byrod/*, collected and cropped from photos of actual Sudokus.

```
# create list of all files ending in .jpg
imlist = [os.path.join(path,f) for f in os.listdir(path) if f.endswith('.jpg')]
# create labels
labels = [int(imfile.split('/')[-1][0]) for imfile in imlist]

# create features from the images
features = []
for imname in imlist:
  im = array(Image.open(imname).convert('L'))
  features.append(compute_feature(im))
return array(features),labels
```

The labels are extracted as the first character of the filename of each of the JPEG files and stored in the *labels* list as integers. The feature vectors are computed using the function above and stored in an array.

Multi-Class SVM

With the training data in place, we are ready to learn a classifier. Here we'll use a multi-class support vector machine. The code looks just as it does in the previous section:

```
from svmutil import *

# TRAINING DATA
features,labels = load_ocr_data('training/')

# TESTING DATA
test_features,test_labels = load_ocr_data('testing/')

# train a linear SVM classifier
features = map(list,features)
test_features = map(list,test_features)

prob = svm_problem(labels,features)
param = svm_parameter('-t 0')

m = svm_train(prob,param)

# how did the training do?
res = svm_predict(labels,features,m)

# how does it perform on the test set?
res = svm_predict(test_labels,test_features,m)
```

This trains a linear SVM classifier and tests the performance on the unseen images in the test set. You should get the following printout from the last two svm_predict() calls:

```
Accuracy = 100% (1409/1409) (classification)
Accuracy = 99.2979% (990/997) (classification)
```

Great news. The 1,409 images of the training set are perfectly separated in the ten classes and the recognition performance on the test set is around 99%. We can now use this classifier on crops from new Sudoku images.

Extracting Cells and Recognizing Characters

With a classifier that recognizes cell contents, the next step is to automatically find the cells. Once we solve that, we can crop them and pass the crops to the classifier. Let's for now assume that the image of the Sudoku is aligned so that the horizontal and vertical lines of the grid are parallel to the image sides (like the left image of Figure 8-8). Under these conditions, we can threshold the image and sum up the pixel values horizontally and vertically. Since the edges will have values of one and the other parts values of zeros, this should give strong response at the edges and tell us where to crop.

The following function takes a grayscale image and a direction and returns the ten edges for that direction:

```
from scipy.ndimage import measurements

def find_sudoku_edges(im,axis=0):
    """ Finds the cell edges for an aligned sudoku image. """

    # threshold and sum rows and columns
    trim = 1*(im<128)
    s = trim.sum(axis=axis)

    # find center of strongest lines
    s_labels,s_nbr = measurements.label(s>(0.5*max(s)))
    m = measurements.center_of_mass(s,s_labels,range(1,s_nbr+1))
    x = [int(x[0]) for x in m]

    # if only the strong lines are detected add lines in between
    if len(x)==4:
        dx = diff(x)
        x = [x[0],x[0]+dx[0]/3,x[0]+2*dx[0]/3,
            x[1],x[1]+dx[1]/3,x[1]+2*dx[1]/3,
            x[2],x[2]+dx[2]/3,x[2]+2*dx[2]/3,x[3]]

    if len(x)==10:
        return x
    else:
        raise RuntimeError('Edges not detected.')
```

First, the image is thresholded at the midpoint to give ones on the dark areas. Then these are added up in the specified direction (axis=0 or 1). The scipy.ndimage package contains a module, measurements, that is very useful for counting and measuring regions in binary or label arrays. First, labels() finds the connected components of a binary array computed by thresholding the sum at the midpoint. Then the center_of_mass() function computes the center point of each independent component. Depending on the graphic design of the Sudoku (all lines equally strong or the sub-grid lines stronger than the other), you might get four or ten points. In the case of four, the intermediary lines are interpolated at even intervals. If the end result does not have ten lines, an exception is raised.

In the "sudokus" folder is a collection of Sudoku images of varying difficulty. There is also a file for each image containing the true values of the Sudoku so that we can check our results. Some of the images are aligned with the image sides. Picking one of them, you can check the performance of the cropping and classification like this:

```
imname = 'sudokus/sudoku18.jpg'
vername = 'sudokus/sudoku18.sud'
im = array(Image.open(imname).convert('L'))

# find the cell edges
x = find_sudoku_edges(im,axis=0)
y = find_sudoku_edges(im,axis=1)

# crop cells and classify
crops = []
for col in range(9):
  for row in range(9):
    crop = im[y[col]:y[col+1],x[row]:x[row+1]]
    crops.append(compute_feature(crop))

res = svm_predict(loadtxt(vername),map(list,crops),m)[0]
res_im = array(res).reshape(9,9)

print 'Result:'
print res_im
```

The edges are found and then crops are extracted for each cell. The crops are passed to the same feature extraction function used for the training and stored in an array. These feature vectors are classified using svm_predict() with the true labels read using loadtxt(). The result in your console should be:

```
Accuracy = 100% (81/81) (classification)
Result:
[[ 0.  0.  0.  0.  1.  7.  0.  5.  0.]
 [ 9.  0.  3.  0.  0.  5.  2.  0.  7.]
 [ 0.  0.  0.  0.  0.  0.  4.  0.  0.]
 [ 0.  1.  6.  0.  0.  4.  0.  0.  2.]
 [ 0.  0.  0.  8.  0.  1.  0.  0.  0.]
 [ 8.  0.  0.  5.  0.  0.  6.  4.  0.]
 [ 0.  0.  9.  0.  0.  0.  0.  0.  0.]
 [ 7.  0.  2.  1.  0.  0.  8.  0.  9.]
 [ 0.  5.  0.  2.  3.  0.  0.  0.  0.]]
```

Now, this was one of the easier images. Try some of the others and see what the errors look like and where the classifier makes mistakes.

If you plot the crops using a 9 × 9 subplot, they should look like the right image of Figure 8-7.

Rectifying Images

If you are happy with the performance of your classifier, the next challenge is to apply it to non-aligned images. We will end our Sudoku example with a simple way of rectifying an image given that the four outer corner points of the grid have been detected or marked manually. The left image in Figure 8-8 shows an example of a Sudoku image with strong perspective effects.

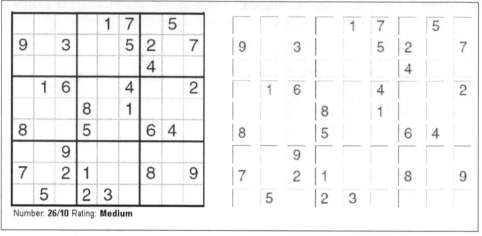

Figure 8-7. An example of detecting and cropping the fields of a Sudoku grid: image of a Sudoku grid (left); the 9 × 9 cropped images of the individual cells to be sent to the OCR classifier (right).

A homography can map the grid to align the edges as in the examples above, all we need to do is estimate the transform. The example below shows the case of manually marking the four corner points and then warping the image to a square target image of 1000 × 1000 pixels:

```
from scipy import ndimage
import homography

imname = 'sudoku8.jpg'
im = array(Image.open(imname).convert('L'))

# mark corners
figure()
imshow(im)
gray()
x = ginput(4)

# top left, top right, bottom right, bottom left
fp = array([array([p[1],p[0],1]) for p in x]).T
tp = array([[0,0,1],[0,1000,1],[1000,1000,1],[1000,0,1]]).T

# estimate the homography
H = homography.H_from_points(tp,fp)

# helper function for geometric_transform
def warpfcn(x):
    x = array([x[0],x[1],1])
    xt = dot(H,x)
    xt = xt/xt[2]
    return xt[0],xt[1]

# warp image with full perspective transform
im_g = ndimage.geometric_transform(im,warpfcn,(1000,1000))
```

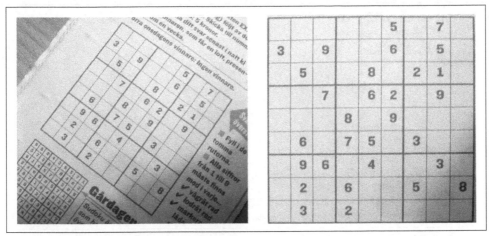

Figure 8-8. An example of rectifying an image using a full perspective transform: the original image with the four corners of the Sudoku marked (left); rectified image warped to a square image of 1000×1000 *pixels (right).*

In most of these sample images an affine transform, as we used in Chapter 3, is not enough. Here we instead used the more general transform function `geometric_transform()` from `scipy.ndimage`. This function takes a 2D to 2D mapping instead of a transform matrix, so we need to use a helper function (using a piecewise affine warp on triangles will introduce artifacts in this case). The warped image is shown to the right in Figure 8-8.

This concludes our Sudoku OCR example. There are many improvements to be made and alternatives to investigate. Some are mentioned in the following exercises; the rest we leave to you.

Exercises

1. The performance of the kNN classifier depends on the value of k. Try to vary this number and see how the accuracy changes. Plot the decision boundaries of the 2D point sets to see how they change.

2. The hand gesture data set in Figure 8-3 also contains images with more complex background (in the "complex/" folders). Try to train and test a classifier on these images. What is the difference in performance? Can you suggest improvements to the image descriptor?

3. Try to vary the number of dimensions after PCA projection of the gesture recognition features for the Bayes classifier. What is a good choice? Plot the singular values S, they should give a typical "knee" shaped curve like the one shown in Figure 8-9. A good compromise between ability to generate the variability of the training data and keeping the number of dimensions low is usually found at a number before the curve flattens out.

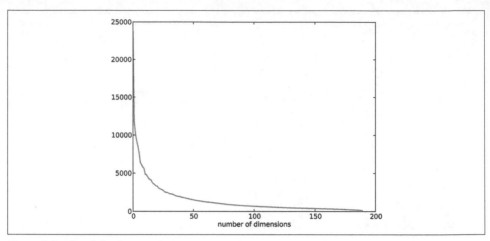

Figure 8-9. Graph for Exercise 3.

4. Modify the Bayes classifier to use a different probability model than Gaussian distributions. For example, try using the frequency counts of each feature in the training set. Compare the results to using a Gaussian distribution for some different datasets.

5. Experiment with using non-linear SVMs for the gesture recognition problem. Try polynomial kernels and increase the degree (using the "-d" parameter) incrementally. What happens to the classification performance on the training set and the test set? With a non-linear classifier, there is a risk of training and optimizing it for a specific set so that performance is close to perfect on the training set, but the classifier has poor performance on other test sets. This phenomenon of breaking the generalization capabilities of a classifier is called *overfitting* and should be avoided.

6. Try some more advanced feature vectors for the Sudoku character recognition problem. If you need inspiration, look at [4].

7. Implement a method for automatically aligning the Sudoku grid. Try, for example, feature detection with RANSAC, line detection, or detecting the cells using morphological and measurement operations from `scipy.ndimage` (*http://docs.scipy .org/doc/scipy/reference/ndimage.html*). Bonus task: Solve the rotation ambiguity of finding the "up" direction. For example, you could try rotating the rectified grid and let the OCR classifier's accuracy vote for the best orientation.

8. For a more challenging classification problem than the Sudoku digits, take a look at the MNIST database of *handwritten digits http://yann.lecun.com/exdb/mnist/*. Try to extract some features and apply SVM to that set. Check where your performance ends up on the ranking of best methods (some are insanely good).

9. If you want to dive deeper into classifiers and machine learning algorithms, take a look at the `scikit.learn` package (*http://scikit-learn.org/*) and try some of the algorithms on the data in this chapter.

## CHAPTER 9

Image Segmentation

Image segmentation is the process of partitioning an image into meaningful regions. Regions can be foreground versus background or individual objects in the image. The regions are constructed using some feature such as color, edges, or neighbor similarity. In this chapter we will look at some different techniques for segmentation.

9.1 Graph Cuts

A *graph* is a set of nodes (sometimes called vertices) with edges between them. See Figure 9-1 for an example.[1] The edges can be directed (as illustrated with arrows in Figure 9-1) or undirected, and may have weights associated with them.

A *graph cut* is the partitioning of a directed graph into two disjoint sets. Graph cuts can be used for solving many different computer vision problems like stereo depth reconstruction, image stitching, and image segmentation. By creating a graph from image pixels and their neighbors and introducing an energy or a "cost," it is possible to use a graph cut process to segment an image in two or more regions. The basic idea is that similar pixels that are also close to each other should belong to the same partition.

The cost of a graph cut C (where C is a set of edges) is defined as the sum of the edge weights of the cuts

$$E_{cut} = \sum_{(i,j) \in C} w_{ij}, \qquad (9.1)$$

where w_{ij} is the weight of the edge (i, j) from node i to node j in the graph and the sum is taken over all edges in the cut C.

The idea behind graph cut segmentation is to partition a graph representation of the image such that the cut cost E_{cut} is minimized. In this graph representation, two additional nodes, a source and a sink node, are added to the graph and only cuts that separate the source and sink are considered.

---

[1] You also saw graphs in action in Section 2.3. This time we are going to use them to partition images.

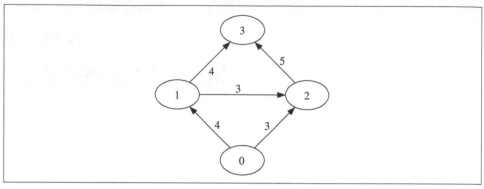

Figure 9-1. A simple directed graph created using `python-graph`.

Finding the *minimum cut* (or *min cut*) is equivalent to finding the *maximum flow* (or *max flow*) between the source and the sink (see [2] for details). There are efficient algorithms for solving these max flow/min cut problems.

For our graph cut examples we will use the `python-graph` package. This package contains many useful graph algorithms. The website with downloads and documentation is *http://code.google.com/p/python-graph/*. We will need the function `maximum_flow()`, which computes the max flow/min cut using the Edmonds-Karp algorithm (*http://en .wikipedia.org/wiki/Edmonds-Karp_algorithm*). The good thing about using a package written fully in Python is ease of installation and compatibility; the downside is speed. Performance is adequate for our purposes, but for anything but small images, a faster implementation is needed.

Here's a simple example of using `python-graph` to compute the max flow/min cut of a small graph.[2]

```
from pygraph.classes.digraph import digraph
from pygraph.algorithms.minmax import maximum_flow

gr = digraph()
gr.add_nodes([0,1,2,3])

gr.add_edge((0,1), wt=4)
gr.add_edge((1,2), wt=3)
gr.add_edge((2,3), wt=5)
gr.add_edge((0,2), wt=3)
gr.add_edge((1,3), wt=4)

flows,cuts = maximum_flow(gr,0,3)
print 'flow is:', flows
print 'cut is:', cuts
```

First, a directed graph is created with four nodes with index 0 . . . 3. Then the edges are added using `add_edge()` with an edge weight specified. This will be used as the

---

[2] Same graph as the example at *http://en.wikipedia.org/wiki/Max-flow_min-cut_theorem*.

maximum flow capacity of the edge. The maximum flow is computed with node 0 as source and node 3 as sink. The flow and the cuts are printed and should look like this:

```
flow is: {(0, 1): 4, (1, 2): 0, (1, 3): 4, (2, 3): 3, (0, 2): 3}
cut is: {0: 0, 1: 1, 2: 1, 3: 1}
```

These two python dictionaries contain the flow through each edge and the label for each node: 0 for the part of the graph containing the source, 1 for the nodes connected to the sink. You can verify manually that the cut is indeed the minimum. The graph is shown in Figure 9-1.

Graphs from Images

Given a neighborhood structure, we can define a graph using the image pixels as nodes. Here we will focus on the simplest case of 4-neighborhood of pixels and two image regions (which we can call foreground and background). A *4-neighborhood* is where a pixel is connected to the pixels directly above, below, left, and right.[3]

In addition to the pixel nodes, we will also need two special nodes: a "source" node and a "sink" node, representing the foreground and background, respectively. We will use a simple model where all pixels are connected to the source and the sink.

Here's how to build the graph:

- Every pixel node has an incoming edge from the source node.
- Every pixel node has an outgoing edge to the sink node.
- Every pixel node has one incoming and one outgoing edge to each of its neighbors.

To determine the weights on these edges, you need a segmentation model that determines the edge weights (representing the maximum flow allowed for that edge) between pixels and between pixels and the source and sink. As before, we call the edge weight between pixel i and pixel j, w_{ij}. Let's call the weight from the source to pixel i, w_{si}, and from pixel i to the sink, w_{it}.

Let's look at using a naive Bayesian classifier from Section 8.2 on the color values of the pixels. Given that we have trained a Bayes classifier on foreground and background pixels (from the same image or from other images), we can compute the probabilities $p_F(I_i)$ and $p_B(I_i)$ for the foreground and background. Here I_i is the color vector of pixel i.

We can now create a model for the edge weights as follows:

$$w_{si} = \frac{p_F(I_i)}{p_F(I_i) + p_B(I_i)}$$

$$w_{it} = \frac{p_B(I_i)}{p_F(I_i) + p_B(I_i)}$$

$$w_{ij} = \kappa \; e^{-|I_i - I_j|^2/\sigma} .$$

[3] Another common option is 8-neighborhood, where the diagonal pixels are also connected.

With this model, each pixel is connected to the foreground and background (source and sink) with weights equal to a normalized probability of belonging to that class. The w_{ij} describe the pixel similarity between neighbors; similar pixels have weight close to κ, dissimilar close to 0. The parameter σ determines how fast the values decay toward zero with increasing dissimilarity.

Create a file *graphcut.py* and add the following function that creates this graph from an image:

```
from pygraph.classes.digraph import digraph
from pygraph.algorithms.minmax import maximum_flow

import bayes

def build_bayes_graph(im,labels,sigma=1e2,kappa=2):
    """ Build a graph from 4-neighborhood of pixels.
        Foreground and background is determined from
        labels (1 for foreground, -1 for background, 0 otherwise)
        and is modeled with naive Bayes classifiers."""

    m,n = im.shape[:2]

    # RGB vector version (one pixel per row)
    vim = im.reshape((-1,3))

    # RGB for foreground and background
    foreground = im[labels==1].reshape((-1,3))
    background = im[labels==-1].reshape((-1,3))
    train_data = [foreground,background]

    # train naive Bayes classifier
    bc = bayes.BayesClassifier()
    bc.train(train_data)

    # get probabilities for all pixels
    bc_lables,prob = bc.classify(vim)
    prob_fg = prob[0]
    prob_bg = prob[1]

    # create graph with m*n+2 nodes
    gr = digraph()
    gr.add_nodes(range(m*n+2))

    source = m*n # second to last is source
    sink = m*n+1 # last node is sink

    # normalize
    for i in range(vim.shape[0]):
        vim[i] = vim[i] / linalg.norm(vim[i])

    # go through all nodes and add edges
    for i in range(m*n):
        # add edge from source
        gr.add_edge((source,i), wt=(prob_fg[i]/(prob_fg[i]+prob_bg[i])))
```

```
# add edge to sink
gr.add_edge((i,sink), wt=(prob_bg[i]/(prob_fg[i]+prob_bg[i])))

# add edges to neighbors
if i%n != 0: # left exists
    edge_wt = kappa*exp(-1.0*sum((vim[i]-vim[i-1])**2)/sigma)
    gr.add_edge((i,i-1), wt=edge_wt)
if (i+1)%n != 0: # right exists
    edge_wt = kappa*exp(-1.0*sum((vim[i]-vim[i+1])**2)/sigma)
    gr.add_edge((i,i+1), wt=edge_wt)
if i//n != 0: # up exists
    edge_wt = kappa*exp(-1.0*sum((vim[i]-vim[i-n])**2)/sigma)
    gr.add_edge((i,i-n), wt=edge_wt)
if i//n != m-1: # down exists
    edge_wt = kappa*exp(-1.0*sum((vim[i]-vim[i+n])**2)/sigma)
    gr.add_edge((i,i+n), wt=edge_wt)

return gr
```

Here we used a label image with values 1 for foreground training data and -1 for background training data. Based on this labeling, a Bayes classifier is trained on the RGB values. Then classification probabilities are computed for each pixel. These are then used as edge weights for the edges going from the source and to the sink. A graph with $n * m + 2$ nodes is created. Note the index of the source and sink; we choose them as the last two to simplify the indexing of the pixels.

To visualize the labeling overlaid on the image we can use the function `contourf()`, which fills the regions between contour levels of an image (in this case the label image). The *alpha* variable sets the transparency. Add the following function to *graphcut.py*:

```
def show_labeling(im,labels):
    """ Show image with foreground and background areas.
        labels = 1 for foreground, -1 for background, 0 otherwise. """

    imshow(im)
    contour(labels,[-0.5,0.5])
    contourf(labels,[-1,-0.5],colors='b',alpha=0.25)
    contourf(labels,[0.5,1],colors='r',alpha=0.25)
    axis('off')
```

Once the graph is built, it needs to be cut at the optimal location. The following function computes the min cut and reformats the output to a binary image of pixel labels:

```
def cut_graph(gr,imsize):
    """ Solve max flow of graph gr and return binary
        labels of the resulting segmentation. """

    m,n = imsize
    source = m*n # second to last is source
    sink = m*n+1 # last is sink

    # cut the graph
    flows,cuts = maximum_flow(gr,source,sink)
```

```
# convert graph to image with labels
res = zeros(m*n)
for pos,label in cuts.items()[:-2]: #don't add source/sink
  res[pos] = label

return res.reshape((m,n))
```

Again, note the indices for the source and sink. We need to take the size of the image as input to compute these indices and to reshape the output before returning the segmentation. The cut is returned as a dictionary, which needs to be copied to an image of segmentation labels. This is done using the *.items()* method that returns a list of (key, value) pairs. Again we skip the last two elements of that list.

Let's see how to use these functions for segmenting an image. The following is a complete example of reading an image and creating a graph with class probabilities estimated from two rectangular image regions:

```
from scipy.misc import imresize
import graphcut

im = array(Image.open('empire.jpg'))
im = imresize(im,0.07,interp='bilinear')
size = im.shape[:2]

# add two rectangular training regions
labels = zeros(size)
labels[3:18,3:18] = -1
labels[-18:-3,-18:-3] = 1

# create graph
g = graphcut.build_bayes_graph(im,labels,kappa=1)

# cut the graph
res = graphcut.cut_graph(g,size)


figure()
graphcut.show_labeling(im,labels)

figure()
imshow(res)
gray()
axis('off')

show()
```

We use the `imresize()` function to make the image small enough for our Python graph library, in this case uniform scaling to 7% of the original size. The graph is cut and the result plotted together with an image showing the training regions. Figure 9-2 shows the training regions overlaid on the image and the final segmentation result.

The variable *kappa* (κ in the equations) determines the relative weight of the edges between neighboring pixels. The effect of changing *kappa* can be seen in Figure 9-3. With increasing value, the segmentation boundary will be smoother and details will be lost. Choosing the right value is up to you. The right value will depend on your application and the type of result you desire.

Figure 9-2. An example of graph cut segmentation using a Bayesian probability model. Image is downsampled to size 54 × 38. Label image for model training (left); training regions shown on the image (middle); segmentation (right).

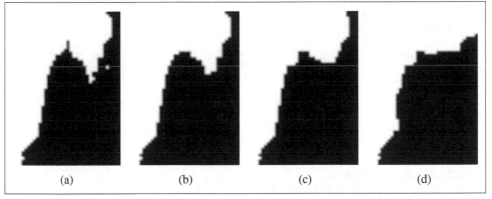

(a)   (b)   (c)   (d)

Figure 9-3. The effect of changing the relative weighting between pixel similarity and class probability. The same segmentation as in Figure 9-2 with: (a) $\kappa = 1$, (b) $\kappa = 2$, (c) $\kappa = 5$, and (d) $\kappa = 10$.

Segmentation with User Input

Graph cut segmentation can be combined with user input in a number of ways. For example, a user can supply markers for foreground and background by drawing on an image. Another way is to select a region that contains the foreground with a bounding box or using a "lasso" tool.

Let's look at this last example using some images from the Grab Cut dataset from Microsoft Research Cambridge; see [27] and Appendix B.5 for details.

These images come with ground truth labels for measuring segmentation performance. They also come with annotations simulating a user selecting a rectangular image region or drawing on the image with a "lasso" type tool to mark foreground and background.

We can use these user inputs to get training data and apply graph cuts to segment the image guided by the user input.

The user input is encoded in bitmap images with the following meaning:

Pixel value	Meaning
0, 64	background
128	unknown
255	foreground

Here's a complete code example of loading an image and annotations and passing that to our graph cut segmentation routine:

```
from scipy.misc import imresize
import graphcut

def create_msr_labels(m,lasso=False):
    """ Create label matrix for training from
        user annotations. """

    labels = zeros(im.shape[:2])

    # background
    labels[m==0] = -1
    labels[m==64] = -1

    # foreground
    if lasso:
        labels[m==255] = 1
    else:
        labels[m==128] = 1

    return labels


# load image and annotation map
im = array(Image.open('376043.jpg'))
m = array(Image.open('376043.bmp'))

# resize
scale = 0.1
im = imresize(im,scale,interp='bilinear')
m = imresize(m,scale,interp='nearest')

# create training labels
labels = create_msr_labels(m,False)

# build graph using annotations
g = graphcut.build_bayes_graph(im,labels,kappa=2)

# cut graph
res = graphcut.cut_graph(g,im.shape[:2])

# remove parts in background
res[m==0] = 1
res[m==64] = 1
```

```
# plot the result
figure()
imshow(res)
gray()
xticks([])
yticks([])
savefig('labelplot.pdf')
```

First, we define a helper function to read the annotation images and format them so
we can pass them to our function for training background and foreground models. The
bounding rectangles contain only background labels. In this case, we set the foreground
training region to the whole "unknown" region (the inside of the rectangle). Next, we
build the graph and cut it. Since we have user input, we remove results that have any
foreground in the marked background area. Last, we plot the resulting segmentation
and remove the tick markers by setting them to an empty list. That way, we get a nice
bounding box (otherwise the boundaries of the image will be hard to see in this black-
and-white plot).

Figure 9-4 shows some results using RGB vector as feature with the original image, a
downsampled mask, and downsampled resulting segmentation. The image on the right
is the plot generated by the script above.

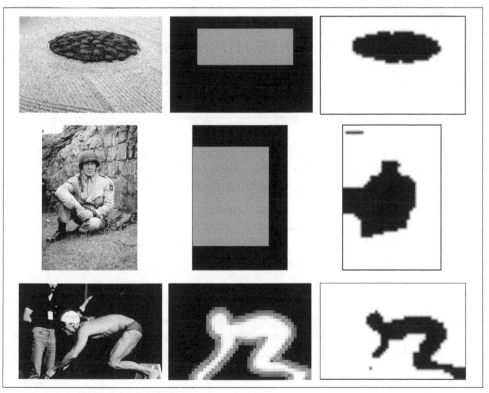

*Figure 9-4. Sample graph cut segmentation results using images from the Grab Cut data set: original
image, downsampled (left); mask used for training (middle); resulting segmentation using RGB values
as feature vectors (right).*

9.2 Segmentation Using Clustering

The graph cut formulation in the previous section solves the segmentation problem by finding a discrete solution using max flow/min cut over an image graph. In this section we will look at an alternative way to cut the image graph. The *normalized cut* algorithm, based on spectral graph theory, combines pixel similarities with spatial proximity to segment the image.

The idea comes from defining a cut cost that takes into account the size of the groups and "normalizes" the cost with the size of the partitions. The normalized cut formulation modifies the cut cost of equation (9.1) to

$$E_{ncut} = \frac{E_{cut}}{\sum_{i \in A} w_{ix}} + \frac{E_{cut}}{\sum_{j \in B} w_{jx}},$$

where A and B indicate the two sets of the cut and the sums add the weights from A and B, respectively, to all other nodes in the graph (which are pixels in the image in this case). This sum is called the *association* and for images where pixels have the same number of connections to other pixels, it is a rough measure of the size of the partitions. In the paper [32], the cost function above was introduced together with an algorithm for finding a minimizer. The algorithm is derived for two-class segmentation and will be described next.

Define W as the edge weight matrix with elements w_{ij} containing the weight of the edge connecting pixel i with pixel j. Let D be the diagonal matrix of the row sums of S, $D = \text{diag}(d_i)$, $d_i = \sum_j w_{ij}$ (same as in Section 6.3). The normalized cut segmentation is obtained as the minimum of the optimization problem

$$\min_{\mathbf{y}} \frac{\mathbf{y}^T (D - W)\mathbf{y}}{\mathbf{y}^T D \mathbf{y}},$$

where the vector $\mathbf{y}$ contains the discrete labels that satisfy the constraints $y_i \in \{1, -b\}$ for some constant b (meaning that $\mathbf{y}$ only takes two discrete values) and $\mathbf{y}^T D$ sum to zero. Because of these constraints, this is not easily solvable.[4]

However, by relaxing the constraints and letting $\mathbf{y}$ take any real value, the problem becomes an eigenvalue problem that is easily solved. The drawback is that you need to threshold or cluster the output to make it a discrete segmentation again.

Relaxing the problem results in solving for eigenvectors of a Laplacian matrix

$$L = D^{-1/2} W D^{-1/2},$$

just like the spectral clustering case. The only remaining difficulty is now to define the between-pixel edge weights w_{ij}. Normalized cuts have many similarities to spectral clustering and the underlying theory overlaps somewhat. See [32] for an explanation and the details.

---

[4] In fact, this problem is NP-hard.

Let's use the edge weights from the original normalized cuts paper [32]. The edge weight connecting two pixels i and j is given by

$$w_{ij} = e^{-|I_i - I_j|^2/\sigma_g} \, e^{-|\mathbf{x}_i - \mathbf{x}_j|^2/\sigma_d}.$$

The first part measures the pixel similarity between the pixels with I_i and I_j denoting either the RGB vectors or the grayscale values. The second part measures the proximity between the pixels in the image with $\mathbf{x}_i$ and $\mathbf{x}_j$ denoting the coordinate vector of each pixel. The scaling factors σ_g and σ_d determine the relative scales and how fast each component approaches zero.

Let's see what this looks like in code. Add the following function to a file *ncut.py*:

```
def ncut_graph_matrix(im,sigma_d=1e2,sigma_g=1e-2):
    """ Create matrix for normalized cut. The parameters are
        the weights for pixel distance and pixel similarity. """

    m,n = im.shape[:2]
    N = m*n

    # normalize and create feature vector of RGB or grayscale
    if len(im.shape)==3:
      for i in range(3):
        im[:,:,i] = im[:,:,i] / im[:,:,i].max()
      vim = im.reshape((-1,3))
    else:
      im = im / im.max()
      vim = im.flatten()

    # x,y coordinates for distance computation
    xx,yy = meshgrid(range(n),range(m))
    x,y = xx.flatten(),yy.flatten()

    # create matrix with edge weights
    W = zeros((N,N),'f')
    for i in range(N):
      for j in range(i,N):
        d = (x[i]-x[j])**2 + (y[i]-y[j])**2
        W[i,j] = W[j,i] = exp(-1.0*sum((vim[i]-vim[j])**2)/sigma_g) * exp(-d/sigma_d)

    return W
```

This function takes an image array and creates a feature vector using either RGB values or grayscale values depending on the input image. Since the edge weights contain a distance component, we use meshgrid() to get the x and y values for each pixel feature vector. Then the function loops over all N pixels and fills out the values in the $N \times N$ normalized cut matrix W.

We can compute the segmentation either by sequentially cutting each eigenvector or by taking a number of eigenvectors and apply clustering. We chose the second approach, which also works without modification for any number of segments. We take the top *ndim* eigenvectors of the Laplacian matrix corresponding to W and cluster the pixels.

The following function implements the clustering. As you can see, it is almost the same as the spectral clustering example in Section 6.3:

```
from scipy.cluster.vq import *

def cluster(S,k,ndim):
  """ Spectral clustering from a similarity matrix."""

  # check for symmetry
  if sum(abs(S-S.T)) > 1e-10:
    print 'not symmetric'

  # create Laplacian matrix
  rowsum = sum(abs(S),axis=0)
  D = diag(1 / sqrt(rowsum + 1e-6))
  L = dot(D,dot(S,D))

  # compute eigenvectors of L
  U,sigma,V = linalg.svd(L)

  # create feature vector from ndim first eigenvectors
  # by stacking eigenvectors as columns
  features = array(V[:ndim]).T

  # k-means
  features = whiten(features)
  centroids,distortion = kmeans(features,k)
  code,distance = vq(features,centroids)

  return code,V
```

Here we used the *k*-means clustering algorithm (see Section 6.1 for details) to group the pixels based on the values in the eigenvector images. You could try any clustering algorithm or grouping criteria if you feel like experimenting with the results.

Now we are ready to try this on some sample images. The following script shows a complete example:

```
import ncut
from scipy.misc import imresize


im = array(Image.open('C-uniform03.ppm'))
m,n = im.shape[:2]

# resize image to (wid,wid)
wid = 50
rim = imresize(im,(wid,wid),interp='bilinear')
rim = array(rim,'f')

# create normalized cut matrix
A = ncut.ncut_graph_matrix(rim,sigma_d=1,sigma_g=1e-2)

# cluster
code,V = ncut.cluster(A,k=3,ndim=3)
```

```
# reshape to original image size
codeim = imresize(code.reshape(wid,wid),(m,n),interp='nearest')

# plot result
figure()
imshow(codeim)
gray()
show()
```

Here we resize the image to a fixed size (50 × 50 in this example) in order to make the eigenvector computation fast enough. The NumPy linalg.svd() function is not fast enough to handle large matrices (and sometimes gives inaccurate results for too large matrices). We use bilinear interpolation when resizing the image, but nearest neighbor interpolation when resizing the resulting segmentation label image, since we don't want to interpolate the class labels. Note the use of first reshaping the one-dimensional array to (*wid,wid*) followed by resizing to the original image size.

In the example, we used one of the hand gesture images from the Static Hand Posture Database (see Section 8.1 for more details) with $k = 3$. The resulting segmentation is shown in Figure 9-5 together with the first four eigenvectors.

The eigenvectors are returned as the array V in the example and can be visualized as images like this:

```
imshow(imresize(V[i].reshape(wid,wid),(m,n),interp='bilinear'))
```

This will show eigenvector i as an image at the original image size.

Figure 9-6 shows some more examples using the same script above. The airplane image is from the "airplane" category in the Caltech 101 dataset. For these examples, we kept the parameters σ_d and σ_g to the same values as above. Changing them can give you

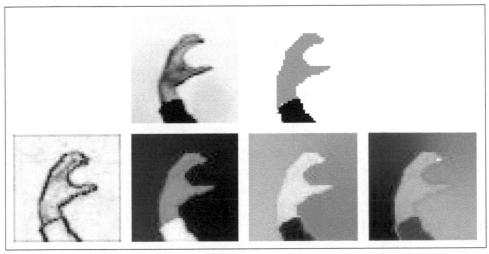

Figure 9-5. Image segmentation using the normalized cuts algorithm: the original image and the resulting three-class segmentation (top); the first four eigenvectors of the graph similarity matrix (bottom).

Figure 9-6. Examples of two-class image segmentation using the normalized cuts algorithm: original image (left); segmentation result (right).

smoother, more regularized results and quite different eigenvector images. We leave the experimentation to you.

It is worth noting that even for these fairly simple examples, a thresholding of the image would not have given the same result; neither would clustering the RGB or graylevel values. This is because neither of these take the pixel neighborhoods into account.

9.3 Variational Methods

In this book, you have seen a number of examples of minimizing a cost or energy to solve computer vision problems. In the previous sections it was minimizing the cut in a

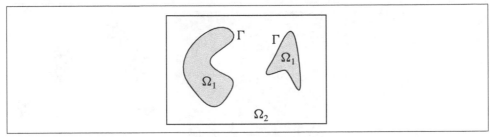

Figure 9-7. The piecewise constant Chan-Vese segmentation model.

graph, but we also saw examples like the ROF de-noising, *k*-means, and support vector machines. These are examples of optimization problems.

When the optimization is taken over functions, the problems are called *variational problems*, and algorithms for solving such problems are called *variational methods*. Let's look at a simple and effective variational model.

The *Chan-Vese segmentation* model [6] assumes a piecewise constant image model for the image regions to be segmented. Here we will focus on the case of two regions, for example foreground and background, but the model extends to multiple regions as well; see, for example, [38]. The model can be described as follows.

If we let a collection of curves Γ separate the image into two regions Ω_1 and Ω_2 as in Figure 9-7, the segmentation is given by minima of the Chan-Vese model energy

$$E(\Gamma) = \lambda \, \text{length}(\Gamma) + \int_{\Omega_1} (I - c_1)^2 d\mathbf{x} + \int_{\Omega_2} (I - c_2)^2 d\mathbf{x},$$

which measures the deviation from the constant graylevels in each region, c_1 and c_2. Here the integrals are taken over each region and the length of the separating curves are there to prefer smoother solutions.

With a piecewise constant image $U = \chi_1 c_1 + \chi_2 c_2$, this can we re-written as

$$E(\Gamma) = \lambda \frac{|c_1 - c_2|}{2} \int |\nabla U| d\mathbf{x} + ||I - U||^2,$$

where χ_1 and χ_2 are characteristic (indicator) functions for the two regions.[5] This transformation is non-trivial and requires some heavy mathematics that are not needed for understanding and that are well outside the scope of this book.

The point is that this equation is now the same as the ROF equation (1.1) with λ replaced by $\lambda |c_1 - c_2|$. The only difference is that in the Chan-Vese case we are looking for an image U that is piecewise constant. It can be shown that thresholding the ROF solution will give a good minimizer. The interested reader can check [8] for the details.

---

[5] *Characteristic functions* are 1 in the region and 0 outside.

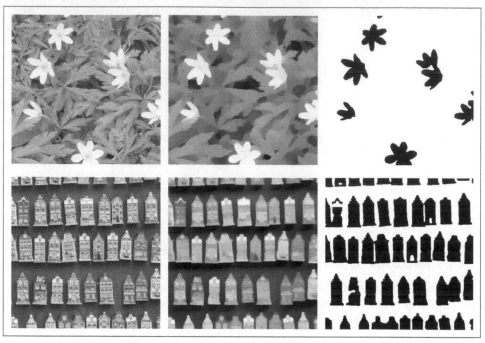

Figure 9-8. Examples image segmentation by minimizing the Chan-Vese model using ROF de-noising: (a) original image; (b) image after ROF de-noising; (c) final segmentation.

Minimizing the Chan-Vese model now becomes a ROF de-noising followed by thresholding:

```
import rof

im = array(Image.open('ceramic-houses_t0.png').convert("L"))
U,T = rof.denoise(im,im,tolerance=0.001)
t = 0.4 #threshold

import scipy.misc
scipy.misc.imsave('result.pdf',U < t*U.max())
```

In this case, we turn down the tolerance threshold for stopping the ROF iterations to make sure we get enough iterations. Figure 9-8 shows the result on two rather difficult images.

Exercises

1. It is possible to speed up computation for the graph cut optimization by reducing the number of edges. This graph construction is described in Section 4.2 of [16]. Try this out and measure the difference in graph size and in segmentation time compared to the simpler construction we used.

2. Create a user interface or simulate a user selecting regions for graph cut segmentation. Then try "hard coding" background and foreground by setting weights to some large value.

3. Change the feature vector in the graph cut segmentation from a RGB vector to some other descriptor. Can you improve on the segmentation results?

4. Implement an iterative segmentation approach using graph cut where a current segmentation is used to train new foreground and background models for the next. Does it improve segmentation quality?

5. The Microsoft Research Grab Cut dataset contains ground truth segmentation maps. Implement a function that measures the segmentation error and evaluate different settings and some of the ideas in the exercises above.

6. Try to vary the parameters of the normalized cut's edge weight and see how they affect the eigenvector images and the segmentation result.

7. Compute image gradients on the first normalized cut's eigenvectors. Combine these gradient images to detect image contours of objects.

8. Implement a linear search over the threshold value for the de-noised image in Chan-Vese segmentation. For each threshold, store the energy $E(\Gamma)$ and pick the segmentation with the lowest value.

## CHAPTER 10

OpenCV

This chapter gives a brief overview of how to use the popular computer vision library OpenCV through the Python interface. OpenCV is a C++ library for real-time computer vision initially developed by Intel and now maintained by Willow Garage. OpenCV is open source and released under a BSD license, meaning it is free for both academic and commercial use. As of version 2.0, Python support has been greatly improved. We will go through some basic examples and look deeper into tracking and video.

10.1 The OpenCV Python Interface

OpenCV is a C++ library with modules that cover many areas of computer vision. Besides C++ (and C), there is growing support for Python as a simpler scripting language through a Python interface on top of the C++ code base. The Python interface is still under development—not all parts of OpenCV are exposed and many functions are undocumented. This is likely to change, as there is an active community behind this interface. The Python interface is documented at *http://opencv.willowgarage.com/documentation/python/index.html*. See Appendix A for installation instructions.

The current OpenCV version (2.3.1) actually comes with two Python interfaces. The old cv module uses internal OpenCV datatypes and can be a little tricky to use from NumPy. The new cv2 module uses NumPy arrays and is much more intuitive to use.[1] The module is available as

```
import cv2
```

and the old module can be accessed as

```
import cv2.cv
```

---

[1] The names and location of these two modules are likely to change over time. Check the online documentation for changes.

We will focus on the cv2 module in this chapter. Look out for future name changes, as well as changes in function names and definitions in future versions. OpenCV and the Python interface is under rapid development.

10.2   OpenCV Basics

OpenCV comes with functions for reading and writing images, as well as matrix operations and math libraries. For the details on OpenCV, there is an excellent book [3] (C++ only). Let's look at some of the basic components and how to use them.

Reading and Writing Images

This short example will load an image, print the size, and convert and save the image in .png format:

```
import cv2

# read image
im = cv2.imread('empire.jpg')
h,w = im.shape[:2]
print h,w

# save image
cv2.imwrite('result.png',im)
```

The function imread() returns the image as a standard NumPy array and can handle a wide range of image formats. You can use this function as an alternative to the PIL image reading if you like. The function imwrite() automatically takes care of any conversion based on the file ending.

Color Spaces

In OpenCV images are not stored using the conventional RGB color channels; they are stored in BGR order (the reverse order). When reading an image the default is BGR; however, there are several conversions available. Color space conversions are done using the function cvtColor(). For example, converting to grayscale is done like this:

```
im = cv2.imread('empire.jpg')
# create a grayscale version
gray = cv2.cvtColor(im,cv2.COLOR_BGR2GRAY)
```

After the source image, there is an OpenCV color conversion code. Some of the most useful conversion codes are:

- cv2.COLOR_BGR2GRAY
- cv2.COLOR_BGR2RGB
- cv2.COLOR_GRAY2BGR

In each of these, the number of color channels for resulting images will match the conversion code (single channel for gray and three channels for RGB and BGR). The last

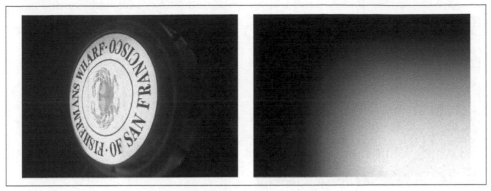

Figure 10-1. Example of computing an integral image using OpenCV's `integral()` *function.*

version converts grayscale images to BGR and is useful if you want to plot or overlay colored objects on the images. We will use this in the examples.

Displaying Images and Results

Let's look at some examples of using OpenCV for image processing and how to show results with OpenCV plotting and window management.

The first example reads an image from file and creates an integral image representation:

```
import cv2

# read image
im = cv2.imread('fisherman.jpg')
gray = cv2.cvtColor(im,cv2.COLOR_BGR2GRAY)

# compute integral image
intim = cv2.integral(gray)

# normalize and save
intim = (255.0*intim) / intim.max()
cv2.imwrite('result.jpg',intim)
```

After reading the image and converting to grayscale, the function `integral()` creates an image where the value at each pixel is the sum of the intensities above and to the left. This is a very useful trick for quickly evaluating features. Integral images are used in OpenCV's `CascadeClassifier`, which is based on a framework introduced by Viola and Jones [39]. Before saving the resulting image, we normalize the values to 0 . . . 255 by dividing with the largest value. Figure 10-1 shows the result for an example image.

The second example applies flood filling starting from a seed pixel:

```
import cv2

# read image
filename = 'fisherman.jpg'
im = cv2.imread(filename)
h,w = im.shape[:2]
```

Figure 10-2. Flood fill of a color image. The highlighted area in the right panel marks all pixels filled using a single seed in the upper-left corner.

```
# flood fill example
diff = (6,6,6)
mask = zeros((h+2,w+2),uint8)
cv2.floodFill(im,mask,(10,10), (255,255,0),diff,diff)

# show the result in an OpenCV window
cv2.imshow('flood fill',im)
cv2.waitKey()

# save the result
cv2.imwrite('result.jpg',im)
```

This example applies flood fill to the image and shows the result in an OpenCV window. The function `waitKey()` pauses until a key is pressed and the window is automatically closed. Here the function `floodFill()` takes the image (grayscale or color), a mask with non-zero pixels indicating areas not to be filled, a seed pixel, and the new color value to replace the flooded pixels together with lower and upper difference thresholds to accept new pixels. The flood fill starts at the seed pixel and keeps expanding as long as new pixels can be added within the difference thresholds. The difference thresholds are given as tuples (R,G,B). The result looks like Figure 10-2.

As a third and final example, we look at extracting SURF features, a faster version of SIFT introduced by [1]. Here we also show how to use some basic OpenCV plotting commands:

```
import cv2

# read image
im = cv2.imread('empire.jpg')

# downsample
im_lowres = cv2.pyrDown(im)

# convert to grayscale
gray = cv2.cvtColor(im_lowres,cv2.COLOR_RGB2GRAY)
```

Figure 10-3. Sample SURF features extracted and plotted using OpenCV.

```
# detect feature points
s = cv2.SURF()
mask = uint8(ones(gray.shape))
keypoints = s.detect(gray,mask)

# show image and points
vis = cv2.cvtColor(gray,cv2.COLOR_GRAY2BGR)

for k in keypoints[::10]:
    cv2.circle(vis,(int(k.pt[0]),int(k.pt[1])),2,(0,255,0),-1)
    cv2.circle(vis,(int(k.pt[0]),int(k.pt[1])),int(k.size),(0,255,0),2)

cv2.imshow('local descriptors',vis)
cv2.waitKey()
```

After reading the image, it is downsampled using the function `pyrDown()`, which, if no new size is given, creates a new image half the size of the original. Then the image is converted to grayscale and passed to a `SURF` keypoint detection object. The *mask* determines what areas to apply the keypoint detector. To plot, we convert the grayscale image to a color image and use the green channel for plotting the keypoints. We loop over every tenth keypoint and plot a circle at the center and one circle showing the scale (size) of the keypoint. The plotting function `circle()` takes an image, a tuple with image coordinates (integer only), a radius, a tuple with plot color, and finally the line thickness (−1 gives a solid circle). Figure 10-3 shows the result.

10.3 Processing Video

Video with pure Python is hard. There are speed, codecs, cameras, operating systems, and file formats to consider. There is currently no video library for Python. OpenCV with its Python interface is the only good option. In this section, we'll look at some basic examples using video.

Video Input

Reading video from a camera is very well supported in OpenCV. A basic complete example that captures frames and shows them in an OpenCV window looks like this:

```
import cv2

# setup video capture
cap = cv2.VideoCapture(0)

while True:
  ret,im = cap.read()
  cv2.imshow('video test',im)
  key = cv2.waitKey(10)
  if key == 27:
    break
  if key == ord(' '):
    cv2.imwrite('vid_result.jpg',im)
```

The capture object VideoCapture captures video from cameras or files. Here we pass an integer at initialization. This is the id of the video device; with a single camera connected this is 0. The method read() decodes and returns the next video frame. The first value is a success flag and the second the actual image array. The waitKey() function waits for a key to be pressed and quits the application if the 'Esc' key (Ascii number 27) is pressed, or saves the frame if the 'space' key is pressed.

Let's extend this example with some simple processing by taking the camera input and showing a blurred (color) version of the input in an OpenCV window. This is only a slight modification to the base example above:

```
import cv2

# setup video capture
cap = cv2.VideoCapture(0)

# get frame, apply Gaussian smoothing, show result
while True:
  ret,im = cap.read()
  blur = cv2.GaussianBlur(im,(0,0),5)
  cv2.imshow('camera blur',blur)
  if cv2.waitKey(10) == 27:
    break
```

Each frame is passed to the function GaussianBlur(), which applies a Gaussian filter to the image. In this case, we are passing a color image so each color channel is blurred separately. The function takes a tuple for filter size and the standard deviation for the Gaussian function (in this case 5). If the filter size is set to zero, it will automatically be determined from the standard deviation. The result looks like Figure 10-4.

Figure 10-4. Screenshot of a blurred video of the author as he's writing this chapter.

Reading video from files works the same way but with the call to VideoCapture() taking the video filename as input:

```
capture = cv2.VideoCapture('filename')
```

Reading Video to NumPy Arrays

Using OpenCV, it is possible to read video frames from a file and convert them to NumPy arrays. Here is an example of capturing video from a camera and storing the frames in a NumPy array:

```
import cv2

# setup video capture
cap = cv2.VideoCapture(0)

frames = []
# get frame, store in array
while True:
  ret,im = cap.read()
  cv2.imshow('video',im)
  frames.append(im)
  if cv2.waitKey(10) == 27:
    break
frames = array(frames)

# check the sizes
print im.shape
print frames.shape
```

Each frame array is added to the end of a list until the capturing is stopped. The resulting array will have size (number of frames, height, width, 3). The printout confirms this:

```
(480, 640, 3)
(40, 480, 640, 3)
```

In this case, there were 40 frames recorded. Arrays with video data like this are useful for video processing, such as in computing frame differences and tracking.

10.4 Tracking

Tracking is the process of following objects through a sequence of images or video.

Optical Flow

Optical flow (sometimes called *optic flow*) is the image motion of objects as the objects, scene, or camera move between two consecutive images. It is a 2D vector field of within-image translation. It is a classic and well-studied field in computer vision with many successful applications in, for example, video compression, motion estimation, object tracking, and image segmentation.

Optical flow relies on three major assumptions:

1. Brightness constancy: The pixel intensities of an object in an image do not change between consecutive images.

2. Temporal regularity: The between-frame time is short enough to consider the motion change between images using differentials (used to derive the central equation below).

3. Spatial consistency: Neighboring pixels have similar motion.

In many cases, these assumptions break down, but for small motions and short time steps between images it is a good model. Assuming that an object pixel $I(x, y, t)$ at time t has the same intensity at time $t + \delta t$ after motion $[\delta x, \delta y]$) means that $I(x, y, t) = I(x + \delta x, y + \delta y, t + \delta t)$. Differentiating this constraint gives the *optical flow equation*:

$$\nabla I^T \mathbf{v} = -I_t,$$

where $\mathbf{v} = [u, v]$ is the motion vector and I_t the time derivative. For individual points in the image, this equation is under-determined and cannot be solved (one equation with two unknowns in $\mathbf{v}$). By enforcing some spatial consistency, it is possible to obtain solutions, though. In the Lucas-Kanade algorithm below, we will see how that assumption is used.

OpenCV contains several optical flow implementations: `CalcOpticalFlowBM()`, which uses block matching; `CalcOpticalFlowHS()`, which uses [15] (both of these currently only in the old cv module); the pyramidal Lucas-Kanade algorithm [19] `calcOpticalFlowPyrLK()`; and finally, `calcOpticalFlowFarneback()` based on [10]. The last one is considered one of the best methods for obtaining dense flow fields. Let's look at an example of using this to find motion vectors in video (the Lucas-Kanade version is the subject of the next section).

Try running the following script:

```
import cv2

def draw_flow(im,flow,step=16):
    """ Plot optical flow at sample points
        spaced step pixels apart. """

    h,w = im.shape[:2]
```

```
    y,x = mgrid[step/2:h:step,step/2:w:step].reshape(2,-1)
    fx,fy = flow[y,x].T

    # create line endpoints
    lines = vstack([x,y,x+fx,y+fy]).T.reshape(-1,2,2)
    lines = int32(lines)

    # create image and draw
    vis = cv2.cvtColor(im,cv2.COLOR_GRAY2BGR)
    for (x1,y1),(x2,y2) in lines:
        cv2.line(vis,(x1,y1),(x2,y2),(0,255,0),1)
        cv2.circle(vis,(x1,y1),1,(0,255,0), -1)
    return vis


# setup video capture
cap = cv2.VideoCapture(0)

ret,im = cap.read()
prev_gray = cv2.cvtColor(im,cv2.COLOR_BGR2GRAY)

while True:
    # get grayscale image
    ret,im = cap.read()
    gray = cv2.cvtColor(im,cv2.COLOR_BGR2GRAY)

    # compute flow
    flow = cv2.calcOpticalFlowFarneback(prev_gray,gray,None,0.5,3,15,3,5,1.2,0)
    prev_gray = gray

    # plot the flow vectors
    cv2.imshow('Optical flow',draw_flow(gray,flow))
    if cv2.waitKey(10) == 27:
        break
```

This example will capture images from a webcam and call the optical flow estimation on every consecutive pair of images. The motion flow vectors are stored in the two-channel image *flow* returned by calcOpticalFlowFarneback(). Besides the previous frame and the current frame, this function takes a sequence of parameters. Look them up in the documentation if you are interested. The helper function draw_flow() plots the motion vectors at evenly spaced points in the image. It uses the OpenCV drawing functions line() and circle(), and the variable *step* controls the spacing of the flow samples. The result can look like the screenshots in Figure 10-5. Here the positions of the flow samples are shown as a grid of circles and the flow vectors with lines show how each sample point moves.

The Lucas-Kanade Algorithm

The most basic form of tracking is to follow interest points such as corners. A popular algorithm for this is the *Lucas-Kanade tracking algorithm*, which uses a sparse optical flow algorithm.

Lucas-Kanade tracking can be applied to any type of features, but usually makes use of corner points similar to the Harris corner points in Section 2.1. The function

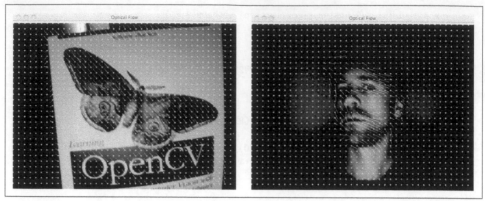

Figure 10-5. Optical flow vectors (sampled at every 16th pixel) shown on video of a translating book and a turning head.

goodFeaturesToTrack() detects corners according to an algorithm by Shi and Tomasi [33], where corners are points with two large eigenvalues of the structure tensor (Harris matrix) equation (2.2) and where the smaller eigenvalue is above a threshold.

The optical flow equation is under-determined (meaning that there are too many unknowns per equation) if considered on a per-pixel basis. Using the assumption that neighboring pixels have the same motion, it is possible to stack many of these equations into one system of equations like this

$$
\begin{bmatrix} \nabla I^T(\mathbf{x}_1) \\ \nabla I^T(\mathbf{x}_2) \\ \vdots \\ \nabla I^T(\mathbf{x}_n) \end{bmatrix} \mathbf{v} = \begin{bmatrix} I_x(\mathbf{x}_1) & I_y(\mathbf{x}_1) \\ I_x(\mathbf{x}_2) & I_y(\mathbf{x}_2) \\ \vdots & \vdots \\ I_x(\mathbf{x}_n) & I_y(\mathbf{x}_n) \end{bmatrix} \begin{bmatrix} u \\ v \end{bmatrix} = - \begin{bmatrix} I_t(\mathbf{x}_1) \\ I_t(\mathbf{x}_2) \\ \vdots \\ I_t(\mathbf{x}_n) \end{bmatrix}
$$

for some neighborhood of n pixels. This has the advantage that the system now has more equations than unknowns and can be solved with least square methods. Typically, the contribution from the surrounding pixels is weighted so that pixels farther away have less influence. A Gaussian weighting is the most common choice. This turns the matrix above into the structure tensor in equation (2.2), and we have the relation

$$
\overline{\mathbf{M}}_I \mathbf{v} = - \begin{bmatrix} I_t(\mathbf{x}_1) \\ I_t(\mathbf{x}_2) \\ \vdots \\ I_t(\mathbf{x}_n) \end{bmatrix} \quad \text{or simpler } A\mathbf{v} = \mathbf{b}.
$$

This over-determined equation system can be solved in a least square sense and the motion vector is given by

$$
\mathbf{v} = (A^T A)^{-1} A^T \mathbf{b}.
$$

This is solvable only when $A^T A$ is invertible, which it is by construction if applied at Harris corner points or the "good features to track" of Shi-Tomasi. This is how the motion vectors are computed in the Lucas-Kanade tracking algorithms.

Standard Lucas-Kanade tracking works for small displacements. To handle larger displacements, a hierarchical approach is used. In this case, the optical flow is computed at coarse-to-fine versions of the image. This is what the OpenCV function calcOpticalFlowPyrLK() does.

The Lucas-Kanade functions are included in OpenCV. Let's look at how to use those to build a Python tracker class. Create a file *lktrack.py* and add the following class and constructor:

```
import cv2

# some constants and default parameters
lk_params = dict(winSize=(15,15),maxLevel=2,
            criteria=(cv2.TERM_CRITERIA_EPS | cv2.TERM_CRITERIA_COUNT,10,0.03))

subpix_params = dict(zeroZone=(-1,-1),winSize=(10,10),
              criteria = (cv2.TERM_CRITERIA_COUNT | cv2.TERM_CRITERIA_EPS,20,0.03))

feature_params = dict(maxCorners=500,qualityLevel=0.01,minDistance=10)


class LKTracker(object):
    """ Class for Lucas-Kanade tracking with
      pyramidal optical flow."""

    def __init__(self,imnames):
      """ Initialize with a list of image names. """

      self.imnames = imnames
      self.features = []
      self.tracks = []
      self.current_frame = 0
```

The tracker object is initialized with a list of filenames. The variables *features* and *tracks* will hold the corner points and their tracked positions. We also use a variable to keep track of the current frame. We define three dictionaries with parameters for the feature extraction, the tracking, and the subpixel feature point refinement.

Now, to start detecting points, we need to load the actual image, create a grayscale version, and extract the "good features to track" points. The OpenCV function doing the main work is goodFeaturesToTrack(). Add this detect_points() method to the class:

```
def detect_points(self):
    """ Detect 'good features to track' (corners) in the current frame
      using sub-pixel accuracy. """

    # load the image and create grayscale
    self.image = cv2.imread(self.imnames[self.current_frame])
    self.gray = cv2.cvtColor(self.image,cv2.COLOR_BGR2GRAY)

    # search for good points
    features = cv2.goodFeaturesToTrack(self.gray, **feature_params)
```

```
# refine the corner locations
cv2.cornerSubPix(self.gray,features, **subpix_params)

self.features = features
self.tracks = [[p] for p in features.reshape((-1,2))]

self.prev_gray = self.gray
```

The point locations are refined using cornerSubPix() and stored in the member variables *features* and *tracks*. Note that running this function clears the track history.

Now that we can detect the points, we also need to track them. First, we need to get the next frame, apply the OpenCV function calcOpticalFlowPyrLK() that finds out where the points moved, and then remove and clean the lists of tracked points. The method track_points() below does this:

```
def track_points(self):
    """ Track the detected features. """

    if self.features != []:
        self.step() # move to the next frame

        # load the image and create grayscale
        self.image = cv2.imread(self.imnames[self.current_frame])
        self.gray = cv2.cvtColor(self.image,cv2.COLOR_BGR2GRAY)

        # reshape to fit input format
        tmp = float32(self.features).reshape(-1, 1, 2)

        # calculate optical flow
        features,status,track_error = cv2.calcOpticalFlowPyrLK(self.prev_gray,
                            self.gray,tmp,None,**lk_params)

        # remove points lost
        self.features = [p for (st,p) in zip(status,features) if st]

        # clean tracks from lost points
        features = array(features).reshape((-1,2))
        for i,f in enumerate(features):
            self.tracks[i].append(f)
        ndx = [i for (i,st) in enumerate(status) if not st]
        ndx.reverse() # remove from back
        for i in ndx:
            self.tracks.pop(i)

        self.prev_gray = self.gray
```

This makes use of a simple helper method step() that moves to the next available frame:

```
def step(self,framenbr=None):
    """ Step to another frame. If no argument is
    given, step to the next frame. """

    if framenbr is None:
        self.current_frame = (self.current_frame + 1) % len(self.imnames)
    else:
        self.current_frame = framenbr % len(self.imnames)
```

This method jumps to a given frame or just to the next if no argument is given.

Finally, we also want to be able to draw the result using OpenCV windows and drawing functions. Add this draw() method to the LKTracker class:

```
def draw(self):
    """ Draw the current image with points using
        OpenCV's own drawing functions.
        Press ant key to close window."""

    # draw points as green circles
    for point in self.features:
        cv2.circle(self.image,(int(point[0][0]),int(point[0][1])),3,(0,255,0),-1)

    cv2.imshow('LKtrack',self.image)
    cv2.waitKey()
```

Now we have a complete self-contained tracking system using OpenCV functions.

Using the tracker

Let's tie it all together by using this tracker class on a real tracking scenario. The following script will initialize a tracker object, detect and track points through the sequence, and draw the result:

```
import lktrack

imnames = ['bt.003.pgm', 'bt.002.pgm', 'bt.001.pgm', 'bt.000.pgm']

# create tracker object
lkt = lktrack.LKTracker(imnames)

# detect in first frame, track in the remaining
lkt.detect_points()
lkt.draw()
for i in range(len(imnames)-1):
    lkt.track_points()
    lkt.draw()
```

The drawing is one frame at a time and shows the points currently tracked. Pressing any key will move to the next image in the sequence. The resulting figure windows for the first four images of the Oxford corridor sequence (one of the Oxford multi-view datasets available at *http://www.robots.ox.ac.uk/~vgg/data/data-mview.html*) looks like Figure 10-6.

Using generators

Add the following method to the LKTracker class:

```
def track(self):
    """ Generator for stepping through a sequence."""

    for i in range(len(self.imnames)):
        if self.features == []:
            self.detect_points()
        else:
            self.track_points()
```

Figure 10-6. Tracking using the Lucas-Kanade algorithm through the LKTrack class.

```
# create a copy in RGB
f = array(self.features).reshape(-1,2)
im = cv2.cvtColor(self.image,cv2.COLOR_BGR2RGB)
yield im,f
```

This creates a generator that makes it easy to step through a sequence and get tracks and the images as RGB arrays so that it is easy to plot the result. To use it on the classic Oxford "dinosaur" sequence (from the same multi-view dataset page as the corridor above) and plot the points and their tracks, the code looks like this:

```
import lktrack

imnames = ['viff.000.ppm', 'viff.001.ppm',
    'viff.002.ppm', 'viff.003.ppm', 'viff.004.ppm']

# track using the LKTracker generator
lkt = lktrack.LKTracker(imnames)
for im,ft in lkt.track():
  print 'tracking %d features' % len(ft)
```

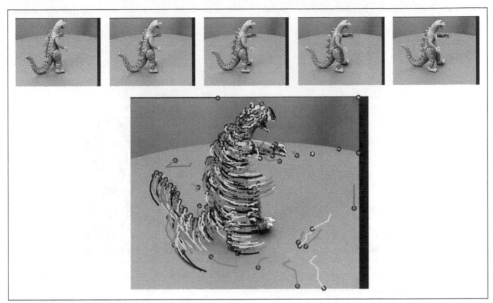

Figure 10-7. An example of using Lucas-Kanade tracking on a turntable sequence and plotting the tracks of points.

```
# plot the tracks
figure()
imshow(im)
for p in ft:
  plot(p[0],p[1],'bo')
for t in lkt.tracks:
  plot([p[0] for p in t],[p[1] for p in t])
axis('off')
show()
```

This generator makes it really easy to use the tracker class and completely hides the OpenCV functions from the user. The example generates a plot like the one shown in Figure 10-7 and the bottom right of Figure 10-6.

10.5 More Examples

With OpenCV comes a number of useful examples of how to use the Python interface. These are in the sub-directory samples/python2/ and are a good way to get familiar with OpenCV. Here are a few selected examples to illustrate some other capabilities of OpenCV.

Inpainting

The reconstruction of lost or deteriorated parts of images is called *inpainting*. This covers both algorithms to recover lost or corrupted parts of image data for restoration purposes as well as removing red-eyes or objects in photo-editing applications.

Figure 10-8. An example of inpainting with OpenCV. The left image shows areas marked by a user as "corrupt." The right image shows the result after inpainting.

Typically, a region of the image is marked as "corrupt" and needs to be filled using the data from the rest of the image.

Try the following command:

```
$ python inpaint.py empire.jpg
```

This will open an interactive window where you can draw regions to be inpainted. The results are shown in a separate window. An example is shown in Figure 10-8.

Segmentation with the Watershed Transform

Watershed is an image processing technique that can be used for segmentation (see Figure 10-9). An image is treated as a topological landscape that is "flooded" from a number of seed regions. Usually, a gradient magnitude image is used since this has ridges at strong edges and will make the segmentation stop at image edges.

The implementation in OpenCV uses an algorithm by Meyer [22]. Try it using the following command:

```
$ python watershed.py empire.jpg
```

This will open an interactive window where you can draw the seed regions you want the algorithm to use as input. The results are shown in a second window with colors representing regions overlaid on a grayscale version of the input image.

Line Detection with a Hough Transform

The *Hough transform* (*http://en.wikipedia.org/wiki/Hough_transform*) is a method for finding shapes in images. It works by using a voting procedure in the parameter space of the shapes. The most common use is to find line structures in images. In that case,

Figure 10-9. An example of segmenting an image using a watershed transform. The left image is the input image with seed regions drawn. The right image shows the resulting segmentation with colors overlaid on the image.

Figure 10-10. An example of detecting lines using a Hough transform. The left image is the source in grayscale. The right image shows an edge map with detected lines.

edges and line segments can be grouped together by them voting for the same line parameters in the 2D parameter space of lines.

The OpenCV sample detects lines using this approach.[2] Try the following command:

```
$ python houghlines.py empire.jpg
```

This gives two windows like the ones shown in Figure 10-10. One window shows the source image in grayscale, and the other shows the edge map used together with lines

---

[2] This sample is currently in the /samples/python folder.

detected as those with most votes in parameter space. Note that the lines are always infinite; if you want to find the endpoints of line segments in the image, you can use the edge map to try to find them.

Exercises

1. Use optical flow to build a simple gesture recognition system. For example, you could sample the flow as in the plotting function and use these sample vectors as input.

2. There are two warp functions available in OpenCV, `cv2.warpAffine()` and `cv2.warpPerspective()`. Try to use them on some of the examples from Chapter 3.

3. Use the flood fill function to do background subtraction on the Oxford "dinosaur" images used in Figure 10-7. Create new images with the dinosaur placed on a different color background or on a different image.

4. OpenCV has a function `cv2.findChessboardCorners()`, which automatically finds the corners of a chessboard pattern. Use this function to get correspondences for calibrating a camera with the function `cv2.calibrateCamera()`.

5. If you have two cameras, mount them in a stereo rig setting and capture stereo image pairs using `cv2.VideoCapture()` with different video device ids. Try 0 and 1 for starters. Compute depth maps for some varying scenes.

6. Use Hu moments with `cv2.HuMoments()` as features for the Sudoku OCR classification problem in Section 8.4 and check the performance.

7. OpenCV has an implementation of the Grab Cut segmentation algorithm. Use the function `cv2.grabCut()` on the Microsoft Research Grab Cut dataset (see Section 9.1). Hopefully you will get better results than the low-resolution segmentation in our examples.

8. Modify the Lucas-Kanade tracker class to take a video file as input and write a script that tracks points between frames and detects new points every k frames.

Installing Packages

Here are short installation instructions for the packages used in the book. They are written based on the latest versions as of the writing of this book. Things change (URLs change!), so if the instructions become outdated, check the individual project websites for help.

In addition to the specific instructions, an option that often works on most platforms is Python's easy_install. If you run into problems with the installation instructions given here, easy_install is worth a try. Find out more on the package website, *http://packages.python.org/distribute/easy_install.html*.

A.1 NumPy and SciPy

Installing NumPy and SciPy is a little different depending on your operating system. Follow the applicable instructions below. The current versions are 2.0 (NumPy) and 0.11 (SciPy) on most platforms. A package that currently works on all major platforms is the Enthought EPD Free bundle, a free light version of the commercial Enthought distribution, available at *http://enthought.com/products/epd_free.php*.

Windows

The easiest way to install NumPy and SciPy is to download and install the binary distributions from *http://www.scipy.org/Download*.

Mac OS X

Later versions of Mac OS X (10.7.0 [Lion] and up) come with NumPy pre-installed.

An easy way to install NumPy and SciPy for Mac OS X is with the "superpack" from *https://github.com/fonnesbeck/ScipySuperpack*. This also gives you Matplotlib.

Another alternative is to use the package system MacPorts (*http://www.macports.org/*). This also works for Matplotlib instead of the instructions below.

If none of those work, the project web page has other alternatives listed (*http://scipy.org/*).

Linux

Installation requires that you have administrator rights on your computer. On some distributions NumPy comes pre-installed, on others not. Both NumPy and SciPy are most easily installed with the built-in package handler (for example Synaptic on Ubuntu). You can also use the package handler for Matplotlib instead of the instructions below.

A.2 Matplotlib

Here are instructions for installing Matplotlib in case your NumPy/SciPy installation did not also install Matplotlib. Matplotlib is freely available at *http://matplotlib.sourceforge .net/*. Click the "download" link and download the installer for the latest version for your system and Python version. Currently the latest version is 1.1.0.

Alternatively, just download the source and unpack. Run

```
$ python setup.py install
```

from the command line and everything should work. General tips on installing for different systems can be found at *http://matplotlib.sourceforge.net/users/installing.html*, but the process above should work for most platforms and Python versions.

A.3 PIL

PIL, the Python Imaging Library, is available at *http://www.pythonware.com/products/ pil/*. The latest free version is 1.1.7. Download the source kit and unpack the folder. In the downloaded folder, run

```
$ python setup.py install
```

from the command line.

You need to have JPEG (libjpeg) and PNG (zlib) supported if you want to save images using PIL. See the README file or the PIL website if you encounter any problems.

A.4 LibSVM

The current release is version 3.1 (released April 2011). Download the zip file from the LibSVM website (*http://www.csie.ntu.edu.tw/~cjlin/libsvm/*). Unzip the file (a directory "libsvm-3.1" will be created). In a terminal window, go to this directory and type "make":

```
$ cd libsvm-3.0
$ make
```

Then go to the "python" directory and do the same:

```
$ cd python/
$ make
```

This should be all you need to do. To test your installation, start Python from the command line and try:

```
import svm
```

The authors wrote a practical guide for using LivSVM [7]. This is a good starting point.

A.5 OpenCV

Installing OpenCV is a bit different, depending on your operating system. Follow the applicable instructions below.

To check your installation, start Python and try the cookbook examples at *http://opencv .willowgarage.com/documentation/python/cookbook.html*. The online OpenCV Python reference guide gives more examples and details on how to use OpenCV with Python at *http://opencv.willowgarage.com/documentation/python/index.html*.

Windows and Unix

There are installers for Windows and Unix available at the SourceForge repository, *http://sourceforge.net/projects/opencvlibrary/*.

Mac OS X

Mac OS X support has been lacking but is on the rise. There are several ways to install from source as described on the OpenCV wiki, *http://opencv.willowgarage.com/wiki/ InstallGuide*. MacPorts is one option that works well if you are using Python, NumPy, SciPy, or Matplotlib, also from MacPorts. Building OpenCV from source can be done like this:

```
$ svn co https://code.ros.org/svn/opencv/trunk/opencv
$ cd opencv/
$ sudo cmake -G "Unix Makefiles" .
$ sudo make -j8
$ sudo make install
```

If you have all the dependencies in place, everything should build and install properly. If you get an error like

```
import cv2
Traceback (most recent call last):
  File "", line 1, in
ImportError: No module named cv2
```

then you need to add the directory containing cv2.so to PYTHONPATH. For example:

```
$ export PYTHONPATH=/usr/local/lib/python2.7/site-packages/
```

Linux

Linux users could try the package installer for the distribution (the package is usually called "opencv") or install from source as described in the Mac OS X section.

A.6   VLFeat

To install VLFeat, download and unpack the latest binary package from *http://vlfeat.org/ download.html* (currently the latest version is 0.9.14). Add the paths to your environment or copy the binaries to a directory in your path. The binaries are in the bin/ directory, just pick the sub-directory for your platform.

The use of the VLFeat command line binaries is described in the src/ sub-directory. Alternatively, you can find the documentation online at *http://vlfeat.org/man/man.html*.

A.7   PyGame

PyGame can be downloaded from *http://www.pygame.org/download.shtml*. The latest version is 1.9.1. The easiest way is to get the binary install package for your system and Python version.

Alternatively, you can download the source, and in the downloaded folder run

```
$ python setup.py install
```

from the command line.

A.8   PyOpenGL

Installing PyOpenGL is easiest done by downloading the package from *http://pypi .python.org/pypi/PyOpenGL* as suggested on the PyOpenGL web page, *http://pyopengl .sourceforge.net/*. Get the latest version, currently 3.0.1.

In the downloaded folder, do the usual

```
$ python setup.py install
```

from the command line. If you get stuck or need information on dependencies, etc., more documentation can be found at *http://pyopengl.sourceforge.net/documentation/ installation.html*. Some good demo scripts for getting started are available at *http://pypi .python.org/pypi/PyOpenGL-Demo*.

A.9   Pydot

Begin by installing the dependencies, GraphViz and Pyparsing. Go to *http://www .graphviz.org/* and download the latest GraphViz binary for your platform. The install files should install GraphViz automatically.

Then go to the Pyparsing project page *http://pyparsing.wikispaces.com/*. The download page is at *http://sourceforge.net/projects/pyparsing/*. Get the latest version (currently 1.5.5) and unzip the file to a directory. Type

```
$ python setup.py install
```

from the command line.

Finally, go to the project page *http://code.google.com/p/pydot/* and click "download". From the download page, download the latest version (currently 1.0.4). Unzip and again type

```
$ python setup.py install
```

from the command line. Now you should be able to import pydot in your Python sessions.

A.10 Python-graph

Python-graph is a Python module for working with graphs and contains lots of useful algorithms like traversals, shortest path, pagerank, and maximum flow. The latest version is 1.8.1 and can be found on the project website *http://code.google.com/p/python-graph/*. If you have easy_install on your system, the simplest way to get python-graph is:

```
$ easy_install python-graph-core
```

Alternatively, download the source code from *http://code.google.com/p/python-graph/downloads/list* and run:

```
$ python setup.py install
```

To write and visualize the graphs (using the DOT language) you need python-graph-dot, which comes with the download or through easy_install:

```
$ easy_install python-graph-dot
```

Python-graph-dot depends on pydot; see above. The documentation (in html) is in the "docs/" folder.

A.11 Simplejson

Simplejson is the independently maintained version of the JSON module that comes with later versions of Python (2.6 or later). The syntax is the same for both modules, but simplejson is more optimized and will give better performance.

To install, go to the project page *https://github.com/simplejson/simplejson* and click the Download button. Then select the latest version from the "Download Packages" section (currently this is 2.1.3). Unzip the folder and type

```
$ python setup.py install
```

from the command line. This should be all you need.

A.12   PySQLite

PySQLite is an SQLite binding for Python. SQLite is a lightweight, disk-based database that can be queried with SQL and is easy to install and use. The latest version is 2.6.3; see the project website, *http://code.google.com/p/pysqlite/*, for more details.

To install, download from *http://code.google.com/p/pysqlite/downloads/list* and unzip to a folder. Run

```
$ python setup.py install
```

from the command line.

A.13   CherryPy

CherryPy (*http://www.cherrypy.org/*) is a fast, stable, and lightweight web server built on Python using an object-oriented model. CherryPy is easy to install; just download the latest version from *http://www.cherrypy.org/wiki/CherryPyInstall*. The latest stable release is 3.2.0. Unpack and run

```
$ python setup.py install
```

from the command line. After installing, look at the tiny tutorial examples that come with CherryPy in the *cherrypy/tutorial/* folder. These examples show you how to pass GET/POST variables, inheritance of page properties, file upload and download, etc.

Image Datasets

B.1 Flickr

The immensely popular photo-sharing site Flickr (*http://flickr.com/*) is a gold mine for computer vision researchers and hobbyists. With hundreds of millions of images, many of them tagged by users, it is a great resource to get training data or for doing experiments on real data. Flickr has an API for interfacing with the service that makes it possible to upload, download, and annotate images (and much more). A full description of the API is available at *http://flickr.com/services/api/*, and there are kits for many programming languages, including Python.

Let's look at using a library called flickrpy, available freely at *http://code.google.com/p/ flickrpy/*. Download the file *flickr.py*. You will need an API Key from Flickr to get this to work. Keys are free for non-commercial use and can be requested for commercial use. Just click the link "Apply for a new API Key" on the Flickr API page and follow the instructions. Once you have an API key, open *flickr.py* and replace the empty string on the line

```
API_KEY = ''
```

with your key. It should look something like this:

```
API_KEY = '123fbbb81441231123cgg5b123d92123'
```

Let's create a simple command line tool that downloads images tagged with a particular tag. Add the following code to a new file called *tagdownload.py*:

```
import flickr
import urllib, urlparse
import os
import sys

if len(sys.argv)>1:
    tag = sys.argv[1]
else:
    print 'no tag specified'
```

```
# downloading image data
f = flickr.photos_search(tags=tag)
urllist = [] #store a list of what was downloaded

# downloading images
for k in f:
    url = k.getURL(size='Medium', urlType='source')
    urllist.append(url)
    image = urllib.URLopener()
    image.retrieve(url, os.path.basename(urlparse.urlparse(url).path))
    print 'downloading:', url
```

If you also want to write the list of urls to a text file, add the following lines at the end:

```
# write the list of urls to file
fl = open('urllist.txt', 'w')
for url in urllist:
    fl.write(url+'\n')
fl.close()
```

From the command line, just type

```
$ python tagdownload.py goldengatebridge
```

and you will get the 100 latest images tagged with "goldengatebridge". As you can see, we chose to take the "Medium" size. If you want thumbnails or full-size originals or something else, there are many sizes available; check the documentation on the Flickr website, *http://flickr.com/api/*.

Here we were just interested in downloading images; for API calls that require authentication the process is slightly more complicated. See the API documentation for more information on how to set up authenticated sessions.

B.2 Panoramio

A good source of geotagged images is Google's photo-sharing service Panoramio (*http://www.panoramio.com/*). This web service has an API to access content programmatically. The API is described at *http://www.panoramio.com/api/*. You can get website widgets and access the data using JavaScript objects. To download images, the simplest way is to use a GET call. For example:

```
http://www.panoramio.com/map/get_panoramas.php?order=popularity&set=public&
from=0&to=20&minx=-180&miny=-90&maxx=180&maxy=90&size=medium
```

where *minx*, *miny*, *maxx*, *maxy* define the geographic area to select photos from (minimum longitude, latitude, maximum longitude and latitude, respectively). The response will be in JSON and look like this:

```
{"count": 3152, "photos":
[{"upload_date": "02 February 2006", "owner_name": "***", "photo_id": 9439,
"longitude": -151.75, "height": 375, "width": 500, "photo_title": "***",
"latitude": -16.5, "owner_url": "http://www.panoramio.com/user/1600", "owner_id": 1600,
```

```
"photo_file_url": "http://mw2.google.com/mw-panoramio/photos/medium/9439.jpg",
"photo_url": "http://www.panoramio.com/photo/9439"},
{"upload_date": "18 January 2011", "owner_name": "***", "photo_id": 46752123,
"longitude": 120.52718600000003, "height": 370, "width": 500, "photo_title": "***",
"latitude": 23.327833999999999, "owner_url": "http://www.panoramio.com/user/2780232",
"owner_id": 2780232,
"photo_file_url": "http://mw2.google.com/mw-panoramio/photos/medium/46752123.jpg",
"photo_url": "http://www.panoramio.com/photo/46752123"},
{"upload_date": "20 January 2011", "owner_name": "***", "photo_id": 46817885,
"longitude": -178.13709299999999, "height": 330, "width": 500, "photo_title": "***",
"latitude": -14.310613, "owner_url": "http://www.panoramio.com/user/919358",
"owner_id": 919358,
"photo_file_url": "http://mw2.google.com/mw-panoramio/photos/medium/46817885.jpg",
"photo_url": "http://www.panoramio.com/photo/46817885"},
  :
  :
], "has_more": true}
```

Using a JSON package, you can get the "photo_file_url" field of the result. See Section 2.3 for an example.

B.3 Oxford Visual Geometry Group

The Visual Geometry research group at Oxford University has many datasets available at *http://www.robots.ox.ac.uk/~vgg/data/*. We used some of the multi-view datasets in this book, for example the "Merton1", "Model House", "dinosaur", and "corridor" sequences. The data is available for download (some with camera matrices and point tracks) at *http://www.robots.ox.ac.uk/~vgg/data/data-mview.html*.

B.4 University of Kentucky Recognition Benchmark Images

The UK Benchmark image set, also called the "ukbench" set, is a set with 2,550 groups of images. Each group has four images of an object or scene from varying viewpoints. This is a good set to test object recognition and image retrieval algorithms. The data set is available for download (the full set is around 1.5 GB) at *http://www.vis.uky.edu/~stewe/ukbench/*. It is described in detail in the paper [23].

In this book, we used a smaller subset using only the first 1,000 images.

B.5 Other
Prague Texture Segmentation Datagenerator and Benchmark

This set used in the segmentation chapter can generate many different types of texture segmentation images. Available at *http://mosaic.utia.cas.cz/index.php*.

MSR Cambridge Grab Cut Dataset

Originaly used in the Grab Cut paper [27], this set provides segmentation images with user annotations. The data set and some papers are available from *http://research .microsoft.com/en-us/um/cambridge/projects/visionimagevideoediting/segmentation/grab cut.htm*. The original images in the data set are from a data set that now is part of the Berkeley Segmentation Dataset, *http://www.eecs.berkeley.edu/Research/Projects/CS/ vision/grouping/segbench/*.

Caltech 101

This is a classic dataset that contains pictures of objects from 101 different categories and can be used to test object recognition algorithms. The data set is available at *http:// www.vision.caltech.edu/Image_Datasets/Caltech101/*.

Static Hand Posture Database

This dataset from Sebastien Marcel is available at *http://www.idiap.ch/resource/gestures/* together with a few other sets with hands and gestures.

Middlebury Stereo Datasets

These are datasets used to benchmark stereo algorithms. They are available for download at *http://vision.middlebury.edu/stereo/data/*. Every stereo pair comes with ground truth depth images to compare results against.

Image Credits

Throughout this book we have made use of publicly available datasets and images available from web services; these were listed in Appendix B. The contributions of the researchers behind these datasets are greatly appreciated.

Some of the reoccurring example images are the author's own. You are free to use these images under a Creative Commons Attribution 3.0 (CC BY 3.0) license (*http://creativecommons.org/licenses/by/3.0/*), for example by citing this book.

These images are:

- The Empire State building image used in almost every example throughout the book.
- The low contrast image in Figure 1-7.
- The feature matching examples used in Figures 2-2, 2-5, 2-6, and 2-7.
- The Fisherman's Wharf sign used in Figures 9-6, 10-1, and 10-2.
- The little boy on top of a hill used in Figures 6-4, 9-6.
- The book image for calibration used in Figures 4-3.
- The two images of the O'Reilly open source book used in Figures 4-4, 4-5, and 4-6.

C.1 Images from Flickr

We used some images from Flickr available with a Creative Commons Attribution 2.0 Generic (CC BY 2.0) license (*http://creativecommons.org/licenses/by/2.0/deed.en*). The contributions from these photographers is greatly appreciated.

The images used from Flickr are (names are the ones used in the examples, not the original filenames):

- *billboard_for_rent.jpg* by @striatic, *http://flickr.com/photos/striatic/21671910/*, used in Figures 3-2.
- *blank_billboard.jpg* by @mediaboytodd, *http://flickr.com/photos/23883605@N06/2317982570/*, used in Figures 3-3.

- *beatles.jpg* by @oddsock, *http://flickr.com/photos/oddsock/82535061/*, used in Figures 3-2, 3-3.
- *turningtorso1.jpg* by @rutgerblom, *http://www.flickr.com/photos/rutgerblom/2873 185336/*, used in Figure 3-5.
- *sunset_tree.jpg* by @jpck, *http://www.flickr.com/photos/jpck/3344929385/*, used in Figure 3-5.

C.2   Other Images

- The face images used in Figures 3-6, 3-7, and 3-8 are courtesy of J. K. Keller. The eye and mouth annotations are the author's.
- The Lund University building images used in Figures 3-9, 3-11, and 3-12 are from a dataset used at the Mathematical Imaging Group, Lund University. Photographer was probably Magnus Oskarsson.
- The toy plane 3D model used in Figure 4-6 is from Gilles Tran (Creative Commons License By Attribution).
- The Alcatraz images in Figures 5-7 and 5-8 are courtesy of Carl Olsson.
- The font data set used in Figures 1-8, 6-2, 6-3 6-7, and 6-8 is courtesy of Martin Solli.
- The Sudoku images in Figures 8-6, 8-7, and 8-8 are courtesy of Martin Byröd.

C.3   Illustrations

The epipolar geometry illustration in Figure 5-1 is based on an illustration by Klas Josephson and adapted for this book.

References

[1] Herbert Bay, Tinne Tuytelaars, and Luc Van Gool. SURF: Speeded up robust features. In *European Conference on Computer Vision*, 2006.

[2] Yuri Boykov, Olga Veksler, and Ramin Zabih. Fast approximate energy minimization via graph cuts. *IEEE Transactions on Pattern Analysis and Machine Intelligence*, 23:2001, 2001.

[3] Gary Bradski and Adrian Kaehler. *Learning OpenCV*. O'Reilly Media Inc., 2008.

[4] Martin Byröd. An optical Sudoku solver. In *Swedish Symposium on Image Analysis, SSBA. http://www.maths.lth.se/matematiklth/personal/byrod/papers/sudokuocr.pdf*, 2007.

[5] Antonin Chambolle. Total variation minimization and a class of binary mrf models. In *Energy Minimization Methods in Computer Vision and Pattern Recognition*, Lecture Notes in Computer Science, pages 136–152. Springer Berlin / Heidelberg, 2005.

[6] T. Chan and L. Vese. Active contours without edges. *IEEE Trans. Image Processing*, 10(2):266–277, 2001.

[7] Chih-Chung Chang and Chih-Jen Lin. *LIBSVM: a library for support vector machines*, 2001. Software available at *http://www.csie.ntu.edu.tw/~cjlin/libsvm*.

[8] D. Cremers, T. Pock, K. Kolev, and A. Chambolle. Convex relaxation techniques for segmentation, stereo and multiview reconstruction. In *Advances in Markov Random Fields for Vision and Image Processing*. MIT Press, 2011.

[9] Nello Cristianini and John Shawe-Taylor. *An Introduction to Support Vector Machines and Other Kernel-based Learning Methods*. Cambridge University Press, 2000.

[10] Gunnar Farnebäck. Two-frame motion estimation based on polynomial expansion. In *Proceedings of the 13th Scandinavian Conference on Image Analysis*, pages 363–370, 2003.

[11] M. A. Fischler and R. C. Bolles. Random sample consensus: a paradigm for model fitting with applications to image analysis and automated cartography. *Communications-of-the-ACM*, 24(6):381–95, 1981.

[12] C. Harris and M. Stephens. A combined corner and edge detector. In *Proceedings Alvey Conference*, pages 189–192, 1988.

[13] R. I. Hartley and A. Zisserman. *Multiple View Geometry in Computer Vision*. Cambridge University Press, ISBN: 0521540518, second edition, 2004.

[14] Richard Hartley. In defense of the eight-point algorithm. *IEEE Transactions on Pattern Analysis and Machine Intelligence*, 19:580–593, 1997.

[15] Berthold K. P. Horn and Brian G. Schunck. Determining optical flow. *Artifical Intelligence*, 17:185–203, 1981.

[16] Vladimir Kolmogorov and Ramin Zabih. What energy functions can be minimized via graph cuts. *IEEE Transactions on Pattern Analysis and Machine Intelligence*, 26:65–81, 2004.

[17] David G. Lowe. Object recognition from local scale-invariant features. In *International Conference on Computer Vision*, pages 1150–1157, 1999.

[18] David G. Lowe. Distinctive image features from scale-invariant keypoints. *International Journal of Computer Vision*, 60(2):91–110, 2004.

[19] Bruce D. Lucas and Takeo Kanade. An iterative image registration technique with an application to stereo vision, pages 674–679, 1981.

[20] Mark Lutz. *Learning Python*. O'Reilly Media Inc., 2009.

[21] Will McGugan. *Beginning Game Development with Python and Pygame*. Apress, 2007.

[22] F. Meyer. Color image segmentation. In *Proceedings of the 4th Conference on Image Processing and its Applications*, pages 302–306, 1992.

[23] D. Nistér and H. Stewénius. Scalable recognition with a vocabulary tree. In *IEEE Conference on Computer Vision and Pattern Recognition (CVPR)*, volume 2, pages 2161–2168, 2006.

[24] Travis E. Oliphant. *Guide to NumPy*. *http://www.tramy.us/numpybook.pdf*, 2006.

[25] M. Pollefeys, L. Van Gool, M. Vergauwen, F. Verbiest, K. Cornelis, J. Tops, and R. Koch. Visual modeling with a hand-held camera. *International Journal of Computer Vision*, 59(3):207–232, 2004.

[26] Marc Pollefeys. Visual 3d modeling from images—tutorial notes. Technical report, University of North Carolina–Chapel Hill. *http://www.cs.unc.edu/~marc/tutorial.pdf*

[27] Carsten Rother, Vladimir Kolmogorov, and Andrew Blake. Grabcut: Interactive foreground extraction using iterated graph cuts. *ACM Transactions on Graphics*, 23: 309–314, 2004.

[28] L. I. Rudin, S. J. Osher, and E. Fatemi. Nonlinear total variation based noise removal algorithms. *Physica D*, 60:259–268, 1992.

[29] Daniel Scharstein and Richard Szeliski. A taxonomy and evaluation of dense two-frame stereo correspondence algorithms. *International Journal of Computer Vision*, 2001.

[30] Daniel Scharstein and Richard Szeliski. High-accuracy stereo depth maps using structured light. In *IEEE Computer Society Conference on Computer Vision and Pattern Recognition*, 2003.

[31] Toby Segaran. *Programming Collective Intelligence*. O'Reilly Media, 2007.

[32] Jianbo Shi and Jitendra Malik. Normalized cuts and image segmentation. *IEEE Trans. Pattern Anal. Mach. Intell.*, 22:888–905, August 2000.

[33] Jianbo Shi and Carlo Tomasi. Good features to track. In *1994 IEEE Conference on Computer Vision and Pattern Recognition (CVPR'94)*, pages 593–600, 1994.

[34] Noah Snavely, Steven M. Seitz, and Richard Szeliski. Photo tourism: Exploring photo collections in 3d. In *SIGGRAPH Conference Proceedings*, pages 835–846. ACM Press, 2006.

[35] Bill Triggs, Philip F. McLauchlan, Richard I. Hartley, and Andrew W. Fitzgibbon. Bundle adjustment - a modern synthesis. In *Proceedings of the International Workshop on Vision Algorithms: Theory and Practice*, ICCV '99, pages 298–372. Springer-Verlag, 2000.

[36] A. Vedaldi and B. Fulkerson. VLFeat: An open and portable library of computer vision algorithms. *http://www.vlfeat.org/*, 2008.

[37] Deepak Verma and Marina Meila. A comparison of spectral clustering algorithms. Technical report, 2003.

[38] Luminita A. Vese and Tony F. Chan. A multiphase level set framework for image segmentation using the mumford and shah model. *International Journal of Computer Vision*, 50:271–293, December 2002.

[39] Paul Viola and Michael Jones. Robust real-time object detection. In *International Journal of Computer Vision*, 2001.

[40] Marco Zuliani. Ransac for dummies. Technical report, Vision Research Lab, UCSB, 2011.

Index

number

3D plotting, 102
3D reconstruction, 116
4-neighborhood, 193

A

affine transformation, 54
affine warping, 57
affinity matrix, 140
agglomerative clustering, 133
alpha map, 58
AR, 89
array, 7
array slicing, 8
aspect ratio, 80
association, 200
augmented reality, 89

B

bag-of-visual-words, 148
bag-of-word representation, 147
baseline, 120
Bayes classifier, 175
binary image, 20
blurring, 16
bundle adustment, 120

C

calibration matrix, 80
camera calibration, 84
camera center, 79
camera matrix, 79
camera model, 79
camera pose estimation, 86
camera resectioning, 109
CBIR, 147

Chan-Vese segmentation, 205
characteristic functions, 205
CherryPy, 162, 164
class centroids, 127
classifying images, 167
clustering images, 127, 137
complete linking, 136
confusion matrix, 174
content-based image retrieval, 147
convex combination, 61
corner detection, 29
correlation, 32
corresponding points, 32
cpickle, 15
cross-correlation, 33
cumulative distribution function, 10
cv, 209, 216
cv2, 209

D

Delaunay triangulation, 62
dendrogram, 137
de-noising, 23
dense depth reconstruction, 120
dense image features, 170
dense SIFT, 170
descriptor, 32
difference-of-Gaussian, 36
digit classification, 183
directed graph, 191
direct linear transformation, 54
distance matrix, 140

E

Edmonds-Karp algorithm, 192
eight point algorithm, 103

epipolar constraint, 100
epipolar geometry, 99
epipolar line, 100
epipole, 101
essential matrix, 113

F

factorization, 83
feature matches, 34
feature matching, 40
flood fill, 212
focal length, 80
fundamental matrix, 100
fundamental matrix estimation, 114

G

Gaussian blurring, 16
Gaussian derivative filters, 19
Gaussian distributions, 177
gesture recognition, 172
GL_MODELVIEW, 90
GL_PROJECTION, 90
Grab Cut dataset, 197
gradient angle, 18
gradient magnitude, 18
graph, 191
graph cut, 191
GraphViz, 48
graylevel transforms, 8

H

Harris corner detection, 29
Harris matrix, 29
hierarchical clustering, 133
hierarchical *k*-means, 145
histogram equalization, 10
Histogram of Oriented Gradients, 170
HOG, 170
homogeneous coordinates, 53
homography, 53
homography estimation, 54
Hough transform, 224

I

`Image`, 1
image contours, 4
`ImageDraw`, 130
image gradient, 18
image graph, 193
image histograms, 4
image patch, 32
image plane, 79

image registration, 64
image retrieval, 147
image search demo, 162
image segmentation, 131, 191
image thumbnails, 2
inliers, 70
inpainting, 223
integral image, 211
interest point descriptor, 32
interest points, 29
inverse depth, 80
inverse document frequency, 148
`io`, 22
iso-contours, 4

J

JSON, 45

K

kernel functions, 180
k-means, 127
k-nearest neighbor classifier, 167
kNN, 167

L

Laplacian matrix, 142
least squares triangulation, 108
LibSVM, 180
local descriptors, 29
Lucas-Kanade tracking algorithm, 217

M

marking points, 7
mathematical morphology, 20
Matplotlib, 3
maximum flow (max flow), 192
`measurements`, 21, 186
metric reconstruction, 100, 112
`minidom`, 65
minimum cut (min cut), 192
`misc`, 22
morphology, 20
`morphology`, 21, 27
`mplot3d`, 102, 118
multi-class SVM, 185
multi-dimensional arrays, 7
multi-dimensional histograms, 137
multiple view geometry, 99

N

naive Bayes classifier, 175
`ndimage`, 57

`ndimage.filters`, 122
normalized cross-correlation, 33
normalized cut, 200
NumPy, 7

O

`objloader`, 96
OCR, 183
OpenCV, ix, 209
OpenGL, 90
OpenGL projection matrix, 91
optical axis, 79
optical center, 81
optical character recognition, 183
optical flow, 216
optical flow equation, 216
optic flow, 216
outliers, 70
overfitting, 190

P

panograph, 78
panorama, 70
PCA, 13
`pickle`, 15, 128, 151
pickling, 15
piecewise affine warping, 61
piecewise constant image model, 205
PIL, 1
pin-hole camera, 79
plane sweeping, 121
plot formatting, 4
plotting, 3
point correspondence, 32
pose estimation, 86
Prewitt filters, 18
Principal Component Analysis, 13, 178
principal point, 81
projection, 79
projection matrix, 79
projective camera, 79
projective transformation, 53
`pydot`, 48
`pygame`, 90
`pygame.image`, 90
`pygame.locals`, 90
Pylab, 3
PyOpenGL, 90
`pyplot`, 27
`pysqlite`, 152
`pysqlite2`, 152
`python-graph`, 192

Python Imaging Library, 1

Q

quad, 92
query with image, 157
quotient image, 27

R

radial basis functions, 180
ranking using homographies, 160
RANSAC, 70, 114
rectified image pair, 120
rectifying images, 187
registration, 64
rigid transformation, 54
robust homography estimation, 72
ROF, 23, 205
RQ-factorization, 83
Rudin-Osher-Fatemi de-noising model, 23

S

Scale-Invariant Feature Transform, 36
`scikit.learn`, 190
Scipy, 16
`scipy.cluster.vq`, 128, 130
`scipy.io`, 22, 23
`scipy.misc`, 23
`scipy.ndimage`, 18, 21, 186, 189, 190
`scipy.ndimage.filters`, 17, 18, 30
`scipy.sparse`, 166
searching images, 147, 155
segmentation, 191
self-calibration, 120
separating hyperplane, 179
SfM, 113
SIFT, 36
similarity matrix, 140
similarity transformation, 54
similarity tree, 133
`simplejson`, 45, 46
single linking, 136
slicing, 8
Sobel filters, 18
spectral clustering, 140, 200
SQLite, 152
SSD, 33
stereo imaging, 120
stereo reconstruction, 120
stereo rig, 120
stereo vision, 120
stitching images, 75
stop words, 148

structure from motion, 113
structuring element, 21
Sudoku reader, 183
sum of squared differences, 33
Support Vector Machines, 179
support vectors, 180
SVM, 179

T

term frequency, 148
term frequency–inverse document frequency,
    148
text mining, 147
tf-idf weighting, 148
total variation, 23
total within-class variance, 127
tracking, 216
triangulation, 107

U

unpickling, 15
unsharp masking, 26
urllib, 46

V

variational methods, 205
variational problems, 205
vector quantization, 128
vector space model, 147
vertical field of view, 91
video, 213
visual codebook, 148
visualizing image distribution, 131
visual vocabulary, 148
visual words., 148
VLFeat, 37

W

warping, 57
watershed, 224
web applications, 162
webcam, 217
word index, 152

X

XML, 65
xml.dom, 65

About the Author

Jan Erik Solem is a Python enthusiast and a computer vision researcher and entrepreneur. He is an applied mathematician and has worked as associate professor, startup CTO, and now also book author. He sometimes writes about computer vision and Python on his blog *www.janeriksolem.net*. He has used Python for computer vision in teaching, research, and industrial applications for many years. He currently lives in San Francisco.

Colophon

The animal on the cover of *Programming Computer Vision with Python* is a bullhead.

Often referred to as "bullhead catfish," members of the genus *Ameiurus* come in three common types: the black bullhead (*Ameiurus melas*), the yellow bullhead (*Ameiurus natalis*), and the brown bullhead (*Ameiurus nebulosus*). These stubborn fish prefer aging, warm-water lakes and are typically found east of the North American continental divide.

Bullheads are known for their obstinacy and tenacity (in fact, people possessing these traits are often characterized as "bullheaded"), and these characteristics have helped them outlive many other species of fish. They can tolerate brackish water and low oxygen and high carbon dioxide levels, making them more resistant to pollutants than most other fish and therefore ideal for lab and medical experiments.

Bullheads are bottom-feeders, prowling in schools at night, on the hunt for clams, insects, leeches, small fish, crayfish, and algae. While doing so, they tend to stir up the bottom of the body of water and destroy aquatic vegetation, which eliminates cover for other species. This, along with their high reproductive rate and subsequent overpopulation, can make them somewhat of a curse for fisheries. For this reason, restrictions are rarely placed on bullhead fishing.

All three types of bullhead are scaleless and average 8 to 10 inches in length. The whisker-like barbells, or feelers, at the corners of their mouth and in a line on the lower chin give them a catfish-like appearance, but they're differentiated partly by the sharp spines at the base of their dorsal and pectoral fins. Like catfish, though, their sense of smell is more developed than that of canines.

The cover image is from Wood's *Animate Creation*. The cover font is Adobe ITC Garamond. The text font is Linotype Birka; the heading font is Adobe Myriad Condensed; and the code font is LucasFont's TheSansMonoCondensed.

O'REILLY®

There's much more where this came from.

Experience books, videos, live online training courses, and more from O'Reilly and our 200+ partners—all in one place.

Learn more at oreilly.com/online-learning